Ukraine

Other Places Travel Guide
Ukraine
Ashley Hardaway

Published by
OTHER PLACES PUBLISHING

First edition
Published October 2011

Ukraine
Other Places Travel Guide
Written by: Ashley Hardaway

Cover designed by: Carla Zetina-Yglesias
Cover photograph by: Aimee Hardaway

Published by:
Other Places Publishing
www.otherplacespublishing.com

All text, illustrations and artwork copyright
© 2011 Other Places Publishing

ISBN 978-1-935850-04-5

The Author

Ashley Hardaway

For months after moving back to America from Eastern Europe, Ashley Hardaway would find herself saying "In Ukraine this one time..." Friends and family became accustomed to this unstoppable annoyance. Editors that she worked with were perplexed as to how she managed to work a Ukraine analogy into seemingly every article she wrote. It seemed, no matter how hard she tried otherwise, that she could not stop thinking about that country.

To everyone's great delight (and/or horror) she got a publishing deal for this Ukraine travel guide. Traveling around the county again and writing about it would either rid her of all her thoughts regarding this country, or provide her with even more stories to torment them with at Christmas time.

So far, all signs point to the latter.

Ashley Hardaway now lives in Florida where she continues to write – about other things as well.

More of Ashley's writing about food, life (and of course Ukraine) can be found at her website: thegluttonouspig.com.

BELARUS

POLAND

Kovel

Korosten

Chernobyl

Chernihiv

KYIV

Rivne

Dubno

Zhytomyr

Berdychiv

LVIV

Ternopil

SLOVAKIA

HUNGARY

Skole

Perechyn

Uzhhorod

Mukachevo

Slavske

IVANO FRANKIVSK

Yaremcha

Kosiv

Verkhovyna

Karnyanets Podilsky

Uman

CHERNIVTSI

MOLDOVA

Ukraine

N

100 km
50 miles

● Designates a city/village
covered in this book

ODESSA

ROMANIA

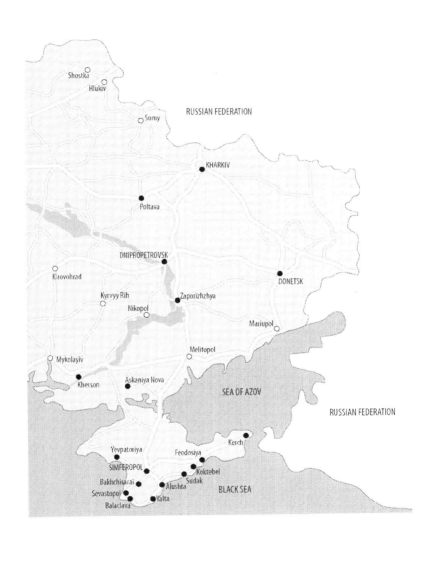

Contents

Acknowledgments

Oh the seldom read acknowledgment section. How good of you to stop by! I'll try to reel this in before it panders into Oscar winning thank-you-speech territory.

Though you may start a journey alone, it seldom ends up that way. The following people hosted me their homes and/or hostels, showed me around their towns, or gave me fantastic suggestions: Jessie Salpeter, Keely Richardson, Jason Boles, Alex Schneider, Roman Terletsky, Ali Kinsella, Betsy Ott, Sylwia Latacz, and Lyuba (and Marcus) Kolomiichuk. The team at Adventure Carpathians was also extraordinarily helpful in planning accommodations in even the most isolated parts of the Carpathians.

Francine Cary, Barbara Trecker, Erica Batres, Danielle Kuczkowski, Devin Davis and Thomas McCloskey: Thank you for penning personal essays for inclusion in this book; it's one of my favorite aspects. Also big thanks to Jay Pusey, Sheila Slemp and Barbara Wieser for sharing invaluable insider knowledge regarding their host sites.

Nick Brown (who wrote the opening history section): Thank you for somehow making the immense, and sometimes depressing breadth of Ukrainian history, seem lively and fun! Sarah (Richardson) Kilchevskyi: Thank you for marrying your Ukrainian sweetheart Volodymyr, and therefore unbeknownst to both of you, becoming my go-to people for all of my "would you say this is an accurate portrayal of…?" questions. Those two when combined with Leah Kumayama and Jocelyn Soto, made up my Peace Corps "core" – coming dangerously close to Oscar territory with that one.

Thanks to my younger sister, Aimee Hardaway, who shot the cover photo in Kyiv. Thank you to Rob Theriot for not writing me off when I said I was leaving the country for a while without him. To my parents and my older sister Aubrey, who have probably spent a vast portion of their income on long-distance phone calls.

Tanya, Valentina and Dima Borchashvili, Natasha, Oleg and Ulia Lyaka (Валентина і Діма Борчашвілі, Наташа, Олег і Юля Ляка): Я вас всіх люблю. Скоро побачимося. Перемога!

Christopher Beale, my editor, thank you for replying to all my late night emails and phone calls with calm, Zen-like, assurance. When I make it to Antigua and Barbuda you better believe I'll have your book with me.

And finally – you're still here? – thanks to Peace Corps Ukraine Group 31 and all the people who have volunteered, or will volunteer in Ukraine. Even if we've never met, we're all bonded together by this place. Like new acquaintances that happen to have dated the same people: we'd definitely have so much to talk about.

Getting Started

Introduction

Far from the snowy tundra most envision, Ukraine is a burgeoning budget tourism mecca replete with sultry beaches, delicate ski resorts, lush forests and posh cities. Having been ensconced behind the Iron Curtain for so long, it's slowly revealing itself as Eastern Europe's premier travel destination. Ease of entry, relaxed visa regulations, and its favorable exchange rates have been raved about by backpackers for years, and it seems the general public is finally catching up.

Having a history that spans back to the fifth century AD, Ukraine hosts a bevy of historical goldmines. From its southern Greek ruins and Odessa's catacombs where soldiers fighting against the Nazi's hid, to Crimea's palaces, mosques, and "secret cities."

Cultural anthropologists will revel in its quaint villages where traditions continue in the form of festivals, *pysanka*, and cleanly spoken Ukrainian. Those searching for their own Walden Pond may find it in the Carpathians where mountainous passages hide villages so picturesque you may consider selling everything to live the "simple life" here.

For the urban cowboys, head to the big cities –Dnipropetrovsk, Kyiv, Odessa, or Kharkiv – where nightclubs rage from dusk till dawn and money falls through fingertips easier than vodka. Adventure seekers can ski, cave dive, mountain bike, and camp for days. Or simply pass out on the beaches of Odessa and Crimea and contemplate why they haven't been here sooner.

Not for the unadventurous, traveling in Ukraine can have its frustrations and its challenges. But for those who are jaded with the conventional experiences most tourists are content with, Ukraine will be a refreshing change. A country that, for better or for worse, holds true to itself, its values, and its culture, Ukraine might not change any time soon, but it might very well change you.

History

Whether Ukrainians are discussing the nationalist sentiments of Cossack Bohdan Khmelnytsky, the origins of Kievan Rus', or the true cause of the Japanese surrender in 1945, Ukrainian history is shrouded in half-truths and guesswork. This author will not pretend to present the undisputed facts of the case: there are few, if any. Rather, the text you find here presents an ambiguous narrative which is as controversial as it is well-known among Ukrainians.

> **Nick Brown**, a Peace Corps Volunteer in Ukraine from 2006 to 2008, wrote this history section. Nick studied history at Colgate University, and continues his passion for the former Soviet Union working for an international development agency in Washington, DC.

KIEVAN RUS

The origins of Ukraine are founded around its modern capital, Kyiv. According to national mythology, Kyiv (Kiev in Russian) was founded by three brothers and their sister in the fifth century AD. While this is disputed, ruins have been found dating to at least the eighth century. By the late tenth century, Kyiv was a burgeoning metropolis, larger than any other city in non-Byzantine Europe. And so, in its attempt to shed its barbaric image as trade with Constantinople grew, Grand Prince Volodymyr the Great converted the entire city of Kyiv to Eastern Orthodoxy in 988, by herding them all into the Dnipro River (Dnieper in Russian) to be baptized (see "Christianity" on page 24). Kievan Rus's rulers married their daughters off to France, Hungary, and Byzantium, making Kyiv an integrated part of Europe's cultural and political identity. To cement that identity, Grand Prince Yaroslav the Wise built the Cathedral of Saint Sophia in the early eleventh century as a "sister church" to Constantinople's venerable Haghia Sophia. This emphasizes the close trading ties between Byzantium and Kievan Rus: fur traders and farmers traveled down the Dnipro River, along treacherous rapids, bandits, and harsh weather, for a chance to trade with the opulent capital of Eastern Orthodoxy. It is no wonder that Volodymyr converted: it was as good for business as it was for Kyiv's faith.

In 1240, however, the Mongol invasion swept all of Kyiv's fortunes away, as it did for so many other Eurasian cultures. A dispute over the subsequent migration of Kievan Rus's rulers has turned into a battle between Russia and Ukraine over Kyiv's cultural heritage. No matter the history of this long-lost empire, for the following 750 years, the vast Central European plain – that is known today as Ukraine – would earn its name as a "borderland" between societies. Kyiv became a football to be passed between the great powers that surrounded it, not a power center in its own right. Until 1648, the history of Ukraine was the history of its neighbors.

THE KHMELNYTSKYI UPRISING

Unlike modern states, there was no clear passport checkpoint or customs guard waiting on the edge of the Russian Empire's jurisdiction, nor that of the Polish-Lithuanian Commonwealth. Travelers had to negotiate a shifting array of bandits, city-states, peasants, and feudal realms to successfully make the trip from Krakow to Moscow. Cossacks, a kind of pirate on horseback who sheltered along the southern portion of the Dnipro River, were a panoply of Tatars, Poles, and various other outcasts from respectable Russian and Polish society. And yet Cossacks, like similar bandits on the high seas of the Caribbean, were strikingly modern. Cossack bands were religiously and ethnically diverse, and surprisingly democratic. These characteristics have made the Cossacks, a quintessential "border" inhabitant, an attractive target for integration into a Ukrainian national myth.

The Dnipro Cossacks, lacking a strong unifying authority, appeared to be nothing more than a nuisance to the Polish-Lithuanian Commonwealth which ostensibly ruled the region. Bohdan Khmelnytsky would change that forever in 1648. Khmelnytsky sought redress from the Polish government after a neighbor raided his lands and killed his son. When Warsaw failed to deliver, Khmelnytsky rallied the Zaporozhian Sich, a Cossack band, and attacked the Commonwealth under alliance with the Tatar Khan of Crimea. He pushed toward Warsaw for the next three years, which resulted in an incredibly bloody struggle that hurt no one more than the peasants inhabiting the farmland on which the wars raged. The rebellion failed, however, in 1651 as the Tatar-Cossack pact disintegrated just after he took Lviv in 1651.

Stuck in the middle of the most volatile and indefensible plain in all of Europe, Khmelnytsky decided to cut a deal with the devil to preserve his precarious hold on power. Fearful of eventual retribution for his insurgency, Khmelnytsky ended his rebellion with the Treaty of Pereyaslav in 1654, a promise of eternal fealty to Tsar Ivan the Terrible. Today, Khmelnytsky remains a controversial figure. Poles depict him as a drunken madman who stole half their kingdom, while Russians see him as the deliverer of their long-lost Kyiv ancestors. Ukrainians, ever ambivalent, cannot decide what to make of him. Khmelnytsky delivered the first semi-independent Ukraine in four hundred years, but his deal with the Russians promised a long-term overlord. Furthermore, his treaty did not deliver the intended peace. For the next thirty years, armies of the Khan, the Tsar, the Cossacks, the Swedes, and the Polish-Lithuanian King rampaged across modern-day Central and Western Ukraine in a period known to Ukrainians as "The Ruin." Finally, in 1686, the Poles signed a peace treaty directly with the Tsar, ceding control of Kyiv to the Russian Empire. Until 1918, Kyiv would be a Russian city.

EUROPEANISM, RUSSIFICATION, & THE RISE OF UKRAINIAN NATIONALISM

For the next two and a half centuries, Ukrainians would see an ongoing tidal shift between Europe and pan-Slavism, liberalism and conservatism, tolerance and

Russification. Depending on the Tsar, the condition of minorities, peasants, and Ukrainians rose and fell on the Left Bank of the Dnipro. Reforms aiming for a modern bureaucracy generally improved the plight of Russian serfdom, but the wars across Ukraine under Catherine the Great destroyed the countryside. Catherine's successor, Alexander I, worked toward political liberalization and an open society, but his younger brother, Nicholas I, instituted draconian "Russification" laws, mandating the use of Russian in all public forums and reducing religious and political freedoms. His successor, Alexander II, freed the serfs and granted democratic local councils, but overturned his own free speech laws when socialist sentiment and Polish rebellions proved to be too much.

Thus, the back-and-forth between peace and war, freedom and servitude, transparency and corruption, was an ongoing saga throughout the eighteenth and nineteenth century. As soon as one Tsar made peace with Poland, the next invaded. While one strove for Europe, the next turned to Slavic brotherhood. This political ping pong exacerbated local tensions and led to increasing frustration among the citizenry. On a local level, important undercurrents had begun that would point the way to Ukrainian nationalism and independence by the 1990s. This nationalism began with a joke.

Specifically, the joke was the use of Ukrainian for tongue-in-cheek references to peasant culture in the plays of the Russian Ivan Kotlyarevsky in 1798. This led to the first Ukrainian grammar book in 1818, and then a dictionary in 1823. By the mid-nineteenth century, the now ubiquitous Taras Shevchenko formalized the language, and was exiled to Kazakhstan for his troubles (see "Literature" on page 34). Shevchenko's influence and contribution to Ukrainian nationalism cannot be overstated, although Ukrainians have certainly tried: finding the western Ukrainian town which lacks a Shevchenko statue is as hopeless a task as opening a window on a *marshrutka* (see "Superstitions" on page 31).

After the partitions of the late eighteenth century removed Poland from the map, the last best refuge for any nationalist movement was the Austro-Hungarian Empire. The very name of this political entity, which had separate capitals in Vienna and Budapest, suggests the more democratic, open society that was the incubus for

The Nationalism of Western Ukraine

While Russia controlled Kyiv at this time, much of modern-day Western Ukraine remained under Polish control until the late eighteenth century, and Lviv was ruled by no Russian until 1939. This at least partially explains the more independent, nationalist streak that travelers will find in Western Ukraine. Because that region has changed hands so often, it has no doubt been easier for citizens of the western regions to form their own cultural heritage, whereas Eastern Ukraine, which was ruled by the Russians almost exclusively from 1654, has had fewer opportunities to wedge an independent language and literary tradition into the breach. Please note, however: if you point out to a Galician that Lviv didn't actually experience the Great Famine (see "Holodomor" on page 17), you'll still get called a jerk, even if you're right.

the modern Polish, Czech, Slovak, Hungarian, German, and, of course, Ukrainian nations. This constituted more effective political representation than anything the Ukrainian people on the Left Bank of the Dnipro saw, despite their smaller numbers in Polish-dominated Lviv (then known as Galicia). The Austro-Hungarian Empire hosted nationalists like the socialist poet Ivan Franko, whom travelers can find on the 20 hryvnia bill, and historian and politician Mikhail Hrushevskyi, who is on the 50 hryvnia bill.

REFORM AND REVOLUTION: THE EARLY 20TH CENTURY

Despite political and economic reforms and improvement at the turn of the century, the early twentieth century was a time of unrest throughout Ukrainian ethnic regions. In 1914, the archduke of Austria, Franz Ferdinand, was assassinated by a Serbian nationalist group. An escalating crisis eventually led to general war in Europe, an event that the modernizing but still primitive Russia was unprepared for. By 1918, the two nations which harbored Ukrainian nationalists had been wiped off the map: Russia by internal revolution, and Austria-Hungary by President Woodrow Wilson and the Treaty of Versailles. Both cases had profound implications for the future of Ukrainian nationalism.

THE TSENTRALNA RADA & THE FIRST INDEPENDENT UKRAINE

When revolution broke out in the late fall of 1917, Ukrainian nationalists scented a chance for an independent state. In response to the total breakdown of government in early 1917, historian and Ukrainian nationalist Mikhail Hrushevskyi became the leader of the *Tsentralna Rada* (Central Council) of Ukraine. Hrushveskyi was responsible for the transition of the assembly from a subunit of the Provisional Government of the Russian Empire to an independent nation, before it was swept away in 1918 by the Red Army and then the Germans, who took effective control of the area after the outbreak of the Russian Civil War. Although short-lived, the one-year independence of Ukraine set a precedent that would prove to be important seventy years later, during the whimpering collapse of Lenin's great project.

Meanwhile, the collapse of the Austro-Hungarian Empire and Woodrow Wilson's rhetoric of the "right of self-determination" for ethnicities in Eastern Europe spurred hope in Lviv that another independent Ukraine might arise from the ashes of Hrushevskyi's failed state. The Ukrainian delegates to the Austro-Hungarian parliament declared independence in November of 1918, but a brief war suppressed this hubris as Poland took back the lands that it, too, historically considered its own. Again, this short rule was a failure in itself, but it helped spur renewed Ukrainian nationalism, which would again appear in the late 1980s.

THE NEW ECONOMIC POLICY & THE HOLODOMOR

After the dust had settled, the eastern and central portions of modern Ukraine were firmly established as the new Ukrainian Soviet Socialist Republic, with a capital in Kharkiv (Kyiv was considered too nationalist to be the capital). The strain of civil war caused Lenin to establish "War Communism," a radical restructuring of the economic system and centralization of state ownership. Upon rampant inflation and chaos, however, leaders decided upon the "New Economic Policy," which established a gold-backed currency and a stock exchange, and this dramatically improved the new state's economic outlook.

Lenin was willing to accept these compromises as a necessary evil on the road to true communism. Stalin disagreed. After Lenin's death, Stalin decided to radically change the status quo in the countryside, in both Ukraine and Russia. He first executed or exiled thousands, if not millions, of "kulaks," a class of wealthy, property-owning peasants, and the state took direct control of their former lands in this "Great Purge" of the middle classes. Citizens could suddenly be punished by death for an act as simple as trying to eat a raw potato upon digging it up. Grain piled in state silos as five million Ukrainians starved to death in the winter of 1932-33. Sources differ as to the true motive behind what is now known as the Holodomor (or the Great Famine): some argue that Stalin wanted to appear economically successful to the West; others call this a deliberate genocide of the Ukrainian people. Still others claim that it was the mere result of bureaucratic mismanagement. Whatever the cause, the effects were clear: entire villages were wiped off the map in this completely unnecessary tragedy.

Radical upheaval did not stop there, however. While the West marveled at Soviet economic progress in the midst of the Great Depression, Stalin was busily herding all of Ukraine and Russia's "intelligentsia" (a term created in tsarist Russia) into the Siberian gulag, a huge system of work projects and prison camps scattered across the vast state. Neighbors turned against each other as tortured "suspects" offered their friends up as political dissidents. The "Red Scare," which would have been almost absurdist if it weren't so tragic, nearly eliminated Ukraine's intellectual and skilled classes. With the Great Purge, the Red Scare, and the Great Famine, Stalin had truly transformed Ukrainian society.

THE GREAT PATRIOTIC WAR

Having terrorized and destroyed almost all of Ukraine's top intellectuals and thinkers in two decades of civil war, chaos, and terror, by 1939, at the end of the Red Scare, it seemed that a renewed war, this time against the anti-Communist Nazis, was the next tragedy awaiting Ukraine. The world therefore greeted with surprise and a sense of betrayal the signature of a pact of non-aggression between Soviet and German forces in August of 1939, just before the Nazi invasion of Poland. The two powers split Poland down the middle, and for the first time, Lviv, Rivne, and Luts'k joined the Ukrainian SSR. The Ukraine that can be seen on the map today was for the first time fully-formed, except Crimea.

Holodomor

Nothing has been a source of more controversy, cover-ups, denials and variations of what occurred in Ukraine than the Holodomor. Coming from the Ukrainian words Голод (hunger) and Мор (plague) Holodomor means "murder by hunger" and is often referred to as the "Great Famine."

The Great Famine was a result of fiercely independent Ukrainian farmers refusing to relinquish their land to Stalin's regime of collectivization. Stalin hoped that government-run farms would produce enough grain to feed their growing numbers of industrial workers while also having enough left over to ship abroad for profit (the proceeds of which would further fuel Soviet industrialization). When the Ukrainian farmers refused to relinquish their land, Stalin began a program to wipe them out all together.

This process took two forms. The first stage began by stripping farmers of their possessions, taking the leaders from their villages and shipping them off to arctic labor camps. Many were never heard from again. Those who were left behind were forced to work on collectivization farms where ever-growing quotas of grain made it impossible to meet the demand. Many were later executed.

During this time, food for the villagers working on the farms were strictly rationed and eventually reduced to nothing as the grain piled up in silos on the edges of villages awaiting export to show the success of the Soviet economic model to foreign lands. Peasants swarmed the train stations in an attempt to flee and find food. However, they were banned from traveling and forced to starve to death in their villages. That year, the Soviet Union exported over thirty million tons of grain.

While the Holodomor was taking place, measures were taken to prevent indication of it at all. A disinformation campaign was launched by the Soviet Union, replete with falsified reports of collected grain numbers and disingenuous census studies. This information was even repeated by New York Times journalist Walter Duranty, a 1932 Pulitzer Prize winner and communist sympathizer. Duranty went so far to dismiss the Holodomor as nothing more than a trivial side effect of collectivization, quoting Stalin by saying, "Conditions are bad, but there is no famine – to put it brutally – you can't make an omelet without breaking eggs." Contrary opinion was hard to come by as the mere mention of "the famine" was criminalized, punishable with a five-year term in the gulag labor camps. Historian Edvard Radzinsky said Stalin "had achieved the impossible: he had silenced all the talk of hunger... Millions were dying, but the nation hymned the praises of collectivization."

Perhaps more surprising is how long it took to grant this catastrophe recognition. While six million people died during the Holocaust, estimates of the death tolls during the 1932-33 man made famine are upwards of seven to ten million. However, Soviet authorities denial that the Holodomor ever happened occurred until 1983. There's still controversy over whether this atrocity "deserved" to be labeled a genocide. Former Russian President Vladimir Putin thought not.

The third Saturday in November is now held as a special remembrance day for the Holodomor in Ukraine and around the world. In November of 2008, the first remembrance ceremony in the U.S. was held in Washington, DC.

The peace which Ukraine enjoyed would be brief. Believing war against the Soviets to be inevitable, Hitler decided to invade the USSR during a lull in the western front in 1941. Hitler believed the rich, black soil of Ukraine and the balmy climate of the Black Sea would be both the breadbasket of Greater Germany and an excellent summer destination for the Aryan race. Many Ukrainians, having endured twenty long years of blood and struggle, welcomed the "Thousand Year Reich" as the end of Ukraine's long wait for stability and peace. Particularly in Western Ukraine, Ukrainians saw Hitler as their last, best chance for a truly independent Ukraine.

Stalin was shocked at the invasion of Germany; he had been quietly preparing for a Nazi attack, but had never expected it to arrive so quickly. Proving that his well of brutalism was yet to run dry, Stalin adopted a "scorched earth" policy, directing his armies to burn all crops, bridges, and resources that the Nazis otherwise might have expected to capitalize upon. This policy, along with strong resistance around Kyiv, Odessa, and especially Sevastopol in Crimea, bogged Reich forces down in the late summer. For their efforts, each of these Ukrainian cities would be declared "hero cities" after the war. Visitors might see concrete monstrosities denoting this honor ("город герой" in Russian) around their city limits. But the Russian winter, as well as Stalin's sheer bloody-mindedness, proved too much even for the Germans. By 1944, exhausted and facing imminent invasion in Western Europe, the German army was steadily pushed back by reconstituted Soviet forces. In less than a year, the Red Army marched from Moscow to Berlin.

KHRUSHCHEV, BREZHNEV, & (ACTUALLY) EXISTING SOCIALISM

After the horrors of civil war, famine, exile and genocide, the postwar Soviet Union was comparatively mild. The Red Army was seen (at least for a while) as a liberator, and Ukrainians, tired of constant chaos, settled in to the great Communist experiment, with few detractors. Stepan Bandera and the Bandery, a rebel group in western Ukraine, plotted terrorist attacks (or patriotic offensives, depending on the Ukrainian you speak with) in the late 1940s, but even that eventually fizzled out. For the next thirty years, Ukrainian political relations were relatively pacific. Stalin's successor, the Ukrainian-born Nikita Khrushchev, most famous for banging a shoe on the podium of the UN General Assembly, was a reformist domestically, denouncing Stalin's rule in his "Secret Speech" to the Party Congress of 1956. From Stalin's death in 1953 to Khrushchev's ouster in 1964, political and economic liberalization led to a legitimate banking system, private property, and the freeing of millions of exiled victims of the arbitrary Stalinist judicial system. The first man ever sent into space, Yuriy Gagarin, was a Ukrainian; a point not lost on any Ukrainian schoolboy or girl you will meet. It was also during this time that Khrushchev gave all of Crimea to Ukraine as a gift on the three-hundredth anniversary of the Treaty of Pereyaslav, a move which seemed at the time to be unimportant considering the wider union of the Ukrainian SSR with the Soviet Union. (After Ukrainian independence, though, Russians, angry at the seemingly arbitrary loss of this long-Russian territory, would be prompted to call Khrushchev an idiot and a drunkard who illegitimately transferred this territory on a whim.)

However, Khrushchev's push for reform of the agricultural system ultimately set the Politburo against him. Tired of radical reform, the Central Committee united behind Leonid Brezhnev, a reactionary consensus-seeker who would lead the USSR until 1982. Chronicles of this period evoke a stagnant political and cultural lifestyle. While the Cold War raged outside the USSR, internally the country failed to move forward. Apartment complexes used architectural styles invented in the 1950s decades later; ten-story high-rises known as "Khruschevs" are ubiquitous across Ukraine. By the mid-1980s, Soviet citizens were again willing to experiment with reform, and Mikhail Gorbachev, a young, intelligent, energetic agricultural secretary seemed to be the man for the job. Elected in 1984, the next seven years would again shake stability and presage revolution, but national spirits were now optimistic for the first time since, arguably, the freeing of the serfs in 1861.

GORBACHEV & GLASNOST

Domestically, Gorbachev's policies of *glasnost* (openness), seeking to draw out the endemic corruption which had been allowed to fester under Brezhnev, initially made him few friends among the party bureaucracy. However, the explosion of a reactor at Chernobyl, in northern Kyiv oblast, highlighted the effects of bureaucratic mismanagement. In the early hours of April 26, 1986, a foolhardy experiment caused one of the reactors to explode, spreading nuclear waste and radioactive materials into the water supply and air. For several days afterward, Communist leaders denied the explosion, costing hundreds of lives and untold exposure to radiation, a tragedy which still affects unsuspecting Ukrainians today. Firefighters worked to stop the fire without any protection from radiation, and the area was not evacuated for at least a week afterward.

This tragedy not only convinced many Ukrainians of the failures of the Soviet experiment; it convinced Gorbachev to further his efforts at openness. Seeking legitimate criticism, he liberalized censorship of state newspapers, and permitted political dissidents to speak freely on the failings of the Soviet leadership. Independent political movements were sanctioned in 1988, and free elections were announced in the same year (albeit with control of one third of seats to the new legislature guaranteed to the Communist Party). Accordingly, a coalition of western Ukrainian political groups allied themselves loosely under the name *Rukh* ("movement" in Ukrainian) and agitated for the end of one-party rule, the KGB, and exile for political beliefs. Direct elections in March 1990 gave Ukrainian nationalists a portion of seats, and the placid Ukrainian Parliament began to see legitimate opposition for the first time.

By 1991, portions of the Politburo had grown tired of Gorbachev's chaotic liberalism. While Gorbachev was on vacation in Crimea in mid-August, they placed him under house arrest and declared a state emergency. Although the leaders lost their backbone upon the shelling of the Russian Duma, the Ukrainian Communist Party leader, Leonid Kravchuk, saw the writing on the wall. He was convinced that the Ukrainian SSR must face either independence from Moscow or revolution by western nationalists. On August 24, 1991, Kravchuk called a vote for independence, and received near-unanimous consent. A Ukrainian state, albeit under bizarre circumstances, had been born.

INDEPENDENCE, KRAVCHUK, & KUCHMA

Independence seemed to surprise no one so much as the very leaders who supported it. Finally untethered from Russian influence, Galician nationalists discovered that they actually were not particularly popular, with *Rukh* winning only 23 percent of the vote in the first presidential elections in 1991. Little changed in the profile of Ukrainian power players; Kravchuk was elected president in the first presidential election. The new state had no independent currency or banking system, as many Ukrainians' bank coffers were seized by Moscow. Inflation peaked in 1993 at ten thousand percent ensuring Kravchuk's presidential defeat to Leonid Kuchma in 1994. Even today, it has been estimated that Ukraine's GDP sits at about 60 percent of what it was in 1989.

Kuchma's two terms involved extensive corruption, as massive portions of state-controlled plants and factories were sold off in shadowy auctions. Parliamentary delegates tailored state laws to suit their own business interests, which were handsomely rewarded for this self-interested legislating. Even today, the overlap between Ukraine's political class and business elite is striking. Conflicts with Russia died down as Russia accepted the territorial integrity of Ukraine, including the disputed Crimea, in exchange for Ukraine's nuclear arsenal and portions of the Black Sea Fleet, as well as a lease on the port of Sevastopol. Kuchma instituted a new currency, the hryvnia, in 1997, as inflation finally tapered off. Political reforms and economic transparency were not forthcoming, however, and Ukraine missed its chance for European integration along with the rest of the former Communist bloc, much of which joined in 2004.

THE ORANGE REVOLUTION

Natalya Dmitruk is perhaps one of the most famous faces of this peaceful political rebellion. Dmitruk, hired to translate the results of 2004 presidential election to some one hundred thousand deaf viewers for the state-owned UT-1 channel, staged a silent revolt when instead of signing what the presenter was saying she signed "I address all deaf viewers. [Challenger Viktor] Yushchenko is our President. Do not believe the Electoral Commission. They are lying."

In the days following, thousands swarmed (some say upwards of one million) Independence Square in Kyiv, protesting the results of 2004 Ukrainian presidential election. Wearing orange (the color of Victor Yushchenko's Our Ukraine Party) the protesters stayed in the streets for six nights, braving November's freezing temperatures and snow, but staying in a controlled and peaceful mood. They were there to rally against what many viewed as a fraudulent election; marred by voter-intimidation, physical assault and torched ballot boxes. Yushchenko himself had been victim of Dioxin poisoning in September with many protesters speculating that it was done as an attack on his life by his political opponents. When a group of student protestors stormed the Ministry of Education building, they were welcomed with tea and cookies and told to stay inside from the cold. It seemed all of Kyiv was participating in the peaceful demonstrations.

After six days, the parliament declared the election results invalid and ordered a run-off. The final results showed a clear victory for Yushchenko, with 52 percent of the votes, trailed by Yanukovych who had merely 44 percent. On January 23, 2005 Yushchenko, his face still pale and scarred by the Dioxin poisoning, took office.

UKRAINIAN POLITICS TODAY

Unfortunately, the optimism that ran through Maidan in that bitter November faded quickly. Shortly after taking power, the new parliamentary coalition elected Yulia Tymoshenko Prime Minister, but this tenuous coalition soon broke down into infighting over corruption and control of cabinet ministers. In a surprising turn of events, Yushchenko accepted a new coalition led by the "villain" of the Orange Revolution, Victor Yanukovych, in August 2006. The subsequent political upheavals and shifts from Tymoshenko to Yushchenko and back again to Yanukovych have made little difference for Ukrainian welfare, other than postponing needed reforms. The end result of these Byzantine power struggles have been nothing more than good television (fistfights and vegetable-throwing are regular occurrences in the chaotic Verkhovna Rada) and the disillusionment of the masses who gathered for modernization, democracy, and an end to corruption in 2004. In early 2010, Victor Yanukovych soundly defeated Yulia Tymoshenko in a free and fair election. When the Tymoshenko camp called the election fraudulent and refused to inaugurate the new president, no crowds materialized on Maidan to protest the result. Ukraine, still a fledgling, chaotic, and decidedly under-institutionalized democracy, has at least gained the privilege of democratically choosing their bandits in regular elections.

Economy

Ukraine's nickname as the "bread basket of Europe" is far from an allegorical expression. It was the second most important component of the former Soviet Union (behind Russia) as it supplied one quarter of their agricultural produce output. It was also the supplier of most of the milk, meat, grain and produce to the other republics. Ukraine's economy was ranked fifty-third in the world in 2009. Its well-developed industrial base, rich farmlands and solid educational system lend itself well to this emerging free market.

After Ukraine declared its independence, the Ukrainian government liberalized most prices and attempted to initiate a legal framework for privatization of business-es to encourage entrepreneurship. Ukraine also encouraged foreign investment in

Ukraine and open trade, but widespread corruption, complex laws, and poor enforcement of contract laws by courts has stymied direct foreign investment growth. By 2000, Ukraine's economy was on the rise again, but eight straight years of economic downturn has had a significant impact on the population. As of February 2010, 35 percent of Ukraine's population lives below the poverty line. This is most evident in smaller villages where relics of former soviet glory are now simply dilapidated and abandoned factories that lie on the outskirts of town. Because of this, many older Ukrainians lament the fall of the Soviet Union. While life has gotten better for many individuals, it has also gotten worse for some. With communism there was the promise of jobs and an expected level of comfort. Now with the unsteadiness that sometimes comes with an open-market economy, many Ukrainians are wary of their nation's integration into the modern business realm. There is a definite line in Ukraine between those who live in the villages and those that live in the cities.

Ukraine's heavy dependence on Russia for energy supplies also makes it increasingly economically vulnerable. Ukraine depends on imports for about three-fourths of its annual oil and natural gas requirements. Most of their natural gas imports come from Turkmenistan, Russia, Kazakhstan and Uzbekistan where it is delivered via pipelines which are owned and controlled by Gazprom, Russia's state-owned gas monopoly. Ukraine owns the pipelines that reside on its territory and their sale is forbidden in the Ukrainian constitution. However, the complex relationship of supplier, deliverer, and middle-man (as Ukraine delivers Russia's product to Western Europe) puts Ukraine in a political and financial tight spot. In January 2006, Ukraine completed a deal with Russia that doubled the rates it pays for its gas. In past disputes, Russia has cut-off Ukraine gas supplies for a short time to remind Ukraine of its power. In March 2008, Russia decided to significantly reduce its gas supply to Ukraine. And in January 2009, it almost completely cut-off gas for a period of three weeks.

By 1999, Ukraine had fallen to less than 40 percent of its output from 1991 levels. In 2000, it experienced a surge of economic growth and expansion but by 2008 a rapid halt to economic growth occurred caused by a lack of global demand for steel exports. In October 2008, a rapid devaluation took place with the hryvnia dropping 38.4 percent from 4.85UAH to every 1 U.S. dollar on September 23rd, to 7.88UAH to every 1 U.S. dollar on December 19th. Ukraine's economy then shrank 15 percent in 2009, making it the worst contraction in fifteen years.

The International Monetary Fund bailed out Ukraine with a 16.4 billion dollar loan and the World Bank also committed over five billion dollars in loans. Ukraine's Central Bank attempted to pacify the nerves of Ukrainians, pointing to the 4.5 percent growth of the second-quarter in 2009 as signs that the economy was improving. However, many analysts point to Ukraine's dependence on steel (a relic of soviet times) as an ongoing weakness and stress that structural reforms must take place or Ukraine's economy will forever be tied with the going rate for metals. Steel is seen as an increasingly bad commodity, as every time there is a global financial crunch, people stop buying houses and cars and therefore demand wanes.

This economic meltdown occurred as the 2010 presidential elections were taking place. Many people were wary of current President Viktor Yanukovych as many of his supporters and donations came from the steel-laden East, and therefore the likelihood of him initiating reforms seemed slim.

Ukraine's economy is expected to make a turn for the better this year with the World Bank and the IMF estimating growth rates from 2.6 to 2.7 percent.

Politics

Ukraine is a semi-presidential representative democratic republic, with executive powers exercised by the Cabinet and legislative powers entrusted in the parliament. Currently (August 2010) the President is Victor Yanukovych and the Prime Minister is Mykola Yanovych.

Ukraine's multi-party system ensures that one political party cannot gain complete power, and parties must work together to form a coalition government. The result is a literal onslaught of various parties, many of which are so obscure they join up with other parties to ratify their voices. As of July 2010 the Kyiv Post reported 182 political parties registered in Ukraine. The ones most often heard about are Party of Regions (*Партія регіонів)*, which is viewed as having a pro-Russian stance; Bloc Yuliya Tymoshenko (*Блок Юлії Тимошенко)*, which collaborates greatly with the Ukrainian Social Democratic Party; and the Our Ukraine party (Наша Україна), which rallied greatly behind former President Viktor Yushchenko.

Ukraine's President is elected by popular vote for one five-year term. The President then nominates the Prime Mister who must be confirmed by Parliament (the Verkhovna Rada).

UKRAINE & NATO

The North Atlantic Treaty Organization (NATO) and Ukraine have been in discussions since 1995. In January 2008 Ukraine was declared as a candidate to join the NATO Membership Action Plan (MAP) and NATO intended to provide assistance to Ukraine to implement the reforms necessary to accede into the MAP. However, Ukraine's involvement with NATO has been downgraded drastically since

So You Want to Talk Politics in Ukraine?

Unlike America, Ukrainian political disagreements do not have their genesis in morality arguments. Ukrainians generally agree, or simply do not bother to care, about such things as religion, abortion, gay marriage or other things so frequently debated in the West. In Ukraine, most political arguments are likely to arise from issues such as possibly joining the EU, their stance on NATO, a national language, or relations with Russia. Some would even argue that without geographical arguments, or language disagreements, there would be no such thing as politics in Ukraine.

the 2010 Presidential Elections. On June 3rd 2010, Ukrainian Parliament excluded the goal of "integration into Euro-Atlantic security and NATO membership." Many people see this as an example of President Yanukovych's close relationship with Russia, as former Russian President Vladimir Putin is fiercely opposed to any eastward expansion of NATO. In fact, in 2008 Russia threatened to point its missiles at Ukraine if they joined NATO and accepted the deployment of a U.S. missile defense shield on Ukrainian soil.

UKRAINE & THE EUROPEAN UNION

According to the Kyiv Post, 53 percent of those 16 years and older favor Ukraine joining the European Union. Not surprisingly, the most supportive regions were Central and Western Ukraine. In 2008 approval was reached to start negotiations on an EU-Ukraine Association Agreement. The EU believes that this Association Agreement will significantly strengthen ties with Ukraine. A solid relationship with Ukraine is of great importance to the EU as 20 percent of the EU's gas consumption is routed to the EU via Ukraine. Also 80 percent of the gas supplied to the EU from Russia is routed through Ukraine; making Ukraine the backbone of gas supplied to Europe. However, this may change in the future as Russia plans to construct new pipelines that will circumnavigate Ukraine.

Religion

Like language, Ukraine can be divided into sections based on religious beliefs. The majority of Ukrainians practice Eastern Orthodoxy. Most adherents of Ukrainian Orthodoxy live in Eastern and Central Ukraine. In Western Ukraine, the Ukrainian Greek Catholic Church prevails. In Crimea, Islam is the minority religion. Sprinkled throughout Ukraine are communities – most notably in Odessa and Uman – where Judaism is highly observed as well. One in ten Ukrainians are not religious, which isn't uncommon in former Soviet states where atheism was once governmentally imposed.

CHRISTIANITY

As with most European countries, Ukraine originally practiced pagan traditions and idol worshipping. Christianity wasn't accepted into the region until 988 AD when Prince Vladimir the Great instated it as the state religion of Kievan Rus'. Vladimir ordered mass baptisms in the Dnieper River and his followers, having to conform to a new religious order, incorporated pagan traditions into their new Christian ones. Many Eastern European Christian traditions, such as the intricately decorated *pysanky*, have their origins in pre-Christian Ukraine.

> After the Great Schism, in 1054, most of Ukraine that was incorporated by Kievan Rus', found itself on the Eastern Orthodox side of the divided Christian world.

When the Union of Lublin, which created a state called The Polish-Lithuanian Commonwealth, was signed in 1569, an acceleration of the Polinization of the Ukrainian church occurred. This was done by levying high taxes on the Orthodox churches and making them susceptible to legal obligations, both of which could be ignored by the Roman Catholic Church. Furthermore, the building of new Orthodox churches was highly discouraged by the government and conversion to Orthodoxy by Roman Catholics was outlawed. Orthodox individuals were also barred from holding high-offices and marriages between the two sects were looked down upon. Because of the persecution and discrimination that they faced, many Orthodox believers fled to the Tsardom of Russia during this time.

As the Polinization of the empire continued, the increasing agitation led to the Khmelnytskyi Uprising of 1648-1657 (see Khmelnytskyi Uprising page 13). The Cossacks targeted all non-Orthodox believers such a Catholics and Jews during their raids which sought to restore their religious freedoms and traditions. The domination of Orthodoxy was again reestablished in Ukraine.

In Ukraine it's worthwhile to notice how the cathedrals and churches change depending on what region you are in. In a country with such a charged history of power struggles and shifting governments, one can tell a city's political past by which churches are present within it.

JUDAISM

Jewish settlements in Ukraine can be traced back to the eighth century. During this time, the Jewish population lived on the banks of the Dnieper River and in the south of Ukraine. Jewish refugees from the Persian and Mesopotamia regions fleeing from Christian persecution came to this area because the Khazar people, who ruled at that time, allowed them to practice their religion in relative peace.

In 1241 the Khazans, and all of Poland, were devastated by the Mongol invasion. In an effort to rebuild and defend its cities, Poland began recruiting men from the West, promising aid and settlements in new towns in return for their service. German Jews, many of whom were victims of the Christian crusades and the Black Death, immigrated to Poland. It was during this time that Yiddish, a combination of Middle German, Polish, and German-Hebrew, was created and implemented as a way for Ukrainian, Polish and German Jews to communicate with one another.

Later, Jews from the western provinces of Poland moved to Ukraine as the economic opportunities created by the Polish-Lithuanian Commonwealth blossomed. By the end of fifteenth century, Jews lived in more than sixty cities and towns across the country.

However, anti-Semitism began to flourish as Jews became increasingly prosperous. When the Cossacks revolted against their Polish landowners in the Khmelnytskyi Uprisings, they also targeted Jews who they saw as supporting members of the oppressive government. It is estimated that upwards of one hundred thousand Jews and three hundred Jewish communities were destroyed during "The Deluge." This anti-Semitic trend continued as the country experienced governmental reform. By the October 1917 Revolution, more than three hundred thousand Jews had left Ukraine for other parts of the Soviet Union. During World War II, parts of the Ukrainian population collaborated with the Nazis with eradicating the Jews from occupied Ukraine.

In 1989 a Soviet Census counted nearly five hundred thousand Jews living in Ukraine. In 2005, the population had disintegrated down to eighty thousand; mostly due to mass relocations after the collapse of the Soviet Union.

Currently, Jewish life is on the upswing in Ukraine. The state now recognizes Jewish cultural and religious institutions including fourteen Jewish Day Schools and seventy Hebrew schools. In 2005, the Egie Kapie synagogue in Yevpatoriya, Crimea was reconstructed and rededicated as a Reform Temple decades after it was closed by the Communist Party. But while Judaism has recently experienced a resurgence in the region, anti-Semitism is still an ongoing problem – one that shouldn't be too readily dismissed.

ISLAM

Muslim settlements in Ukraine are predominately concentrated in its southern half, although there were Lipka Tatars colonies in other regions like Volhynia and Podolia.

The Crimean Tatars established the Crimean Khanate in Crimea during the fifteenth century. The Tatars, being the descendants of Turkic and non-Turkic people, had settled in the area around the seventh century and Bakhchisarai was their capital. Through the fifteenth and into the eighteenth century, the Tatars frequently raided Eastern-European lands bringing back slaves, most of which were Ukrainian, to the area. It is estimated that they enslaved roughly three million people during this time.

In the eighteenth century Russia conquered the area and forced out over one hundred and fifty thousand Tatars. During this time, there were over eighteen mosques in the capital.

Crimean Muslims were once again subjected to deportation in 1944 when Stalin accused them of collaborating with the Germans during World War II. This false accusation gave him the credence needed to commit ethnocide as an estimated 45 percent of the two hundred thousand Crimean Muslims perished after their relocation to Uzbekistan, Kazakhstan and other parts of the Russian SFSR. The land they left behind was sequestered by the Russians who took over settlement of the area with the help of Soviet authorities. The charges against them were lifted in 1967 by a Soviet decree, but nothing was done to aid them in reclaiming the land that was wrongfully taken from them. Restitution wasn't attempted until 1989 when Crimean Tatars were allowed back on their homelands.

After Ukraine declared independence in 1991, more Crimean Tatars have returned to the area. In Crimea, Muslims make up 12 percent of the population, and throughout Ukraine they are present in more than three hundred communities. Currently there are over one hundred and fifty mosques in Ukraine with the most well known being in Donetsk, Bakhchisarai, and Mariupol (see Tatar sidebar, Crimean Section, page""").

Language

The Ukrainian language is a part of the Eastern-Slavic subgroup of the Slavic Languages. It is the official state language of Ukraine. A 2001 census puts 87.8 percent of the population able to communicate in Ukrainian. Admittedly, depending on what part of the country you are traveling in, you might hear more Russian than Ukrainian. In Crimea, Russian is primarily spoken, but Ukrainian can be understood, if somewhat humorously by locals.

In Central Ukraine and in eastern parts, Ukrainian has been blended with Russian to make "*Surzhyk*," the Spanglish of the East. In the villages of western Ukraine and in larger western cities like Lviv, clean Ukrainian is heavily enforced by patriotic locals selling shirts that translate to "Thank God I'm Not a Moscovite!" and driving buses that have "Here We Speak UKRAINIAN!" stickers on them. It's not a coincidence that the language you speak has a political connotation to it.

Unlike many countries, Ukraine hasn't been inflicted with globalization to the point where it's easy for visitors to get by on English alone. While some younger students might take pity on you, generally you will be met with a blank stare when rattling off English. If you don't speak Russian or Ukrainian, be sure to bring a great phrase book with you and learn the Cyrillic alphabet. And never underestimate the value of great pantomime skills.

"The Most Melodious Language in the World"

You will undoubtedly hear, as you travel throughout Ukraine, Ukrainians proclaiming their language to be "the most beautiful language in the world." They back this up with one lone, often cited but oddly enigmatic study done in Paris in 1934. Ukrainian supposedly won second in "the most melodic" category behind Italian and third for the overall most beautiful language behind French and Persian. So get ready, because when you are asked what you think of Ukrainian, it's usually just a set-up so they can cite this study.

THE DEVELOPMENT OF UKRAINIAN

Until the end of the eighteenth century, written Ukrainian varied greatly from spoken Ukrainian. Because of this, it's very hard to trace its origins throughout history.

Various hypotheses exist as to why Ukrainian developed apart from Russian. One of the earliest hailed from Mikhail Lomonosov in the middle of the eighteenth century. Lomonosov proposed what has become known as the "Polinization" theory which attempts to explain the differences between Ukrainian and Russian on the influence of the Polish language between the thirteenth and seventieth centuries. Believers in this theory point to Ukrainian words that were borrowed from Polish. For instance, the Ukrainian words *zavzhdy* (always, from Polish *zawsze)* and *obitsiaty* (to promise, from Polish *obiecac*). However convenient this theory is, it is generally dismissed by modern linguists citing that the most characteristic features of modern Ukrainian are found in neither Polish nor Russian. Furthermore, all Slavic languages tend to share a comparable vocabulary, so alluding to their similarities is not proof enough.

The most common consensus is that there was a common Eastern-Slavic language which somehow evolved over time to form Belarusian, Ukrainian and Russian. The period in which these developed are still heavily debated. Some surmise Ukrainian language's genesis dates back to the time of Kievan Rus' (ninth to thirteenth century) while Russian theorists favor the belief that the language from that time was the beginning of "Old Russian."

What is known is that during the thirteenth century, southwestern areas of Rus' (including Kyiv) were integrated into the Grand Duchy of Lithuania where Old Ukrainian (also known as Ruthenian and East Slavonic) was recognized as the official language.

In 1569 the Polish-Lithuanian Commonwealth was formed. During this time, many Ukrainians adopted Catholicism and language became associated with religion: Catholics spoke Polish and Orthodox individuals spoke East Slavonic. The developing Ukrainian language flourished during this time with the opening of Kyiv-Mohyla University. However, the assimilation by the upper-classes into the culture of Poland alienated lower-class individuals and created distinctive cultural differences between upper-class and lower-class Ukrainians.

Cultural and religious distinctions led to the Khmelnytsky Uprising (see page 13). In the aftermath, Ukrainians were again subjugated to heed the orders of whoever held power over their territory. Kyiv-Mohyla University was now under control of the Russian Empire and most Ukrainian schools were closed or under Polish or Russian jurisdiction.

The development of the Ukrainian language became threatened. It was, however, not lost. In the 1830s, the Brotherhood of Saints Cyril and Methodius was formed, among which Ukrainian poet Taras Shevchenko (see Literature, page 34) was thought to be a member. The Brotherhood believed that a federation of Slav people should include Ukrainians. The group, and its ideas, was suppressed by the authorities and its members subsequently went into exile. However, many writers during this time purposefully constructed their stories in clean Ukrainian to demonstrate that it wasn't merely the "little Russian language," but one capable of conveying artistic and cultural ideas. Soon, the Russian Empire became threatened by these self-aware expressions, fearful that this burgeoning growth of individuality could threaten the solidarity of the Empire. Expressions of Ukrainian culture and literature were persecuted and in 1863 Tsarist Interior Minister Pyotr Valuyev proclaimed "there never has been, is not, and never can be, a separate Little Russian language." The tyrannical assault on Ukrainian culture escalated in 1878 when Alexander II issued the *Ems Ukase,* a secret decree which banned the use of the Ukrainian language and outlawed Ukrainian publications. During this time, the development of Ukrainian culture and language practically ceased.

The ban was never fully lifted, but it was voided after the February Revolution in 1918, in which many other imperial laws were also lifted. With the collapse of Austro-Hungary in 1918, "Little Russians," were now ready to initiate a Ukrainian language education system and Ukrainian was accepted as a language in its own right.

Of course, Ukrainian would have to struggle through the onslaught raged against it by Stalinism, the Great Purge and the Great Famine until Ukraine could amass its Independence in 1991. With such vast historic challenges against it, it should be no surprise then why so many Ukrainians adamantly state that they speak Ukrainian and not Russian. While locals will speak a mixture of the two, outsiders should be aware that the language one chooses to speak does have political connotations and should respect that Russian and Ukrainian are two vastly different languages.

Culture, Etiquette, & Faux Pas

Ukrainians will spend their last dime cooking you a welcome dinner! But they'll also cut you in line at the bus stop and ignore you in their shops. Patience is a virtue that can't be stressed enough in Ukraine.

CULTURAL NORMS

Ukraine observes some customs and protocol that might seem very peculiar to a foreigner. Generally when a visitor "breaks" one of these traditional behaviors they are gently informed that that's not how it's done in Ukraine. Of course the best thing is to know in advance so you don't embarrass yourself.

Shaking Hands....
Feminists may have a hard time accepting this one, but in Ukraine men and women generally do not shake hands. In business situations it is not uncommon for men to go around the table shaking other men's hands, but when they reach a woman, pass over her. This is not a diss! Just an engrained cultural rule that is almost impossible to banish. If you're a woman and doing business in Ukraine and you want to assert yourself, then offer a handshake, but don't be surprised if you get a few odd looks.

With Your Gloves On
In Ukraine it is considered incredibly rude to shake someone's hands with your gloves on. Women are sometimes granted a pardon on this one because of their "sensitivity to cold," but men should always remove their gloves when shaking hands. To not do so is considered a sign of disrespect.

Over the Threshold: If you're going to a Ukrainian's house do not greet them over the threshold. Ukrainians believe that to kiss, hug, or shake hands over the threshold of a door is bad luck, so they will wait until you are inside to do this.

Slipper Time

When entering a Ukrainian's home remove your shoes (Ukrainians generally have a front parlor or room where shoes are left) and put on slippers (тапочки, *tapochky)* which your host is likely to provide.

Flowers

Ukrainians love giving flowers and generally use any excuse to do so. However, the notion of "a dozen roses" doesn't fly in Ukraine as even numbers are only given to convey condolences (generally at funerals). Bouquets in odd numbers are the only flowers given to living individuals in happy situations and this is observed with gusto. If you try to buy a half dozen flowers, don't be surprised if the flower vendor absolutely refuses to sell it to you, or asks who died. Also be wary of giving yellow flowers to a lover as this conveys that the love-affair is over!

Carrying Things

Ukrainian men never allow Ukrainian women to carry *anything*. If you're a man and find yourself with a Ukrainian woman that you know, and you have not offered to carry her things, don't be surprised if another woman approaches you to berate you. It is not uncommon for an elderly woman, commonly referred to in Ukraine as a *babushka (baba),* to cross roads to smack a non-obliging boy over the head before giving him the girl's bag. They will literally beat this idea into men's heads.

Ukrainians also consider it very tacky to carry things (books, folders, food) in their hands. This just "doesn't look nice." Don't be surprised if someone is insistent you put your books or folders into a plastic bag to carry instead.

Appearance is Everything

In Ukraine there is no such thing as running out of the house in the morning in a zip up jacket and sweatpants. Ukrainians would never do this. It is of utmost importance to always look presentable in public. For this reason, do not be surprised if you are

---

Ukrainian Clubs

Dance clubs in Ukraine are in nearly every major city or small town. In Kyiv, these can be monolithic venues that boast expensive covers and outrageous drink prices. Generally every "good" dance club will have what would be deemed a strip show in the West. Don't be surprised if you are dancing and then suddenly told to clear the dance floor so a costumed girl (usually dressed as a hyper-sexualized fairy tale character) can perform a risqué choreographed dance. Some or all clothes are removed and occasionally a male member of the dance club will be pulled on stage to partake in an impromptu lap dance. Then the music comes back on and everyone goes back to dancing. If you go to a club, and this does not happen, then it wasn't a very "good" club.

"comfortably" dressed and given a few odd looks. They are judging you.

If living or working in Ukraine, pay attention to the cleanliness of your shoes; Ukrainians shine their shoes daily and if you are working in a professional environment, they will expect you to do the same. Many Ukrainians keep an extra set of clean and shined shoes at work that they change into after their morning commute.

Looking good in Ukraine's largest and best night clubs is a must. Clubs in larger cities enforce strict "face control" so if you plan on going to any of these nightspots (see "Ukrainian Clubs" box on page 30) it's very important that you bring a nice outfit and great shoes as they will not let you in without the right dress (i.e. no jeans and no sneakers). Sometimes being a foreigner is enough to get you in without the right dress, but the best ones hold fast to their rules.

Women's Clothing

Ukrainians pride themselves on personal appearance and are very upfront with the fact that their country is known for having "the most beautiful women in the world." In Ukraine sexuality is not such a taboo subject as it is in the West. Ukrainian women embrace their bodies and show them off. It's not uncommon for young girls to wear what would be deemed risqué outfits in front of their family or to school. And professional women in Ukraine sometimes don outfits that would be considered inappropriate business attire in the West. Don't make assumptions about a woman because of her dress.

SUPERSTITIONS

Ukraine is perhaps best appreciated through its slightly bizarre beliefs. You'll soon grow tired of trying to convince Ukrainians otherwise. It's simply best to smile and nod and join in on implementing these practices into your everyday life in Ukraine.

Sitting on Cold Concrete

In Ukraine, you'll observe that outside seating is not that plentiful; especially at bus stops. Thus you'll see amazing displays of dexterity performed by men of all ages in various squatting positions. Women will never do this, nor will they sit if a stoop is available. Why? Because if a woman sits on cold concrete, their ovaries will freeze. The truth in this is undeniable to Ukrainians and worrisome *babas* will rush to shoo women off railings and concrete platforms. Keep this in mind if you're waiting for a bus and considering sitting on the ground or the stoop of some stairs. Think of your future children!

Sitting on the Corner of Tables

If you're an unmarried woman, don't be surprised if the whole table moves around so you can sit in the middle. Ukrainians consider it unlucky for unmarried women to sit at the corners of tables. The theory is they will never get married; which in Ukraine is one of the saddest things imaginable.

The Draft

In the summertime, it can be swelteringly hot on buses and trains and sweet relief is just a rise of a windowsill away. Yet, Ukrainians will sit there with sweat beading down their faces, and perspiration fogging up the windows and refuse to open the windows. If you're brave enough to attempt a mere crack, the window will be forcefully closed seconds later by an insistent *baba* who claims you want to kill everyone on the bus, train or trolley. The reason for this is Ukrainian's "fear of the draft." A windy draft is blamed for countless deaths a year and this evil force is fought off by never opening a window…ever. Even in the summertime. Bringing a battery-operated mini fan with you may not be such a ridiculous thought after all.

Whistling

To whistle in Ukraine, in a covered place, is a foolhardy activity that only solidifies your economic fate. Ukrainians believe that whistling indoors ensures that your money goes "flying out the window," and you also endanger those around you to experience the same bad luck. So whistle at your own peril and only while alone.

From Those in the Know - The Chill

"You may want to wait a while, the bus will be hot." My Ukrainian colleague advised me as I stood outside the bus station.

Ten minutes before it was scheduled to depart, I climbed in anyway and immediately recognized the depth of my misjudgment. With each step, I moved further into the steam box which contained passengers in various states of consciousness sitting motionless in the collective bus sauna as it gradually warmed in the direct sun. I surveyed my surroundings: all windows shut.

The bus filled up and then filled up more. People crowed into the aisle and into each other until the collective mass of passengers prevented the door from completely closing. And then we were off. As the bus poked out of the station, I felt the first breeze of air. But the relief was short lived. A woman, by all appearances in solid frame of mind, turned to the man across of the aisle from her and murmured something to him. The colorless man, who was likely suffering from advanced heat stroke, obediently closed the window and sealed us in.

I looked frantically at my neighbors for the outcry but the only movement in response came from the twenty-something next to me who pulled out a napkin to stop the stream of sweat threatening to short-circuit his iPod. The next twenty minutes were spent in the haze of back and forth between passengers over "The Chill." The Chill, I later learned, is a sickness that one can catch in Ukraine with cool breezes, even in desperately hot times.

It took me many months to slow down and accept this cultural antagonistic relationship towards wind. Fresh air just always seemed preferable to stuffy recycled hot air. And though I never truly embraced closed confined hot spaces, sometimes, when I find myself on an ice-cold air-conditioned bus squealing along the streets of New York City, I have to ask, "Can't this thing be turned down? Someone's gonna catch a cold in here."

- Danielle Kuczkowski

Dining

Like any culture where social activities tend to happen around the kitchen table, Ukraine has developed all sorts of superstitions that revolve around utensils. When dining, if you drop a fork, someone hungry is coming from the direction the fork is pointing towards. If you drop a knife, someone angry is coming from the direction the knife is pointing towards. Dropping a spoon, however, is good news as that means someone happy is coming from that direction.

When you're drinking with Ukrainians, the amount of bottles consumed can reach staggering amounts. You'll notice that after every last pour of a bottle, the bottle is then promptly placed on the floor. Some Ukrainians will also make a wish by blowing into the bottle before placing it on the floor. But the rule is always the same: empty bottles are never allowed on the table.

Body

If you're right palm suddenly starts itching, Ukrainians will tell you that you will soon meet a friend. If it's your left palm, you'll soon receive some money. If you sneeze, whatever was said right before that is true.

Getting Dressed

When getting dressed, if you accidentally put something on inside out, then you must take it off and step on it three times to reverse the bad luck (I've heard of this, but few people have actually witnessed this amazing belief).

Crossing the road...

Like Americans, Ukrainians believe that it is bad luck for a black cat to cross in front of you. However, Ukrainians also believe if someone with an empty bucket (and

When You Smile

Looking back through all my photos taken throughout Ukraine, its easy to spot the non-Ukrainian – they're the ones smiling. Birthday parties, school openings, family portraits... the Soviet faces remain the same; serious with a resigned look about them.

I used to think it was odd and frustrating. Accidentally making eye-contact with someone in the metro I would have to force myself to look away and not, by instinct alone, flash a smile.

In Ukraine you have to earn a smile, earn the trust needed to open up to someone and let your guard down. My friend Natasha would always ask "why do you lie? Whenever someone ask you how your day was, you always say 'good,' even when it was bad. Why?" When I would reply its because I thought it was the "nice" thing to do she would explain "here we don't ask if we don't want to know. They really want to know how it was: good or bad. We don't ask, simply to ask."

So perhaps Westerners do smile too much. I smile to the postman, the grocery-store lady, the guy that just cut me off in traffic. Smile, smile, smile. In Ukraine, they'd think that was creepy, and maybe it is. Think about: A Ukrainian coming to America and wandering through the airport; greeted by all these creepy foreigners just beaming away at them for no reason. Terrifying.

So when you come to Ukraine, try and get your "metro, serious face" on and save the smiles for the people who've earned them.

people wielding buckets are plentiful in Ukraine, so this happens often) crosses in front of you, you will lose money. If the bucket is full however, you will gain money.

Stepping...

Stepping over someone (like a child lying on the ground) makes them stop growing unless you step back over them. Stepping on dog poo in the road is good luck – dog poo is everywhere in Ukraine so your chances of getting some extra luck are very good!

Music, Art, & Literature

MUSIC

Ukrainian music is heavily influenced by the unique mix of ethnic groups that surround Ukraine. Recently the Kobza (a gut-strung, hollowed body instrument similar to a lute) has begun a resurgence. This instrument was traditionally played by the Kobzari. Their repertoire dates back to the seventieth century when their songs depicted the struggles of the Kozacks under various foreign oppressors.

> At the beginning of the nineteenth century, the *Kobzari* formed guilds or brotherhoods. Three-year apprenticeships were developed and then final exams were given to officially become a *kobzar*.

During the Soviet era, almost all the Kobzari perished under Stalin's "purge" of ethnic minorities. Even their instruments, like the Kobza, became illegal and were confiscated and destroyed. In 1991, the Kobzar Guild was reestablished in Ukraine with hopes of fostering the tradition again.

In the Carpathians, the Hutsuls are known for their use of the Trembita (a wooden alpine horn) as a signaling device to announce deaths, weddings and funerals. They also implemented the use of flutes into much of their traditional music. Ruslana Lyzhichko won the Eurovision 2004 competition with her song "Wild Dances" that was heavily influenced by this ethnic style of music. Following her performance, the country went a little mad for Ruslana thus making the Trembita more popular than ever.

Pop-music is the current fad, with the airwaves overtaken by the latest imports from Britain and America. Artists from Russia are also popular in Ukraine, but recently a new wave of artists that sing in "clean Ukrainian" has emerged. The most popular Ukrainian group is Okean Elzy (check out their album "Gloria").

Verka Serduchka might be the most easily recognizable Ukrainian superstar as this pudgy, short, cross-dressing singer likes to wear giant sequined stars on his head. Foreigners generally don't get Verka Serduchka, as evident by his defeat at the 2007 Eurovision.

LITERATURE

Literature is a highly respected art form in Ukraine. Traditionally, oral literature, such as the Cossack's epic songs, were passed down through generations by specific retellings. Eventually they were committed to paper. Because of this, many old Ukrainian legends and characters are still a mainstay in Ukrainian plots.

In 1574, the first Ukrainian textbook was printed by Ivan Fyoderov. He also produced the first Church Slavonic Bible as well as the first printed Russian calendar and poem. Born in Moscow, Fyoderov studied in Krakow and when he was asked to retire to a farm, he declined saying he was "better at sowing words than seeds." He died in Lviv in 1573 and was buried at Onufriev Monastery. His gravestone read "printer of books not seen before." A statue of Ivan Fedorov now stands along the street named after him in Lviv. A used book market sets up there daily (see page 111).

Ivan Kotlyarevsky (1769-1838) is regarded as the pioneer of modern Ukrainian literature. He penned *Eneyida* which is considered to be the first literary work published entirely in the modern Ukrainian language. Although Ukrainian was the everyday language of many people, it was discouraged in its use by Imperial Russia. *Eneyida* parodied Virgil's *Aeneid* by transforming the original Trojan heroes into Ukrainian Zaporozhian Cossacks.

Taras Shevchenko (1814-1861) is Ukraine's most revered national poet, artist and practitioner of humanism. Born into a serf family and orphaned when he was eleven years old, he was taught to read by his village's precentor. A Russian aristocrat, Lord Pavel Engelhardt, took him to St. Petersburg and there noticed his artistic talent. He brought him into the artistic underbelly of the city, through which he became acquainted with one of the empire's most revered artists, Karl Briullov.

Shevchenko made many trips back to Ukraine after his first successes, among which was his critically acclaimed first book of poems *Kobzar* in 1840. The hardships under which the Ukrainian peasantry lived had a significant impact on the young artist. He began to talk with other intellectuals about politically liberalizing the empire and recognizing the rights of the lower-classes.

During this time he penned a poem which was seen as inflammatory (denigrating the Tsar's wife and criticizing imperial rule). To make things worse, the poem, "The Dream," that had caused the snub was written in Ukrainian; a language that had been heavily discouraged in its use.

Shevchenko was exiled into the Russian military Orrenburg garrison, near the Ural Mountains. The Tsar commanded that he be heavily watched and not allowed to paint or write. In 1857, Shevchenko returned from exile with plans of moving to Ukraine, however he was ordered to return to St. Petersburg. In 1861 he fell victim to an illness, which proved to be too much to overcome after the hardships of his exile. He died in St. Petersburg on March 10, 1861 – the day after his forty-seventh birthday and just seven days before the Emancipation of the Serfs was announced. He's now buried in Kaniv, Ukraine in what is now known as Taras Hill.

Taras Shevchenko's legacy continues. An iconic symbol in Ukraine, his portrait is currently on the 100 hryvnia note. There's also a metro and university named after him in Kyiv, and statues and monuments to him are erected all across the country. So if Ukrainians are aghast when you ask them who he is, now you know why.

ARTS &CRAFTS

On the zigzagged street of Andreevsky Spusk in Kyiv and amidst the bustle of Market Square in Lviv, you'll see vendors selling brightly colored eggs and embroidered cloths of all sorts. These two crafts, the former known as *Pysanka* and the latter known as *Rushnyky*, are the oldest traditional crafts in Ukraine.

Pysanka

Pysanka (plural: *Pysanky*) are ornamental eggs, traditionally made during the weeks before Easter, that are decorated using a wax-resist method in traditional Ukrainian designs. Traditionally, real eggs were used and in most homes this tradition continues. However, in the markets and stores most foreigners will come across wooden variations as they travel better than their fragile counterparts.

Some date this folk art back to the pre-Christian era, when eggs were associated with the rebirth of the earth after winter and the arrival of spring. When Christianity was adopted into the region, this tradition (like most pre-Christian traditions) became an integral part of the Easter service. Ukrainians now make the infamous red dyed eggs, elaborately decorated, in the forty days leading up to Easter when they are taken to the church to be blessed by the priest. This practice was later banished by the Soviet regime as it was a Ukrainian tradition and, furthermore, a religious one. It was only saved by brave community members who carried on the tradition in secret and those who fled the country, carrying the tradition with them overseas. Since Ukraine declared its independence, this art form has again flourished. It's impossible to attend a craft market or walk anywhere around Easter and not come across this fragile art form.

Ukrainian Embroidery, *Vyshyvka*

The national garb of Ukraine is a heavily embroidered costume consisting of a white tunic with intricate red patterns. Excavations of sites in Ukraine from the first century AD have produced embroidered clothing and in Kyiv, at St. Sophia, there are eleventh century examples of this on tapestries. Some locals claim that they can tell which part of the country an item was embroidered in depending on the stitch and design used. Apart from the traditional dress, embroidery is most seen on *Rushnyky*, a highly ornamental and decorated towel. These towels are used as the base for the bread in the Bread and Salt greeting (see "Bread and Salt" on page 53) as well as used to decorate the pictures of religious icons that some have hanging in their houses. During a wedding ceremony, a bride will drag a *pidnozhnyk* behind her while her bridesmaids follow. The idea being that they will soon follow in her footsteps and become married.

Special Considerations

Ukraine, like any country that has recently undergone a radical political change, has some unpleasant issues. Most of these have been addressed by the government in an attempt to initiate positive change. But change, like most things in Ukraine, is painfully slow and one often has to remind themselves that an unbelievable amount of patience must be exercised in this country where "in due time," seems to be the mantra.

DRUGS AND HIV/AIDS

Situated at the crossroads of Asian suppliers, and European consumers, Ukraine's Black Sea port of Odessa has become the entry-point for illicit drugs into the country. The trafficking of drugs into the area has compounded political and economic problems and escalated the HIV/AIDS problem in Ukraine. UNAIDS estimates that there are currently six hundred thousand injecting drug users in Ukraine.

In 2002, Ukraine registered the highest and fastest growing HIV rates in all of Eastern Europe with an estimated 1.6 percent of the adult population being HIV positive. The epidemic afflicts mostly intravenous drug users and their partners, sex workers and, by a much lesser but growing extent, young people who practice unsafe sex.

Currently, the epidemic is being addressed by the government. A rising number of HIV drug reduction centers have opened throughout Ukraine and in 2006 the government approved the methadone-based opioid substitution therapy for injecting drug users. Organizations such as Alliance, UNICEF and Peace Corps currently lead projects and initiatives throughout the country to combat this epidemic and spread lifesaving information. It is estimated that only 44 percent of Ukraine's population have correct information about HIV prevention and how it can be spread.

Because of the HIV/AIDS situation in Ukraine, it is of paramount importance to diligently exercise caution when engaging in sexual activities. If you are planning to be sexually active during your stay, make sure to bring condoms and practice only safe sex.

HUMAN TRAFFICKING

Ukraine is currently on the U.S. State Department's Tier Two Watch List, meaning that it is does not fully comply with the minimum standards for the elimination of trafficking but is making a significant effort to do so. More people from Ukraine have been trafficked abroad than from any other former communist country.

Approximately 117,000 Ukrainians have been forced into exploitive labor abroad since the Soviet breakup. An estimated 48 percent of these victims are women and children that are forced into the commercial sex industry.

Ukrainian authorities site low salaries and high rates of unemployment as the reasons for its increased vulnerability amongst citizens to be victims of human trafficking. Generally, trafficking groups have liaisons that work in smaller communities and towns (i.e. poorer economic regions within Ukraine) where they work to lure young women (or men, or children) with "promising job opportunities" overseas. Often times they win over their trust by "lending" them money for visas and travel arrangements which they can "pay back later." When the victim leaves their town and reaches their destination across the border, typically their documents are seized and they are brought to their new "home" which often houses other victims. What happens next depends on the situation.

Women are often told that to get their documents back they must "earn them" by working in the commercial sex industry. Men are victims of slave labor – often forced into working in the commercial fishing industry, or in construction for little or no pay – and children are often initiated into begging rackets abroad.

Common destinations include Israel, Turkey, Japan, Germany, Greece, Russia, and the United States. The Office for Democratic Institutions and Human Rights (ODIHR), U.S. Association for International Migration (USAIM), and the International Organization for Migration (IOM) all have programs and hotlines that are currently combating this problem in Ukraine by disseminating information and providing aid for victims. In 2007, the Ukrainian government began broadcasting public service announcements warning citizens to exercise caution when regarding overseas job opportunities.

ENVIRONMENTAL CONCERNS

Ukraine is perhaps most infamously known for its Chernobyl disaster in which one-tenth of Ukraine's land was affected by the resulting radiation. According to the UN, approximately one million people were exposed to unsafe radiation levels through food contamination. Construction for a new shelter around the "sarcophagus" – the concrete shell that was hastily built around the damaged reactor after the explosion – has begun with the goal of a 2012 completion.

For visitors looking for a better understanding of what happened at Chernobyl and the aftermath, be sure to visit the Chernobyl Museum in Kyiv (page 78). For thrill seekers, check out Chernobyl Tours (page 96).

Fear of exposure to radiation is not something that should deter travelers. Radiation levels are continuously monitored, and the Ukrainian government has a highly effective program for monitoring the fresh foods and meats sold in grocery store. Visitors should, however, be wary of berries, mushrooms and wild game as these generally have higher levels of radiation absorption and should not be purchased on the street.

Pollution from other sources is a big concern in the country, too. Ukraine releases organic compounds, polluted water, heavy metal and oil-related pollutants into the Black Sea. Air quality is also a problem in the East due to carbon-monoxide emissions from the many factories. Ukraine has established a Ministry of the Environment which has enacted a pollution fee system, the revenue of which is supposed to be channeled into environmental protection activities. The system is supposed to impose taxes on air and water pollution as well as waste disposal. While enforcement of these penalties has been lax, it is gradually improving.

If interested in keeping your trip as green as possible, check out the eco-tourism options on page 65.

The Accidental Racist

"Have you ever met a Jewish person?" I said to the young Ukrainian guy, Sasha, that I got a ride from. Halfway through our four hour journey over the Carpathian mountains he had revealed to me that he "didn't want them here."

"Yes," he said, "but I didn't talk to them." Here was this twenty-two year old, brilliant guy, who knew how to waltz, play the piano, loved Ben and Jerry's Ice Cream, and spoke English incredibly – and he was an open anti-Semite. What? Unfortunately in this part of the world his sentiment is not really shocking. At the time, Mel Gibson's rants were being blasted all over the airwaves back home, but here, nobody cared.

Arguing with him wouldn't have change his mind, so I just let him talk, desperately trying to sort out how he came to form this viewpoint.

His *babushka*, who practically raised him, had lived through World War II. She told him stories about German officers who came through their village. When they came, she said, they brought tea and jam and asked if they could enter their home to talk. She told him later that when the Russians came through, they raped all the girls, ransacked their village, and burned many homes so there would be nothing left to take.

Because of these stories, and his village's location in the west of Ukraine, Sasha is a fiercely nationalist and demonstrably anti-Russian. His political beliefs border on radical as he fears for his country's independent status. He wants a strong leader, one who will do anything to "serve" his people. Because of this, he views Hitler as an authoritarian who wanted a strong "clean" country and nothing more – no better and unfortunately, no worse.

"It's not that I hate Jewish people," he justified, "I just think they shouldn't come here." He ended with that as we pulled over at the road leading to the town where I was staying.

As the car came to a stop it suddenly came to me, and I said "Sasha, you already know I don't agree with you on all of this," he looked at me with an almost apologetic glance, "but I have to tell you something." I paused. "You know Ben and Jerry's, that ice cream you love so much? Well, it was definitely created by Jews."

The way his face fell, I wouldn't be surprised if his love for that ice cream made him reevaluate some things.

Because Ukraine was located behind the "Iron Curtain" for such a long time, foreign visitors of different ethnicities are still a novelty. Don't be surprised if you are stared at, or asked seemingly "inappropriate" questions by strangers. Generally, they are not intending to offend or come off as rude, they are just genuinely curious, especially in rural areas. In Kyiv and larger cities it isn't so much an issue, but if you're traveling to smaller villages and towns, it's very possible that they've never met a person of different ethnic descent before. Offensive Ukrainians, for the most part, aren't intentionally being racist, they just lack the exposure much of the EU and the West has had to different cultures and so all their generalizations about minorities come from television shows and movies. Westerners are likely going to be asked about their encounters with other races, as this is very interesting to dwellers of this formerly closed-off country. Don't be offended. Use this chance to demystify and perhaps eradicate any incorrect ideas they might have. Don't assume, however, all Ukrainians share these thoughts and notions regarding race. Many Ukrainians are open-minded citizens who have travelled the world and are very progressive.

MINORITIES

Generally Ukraine is more welcoming to minorities of Asian, African or Caribbean appearance than one would assume. However, minorities do need to exercise special caution. Violent, unprovoked attacks on minorities have occurred by neo-Nazi and "skinhead" groups in Kyiv. Organized rallies by racist groups have also occurred in the capital city. Ukrainian officials have condemned hate-crimes, yet law enforcement is lacking and the U.S. Embassy has had reports that police were present during some attacks and yet did nothing to stop it or aid in the prosecution of the perpetrators. The Ukrainian government has recently established a special law enforcement unit responsible for the prevention and prosecution of hate crimes, yet problems persist. It's wise for minorities visiting Ukraine to be extra cautious of their surroundings.

The Basics

When to Visit

The average temperature in Kiev in January is -6°C (21°F) and even in sunny Crimea the unpredictable weather can cause quite a bit of problems (an unexpected snowstorm that blasted the Sevastopol area in March of 2010 wreaked havoc, causing blackouts and practically shut down all transportation). If you're heading to Ukraine during the winter months (January to March), it's best to head to the ski resorts of the Carpathians where the heavy blankets of snow are welcomed by locals and tourists alike. If you're planning to fly into Kiev and then take another plane from there (most likely to Uzhhorod), it's best to find another option. Smaller flights are often cancelled as heavy winter storms make it impossible to navigate into the West. Hiring a driver or taking a bus or train is the safer and cheaper option (see "Transportation" page 45).

In the spring, Ukrainians are wrapped up in preparations for Orthodox Easter (which generally falls between late March and late April). In April, the average temperature in Kiev is 11°C (52°F) while in Crimea the average temperature is 15°C (59°F). This is a great time to visit as numerous festivals abound and the beer tents (which were solemnly retired during the winter) are triumphantly raised. Bring an umbrella or a poncho if you're traveling out west though as this is the rainy season. By the end of May the temperatures are back to stifling and "Last Bell" ceremonies welcome the beginning of summer break for schools across Ukraine.

Traveling in the summertime (June through August) has its benefits and downfalls. Train tickets and hotels are best booked in advance for the Crimean region as locals flock to its shores. Yalta is a madhouse during this time as it has become the Hamptons of Ukraine with wealthy Ukrainians and Russians alike booking its best rooms far in advance. Bus and train travel can also be an exercise in discomfort as non-air-conditioned compartments, combined with locals who fear the draft an open window causes (see "The Draft" on page 32), can reach stifling temperatures. It's best to book *kupe* or *SV* class on a train if you're traveling during this time and worried about comfort level, as *platskart* (see the following Transportation section for more on train classes) can feel much like a death trap. The summer months though provide the luxury of packing light and easy travel. Buses run constantly and merchants crowd the streets of Kiev's Andreevsky Spusk and Lviv's Market Square.

September and October are possibly the most comfortable months to travel throughout Ukraine as the scorching summer sun has subsided and winter has yet to appear. In late October the rains usually begin which can make for an incredibly muddy experience. The average temperature in Kiev during this time is 10°C (50°F) with temperatures hovering around 17°C (62°F) in the South. Buses and trains still are numerous and platskart tickets on trains are again a cheap, and comfortable, option.

Getting There

Getting into Ukraine is a fairly simple, if time consuming, process. Expect your passport to be heavily scrutinized and possibly even momentarily taken away to be reviewed (I was pulled off the bus at the Polish-Ukrainian border, my Blockbuster card with my name on it got me back on). Getting out of the country and into EU territory can be a lengthy affair as these routes are popular with smugglers who make their money on the alcohol and cigarette trade. Be prepared for long wait times at border crossings. That being said, there's nothing to fear but immense boredom (wait times at the Polish-Ukraine border are known to last an average of four hours but have gone up to nine hours).

Smuggling

Smuggling is a fact of life in Ukraine and for many people it's their full-time job. You are legally allowed to take two packages of twenty cigarettes and one liter of alcohol into the EU. It can be fascinating to see how this law is abused. Don't be alarmed if during routine custom searches at the border, Patrol Guards pull up a tile from the train ceiling and cigarettes start falling, or packages of plastic-wrapped cigarette cartons are found taped to the bottom of the luggage compartment or bus seats. Exercise commonsense. If someone asks you to carry something for them, politely decline. If you're a Westerner, Patrol Guards are likely not going to accuse you of anything. If you're asked if you saw anything say that you were sleeping. Then simply sit back and be amazed at the amount of smuggled goods one bus or train compartment can hold!

TRAIN

Numerous trains connect Ukraine to its neighboring countries. At the Polish-Ukrainian border, the train is shunted into the gauge changing shed to have its wheels changed from the standard European gauge to Russian gauge. Passengers remain on board during the change. Because of this necessary changeover, tickets from Europe into Ukraine, and vice-versa, are often twice as expensive as fares within Europe. On some routes into Ukraine (for instance the Krakow-Lviv train) they tired of doing this labor-intensive procedure and so now instead of changing gauges, they simply stop the train at the border and have all passengers transfer to another train on the other side. Oh progress!

International train tickets can only be bought from certain ticket counters. In Kiev they're only available at the Central Ticket Office which is a ten minute uphill walk from the Central Train Station. The ticket counters that sell them, #42 and #43, are located in the side room to the left of the main hall. The hours (and these are always variable as "breaks" occur often) are from 7:00 to 23:00 on weekdays and from 8:00 to 20:00 on weekends.

Estimated minimum travel times from Kyiv to other major cities:

Belgrade: 32 hours

Berlin: 24 hours

Bucharest: 27.5 hours

Budapest: 20 hours

Krakow: 16 hours

Lisbon: 69 hours

London: 37.5 hours

Madrid: 55 hours

Moscow: 9.5 hours

Paris: 34 hours

Prague: 29 hours

St. Petersburg: 20 hours

Warsaw: 22.5 hours

Zurich: 32.5 hours

> If your train passes through Belarus, Moldova or Russia, you may need a special visa, even if your final destination is in some other country (i.e: Romania).

A great website to check for trains running from various countries into Ukraine is Bahn.com. Travel-2-Ukraine (www.travel-2-ukraine.com) can buy your train tickets for you and have them delivered to you at home (for a fee of course).

Kyiv Central Railway Station *Vokzal'na Square (Вокзальна площа); Tel: 005 / +380 (44) 503-70-05; www.uz.gov.ua (only in Russian and Ukrainian)*

Central Ticket Office *Kyiv, T.Shevchenka Str. (Т. Шевченка, вул), 38/40; Tel: 050 / 465-19-17 / 503-60-51; There is also a Ticket Office at Boryspil Airport.*

BUS

Most travelers coming to Ukraine from Europe will be crossing from the Polish border. There are daily bus routes that depart from Polish cities such as Warsaw, Przemysl, Lublin, Wroclaw, Krakow, Lodz, Katowice, Rzeszow, Tomaszow and Lubelski that head to the Stryiskyi Bus Station (Стрийський автовокзал) in Lviv.

From the Krakow bus station there's an overnight bus that departs at 21:50 from Krakow and usually arrive at 6:00 in Lviv (dependent on wait times at the border).

From Przemyśl, just outside the train station, it's possible to take a privately owned bus to the Ukrainian border, get out, walk through border control, and take another bus to Lviv once you reach the Ukrainian side (walk up the main strip, through all the shops, and on the main road to the left you'll see the private buses lined up to make the 2 to 3 hour drive to Lviv). These buses can be crowded and uncomfortable but they are also incredibly cheap. For border crossing enthusiasts who love a story, this is the way to go.

AIR

Flying into Ukraine is easy and convenient. Direct flights to Kyiv are available from New York with Delta airlines as well as numerous flights into Lviv, Odessa, Dnipropetrovsk, Donetsk, Kharkiv and Simferopol from a variety of European cities. Be careful if you have a layover in Russia for more than four hours, or if your departing plane takes off from another terminal (for example arrives at SVO1 and departs from SVO2), as you might be required to obtain a Russian Transit Visa.

Special Notice!
Lviv is hosting the European Football Cup of 2012. In preparation for this event, Lviv's airport may be partially closed in 2011. Check with your airline provider to ensure that your final destination is in fact Lviv, and not another nearby city such as Lutsk or Ivano-Frankivsk!

Ukrainian Airlines

AeroSvit *Tel: +38 044 490 3 490; www.aerosvit.ua/eng.html*

Ukraine International Airlines *Address: Bohdana Khmel'nyts'koho Street, 63A; Tel: +38 044 461 50 50; www.flyuia.com*

Ukraine National Airlines *Address: Povitroflotsky Prosp., 90; Tel: +38 044 245 98 72*

Other Airlines with Service to Ukraine

Aeroflot *Saksagans'kogo Street, 112a; Tel: +38 044 245 43 59; www.aeroflot.ru*

Air Baltic *Bohdana Khmel'nyts'koho Str., 52; Tel: +38 044 238 26 49; www.airbaltic.com*

Air France *Velyka Zhytomyrs'ka Street, 6/11; Tel: +38 044 464 10 10; www.airfrance.com*

Austrian Airlines *Velyka Vasyl'kivs'ka Street, 9/2; Tel: +38 044 244 35 40; www.austrian.com*

British Airways *Yaroslaviv Val Street, 5; Tel: +38 044 490 60 60; www.britishairways.com*

Czech Airlines *Ivana Franka Street, 36;Tel: +38 044 288 10 60 (61)*

Delta *Tarasa Shevchenka Blvd., 10; Tel: +38 044 246 56 56 / +38 044 246 38 48; www.delta.com*

Egypt Air *Khreschatik Street, 14; Tel: +38 044 228 23 43; www.egyptair.com*

Estonian Airlines *Velyka Vasyl'kivs'ka Street (former Chervonoarmiys'ka Str.), 9/2; #14; Tel: +38 044 220 05 20; www.estonian-air.ee*

Finnair *Velyka Vasyl'kivs'ka Street (former Chervonoarmiys'ka Str.), 9/2; #6; Tel: +38 044 247 57 77; www.finnair.com*

KLM *Ivana Franka Street, 34/33; Tel: +38 044 490 2 490; www.klm.com*

LOT *Ivana Franka Street, 36; Tel: +38 044 246 56 20; www.lot.com*

Lufthansa *Bohdana Khmel'nyts'koho Street, 52; Tel: +38 044 490 38 00; www.lufthansa.com*

Malev *Pushkins'ka Street, 45/2; #22; Tel: +38 044 490 73 42; www.malev.com*

Swiss Air *Velyka Vasyl'kivs'ka Street, 9/2; #53; Tel: +38 044 490 65 00; www.swiss.com*

Turkish Airlines *Pushkins'ka Street, 19; Tel: +38 044 490 59 33; www.turkishairlines.com*

Wizz *Air Grishka Street, 3-A; www.wizzair.com*

FERRY

While there used to be many ferries that ran between Ukraine's port cities (Odessa, Yalta, and Kherson) to other countries like Turkey, it seems that the recent economic downturn has affected these too. Ferries are subject to being cancelled last minute, and information regarding their exact schedule is almost nonexistent. You're better off booking your tickets through a travel agency.

For mildly up-to-date info check the Ukrferry Shipping Company website (www.ukrferry.com). Leges Tourism is a good travel agency based in Istanbul that can also help arrange ferry transfers. You can reach their English-speaking staff via email at legesturizm@doruk.net.tr.

Transportation in Ukraine

Getting around Ukraine can be a daunting process, but far from impossible. Ukraine has well-developed systems of public transportation in place as Ukrainians are less dependent on personal vehicles than Americans and Western Europeans. Every large city and Oblast capital is connected by a railway network. From there, minibuses (marshrutkas, маршрутки), trolleybuses (тролейбусів), and private taxis are available for inner-city and short commute routes. It's also possible to travel long distances by bus (автобус), but this is sometimes more expensive and less comfortable than by train. In the East, it's generally easiest to travel by train, while in the West marshrutkas are the way to go.

TRAIN

Trains are the best way to travel long distances in Ukraine. Every major city has a train station (вокзал, *voksal*). Trains can vary from express (Швидко, *shvydko*) trains to depressingly slow *electrichkas* (commuter trains). Train tickets can be bought up to 42 days in advance. During the high season, it's especially recommended to buy tickets in advance (especially if you're traveling to resort destination cities). Trains usually have three classes of seating available and prices can vary from US$10 to US$60 dollars a ticket (which include taxes, linen and baggage fees) depending on the length of the trip and the class of ticket.

1st class, *SV* (CB), sleeper

This is the best (and most expensive) class of ticket available. Every train car is divided into nine cabins; with two beds in each cabin (therefore women traveling alone may not be comfortable staying in *SV* as they might have to room with a creeper). Luggage can be stored underneath the bed which lifts up, or in the storage compartment above the entrance door. Every compartment can lock from the inside (a decidedly double-edged sword for woman travelling by themselves) and every car is equipped with two bathrooms, one on either side. *SV* cabins are also air-conditioned when the train is moving and heated in the wintertime. As pricey as a *SV* ticket is, it's not really worth it. You're better off saving a few dollars and going with *kupe* instead.

2nd class, *Kupe* (купе), Sleeper

Kupe is a nice middle ground for travel, providing comfort while saving a buck or two. Just like *SV*, *kupe* is divided into nine cabins, except every cabin has four beds – two lower (Нижній, *nyzhche*) and two upper (Верхній, *verkhniy*) beds. If you're traveling with two people, it's sometimes cheaper to just buy out a whole *kupe* cabin, rather than pay for two *SV* tickets. Luggage storage is located beneath the lower beds and in a compartment over the door frame. Every compartment has a lock on the inside and every car has a bathroom. Generally, *kupe* is air-conditioned, but this is not always the case. It is, however, heated in the wintertime.

3rd class, *Platskart* (плацкарт), Sleeper

For those traveling alone, or interested in meeting people, *platskart* can be quite the adventure. It's safer in some ways than *kupe* or *SV* because you won't be stuck in a compartment with someone you don't know for hours. That being said, it can also be harder to keep an eye on your valuables as there are no locks or privacy. Every car has 56 beds, 36 of which are grouped by fours along open "cabins" and 18 of which are stacked along the passageway. *Platskart* is non-air-conditioned which can make for a tortuously hot journey. However, these cars can be the most jovial with passengers sharing drinks and food and telling stories with one another. The new public ban on alcohol on public transportation might destroy this amazing sub-culture with time though.

Tips for Non-Ukrainian Speakers

Buying transportation tickets can be amazingly difficult if you speak no Ukrainian or Russian. Attendants at bus and train stations are not exactly known for their patience or courtesy, and those in line around you are not likely to assist. It's best to learn Cyrillic so that you can read the timetables posted at the station. From there, simply write down the train number you need tickets for, the destination city and how many seats you want. It also helps to write out which class of ticket you want if you're taking a train.

Websites such as Seat 61 (www.seat61.com/Ukraine.htm) and Travel 2 Ukraine (www.travel-2-ukraine.com) have good, updated train schedules from major cities available on their sites in English. Poezda (www.poezda.net/en/index) also has a searchable timetable in English but the spellings can be infuriatingly odd. For those wary of buying tickets unassisted, several online agencies exist that will buy the tickets for you and deliver them to you in Kyiv, or mail them to your home for a slight fee (it's best to have them deliver your tickets to you in Kyiv). Hotels and hostels will often assist you with buying tickets as well.

Upper or Lower? (Верхня або нижня, Verkhnya abo Nyzhnya?)

Train connoisseurs have lengthy debates about which seat to request when buying your train tickets. Upper or lower? While each seat has its merits, there are some points to consider. In *kupe* and *platskart* the top seat affords individuals the right to go to bed whenever they want. The bottom seat is usually shared, until the person who has the top seat decides to go to bed (or until the person with the bottom seat blatantly starts to make their bed as an obvious hint). That being said, the top seat in *platskart* is so tight, that it's impossible to fully sit up. One must also possess the acrobatic skills necessary to propel oneself into it. So, just as a recommendation: top seat in *kupe*, bottom seat in *platskart*.

Basics

BUS
АВТОБУС, *AVTOBUS*

In larger cities, buses leave from a bus station (автовокзал, *avtovoksal*). In the smaller ones, they leave from the side of the road. You can buy tickets from the ticket counter (каса, *kasa)* in the bus station, or from the driver if you're catching it roadside. Inside most bus stations they also have a timetable (розклад, *rozklad)* posted of the bus schedules. Schedules are available online in Ukrainian (www.bus.com.ua) but it's often incorrect. You're better off checking at the station. Buses make a great substitution for train rides if the cities are close by. It's also possible to take overnight buses from one side of the country to the other side or into a bordering country (although these tickets should be bought in advance). Prices vary depending on the length of the trip (generally 100 to 180UAH). Gunsel (www.gunsel.com.ua) and Avtolux (www.autolux.ua/English) are the nicest shuttle bus companies. Both have schedules available online in English and have offices located inside Borispol airport making buying tickets with them a breeze.

MARSHRUTKAS
МАРШРУТКА

You cannot escape Ukraine without traveling in these buses that resemble the VW vans of the sixties. These can seat 12 to 20 passengers and with standing room can accommodate countless more (and usually do). Generally they are numbered and marked with a sign that says the beginning and end of their route. For inner-city transport the cost is generally 20 cents to US$1 a person. For travel from one nearby city to another the cost is usually US$1 to US$10 a person. Advance ticket purchases are not needed (but you will occasionally need to lose your inhibitions and jam yourself into a crowded bus to catch it). Generally you pay the driver, or pass the money up through the passengers to the driver. The trauma afflicted by a ride in these, what some call "death machines," is part of the charm. For passengers wary of barreling down a road in a full-on cramped metal box, may we suggest not looking out the front window as the images of barely missed pedestrians and oncoming vehicles might soon become overwhelming.

TROLLEYBUSES
ТРОЛЕЙБУСІВ, *TROLEYBUSIV*

Every larger city has a trolleybus that runs through the downtown area and around the perimeter. The 86-kilometer (just under 54 miles) trolleybus ride from Simferopol to Yalta is currently the longest and the most boring trolleybus ride in the world (the first five miles is a leisurely amusement, after that it's just agonizingly slow). Tickets can be bought on the trolleybuses for 20 cents to US$1 a person. Sometimes you will purchase the ticket from a driver and other times an attendant will be selling them. Look to see if they have a stamp validation machine on the bus (often times this will be the rusty box in the corner). Make sure to use it, even if no one else does, as it's not uncommon for foreigners to get "fined" for not validating their ticket, especially in Lviv.

TAXIS

Taxis in Ukraine usually lack meters, therefore it's best to agree on a price before starting your journey. Be prepared to haggle for a good rate as your accent will undoubtedly set you up for an overpriced quote. A good rule of thumb is about 2 to 3UAH per kilometer.

However, in Ukraine, any car is a potential taxicab. It's considered normal to simply put your hand out, palm down (note: not your thumb) and wait for an unlicensed community member interested in making a quick dollar to stop. It's sort of like hitch-hiking: but you will always pay your driver. As with everything exercise caution if you're traveling alone, and reconsider this form of travel if you're traveling to someplace other than within the city limits.

PRIVATE TRANSPORT

For daredevils over 25 years of age (ones with nerves of steel and an amazing portable GPS), it's possible to rent a car quite easily. Budget (www.budget.ua.en), Hertz (www.hertz.ua) and Europcar (www.europcar.com) all have car rental agencies in Kiev, Donetsk, Lviv, and Simferopol. Budget and Hertz also have offices located in other major cities. Issues such as poorly lit roads at night, potholes, uneven roads, and unmarked streets are a common complaint among foreign drivers. Add to that the fact that Ukraine was named the second highest country in the world for motor vehicle related deaths in 2008 by Forbes, and you have quite a challenge ahead of you. A safer option is hiring a driver. Hiring a driver can be an expensive luxury costing anywhere from US$60 to US$100 dollars a day. If you can afford it though, it can make for an amazing investment. Arrangements can be made through most travel agencies, hotel desks or airports. Hostel workers are also known to help out as they most likely have friends or family with a car who wouldn't mind the extra money.

Police

It's very common for police to stop cars for no apparent reason. Even locals will admit that their underpaid police officers are a bit corrupt. If stopped, police will ask to see your passport (to check for an entry stamp), vehicle registration certificate and driver's license. Police have been known to check for random things like first-aid kits and warning triangles, which every car is required to have, in an attempt to solicit a bribe.

Food & Drink

Food is a big aspect of Ukrainian life. As a foreigner you will no doubt be treated very kindly in-regards to food. If you're having dinner with a Ukrainian family, don't be shy about expressing when you are full. You will literally have to insist that you cannot eat anymore.

Many Ukrainians still have family members alive who lived through the Great Famine (see the following Holodomor box). Because of this, Ukrainians do not waste food by throwing it away and always seek to ensure that their guests are not going hungry. In restaurants, it's not considered rude to leave food behind, but when eating at a Ukrainian home, be mindful about throwing away food scraps. Generally Ukrainians have a bucket located next to the trash can where these scraps are gathered and then fed to dogs or livestock.

In Kiev and larger cities, it's not hard to find "ethnic" food (if your culinary hopes aren't too high). But generally, you're likely to run into the same food over and over again. Not to fear, Ukrainian food is far from the bland boiled potatoes and beets popular culture has made it out to be. Furthermore, it's possible to be a vegetarian (вегетаріанський, *vehitarianets (m) / vehitarianka (f)* – See they even have a word for it!) and not starve to death.

Tipping

The Western notion of tipping has spread to Ukraine. In smaller villages and towns this is still a novel concept, but in larger cities it's now the standard. The typical tip in Ukraine is 5 to 10 percent of the total bill. Look over your bill to see if a tip has already been included. You need not tip at bars or cafés where you place your order at a counter.

Here are the dishes you will likely see on menus and served in Ukrainian homes. As you can see, sour cream (сметана, *smetana*) is practically its own food group.

Borsch (борщ): Soup made out of beets, cabbage, potatoes, tomatoes, carrots, onions, garlic, dill, and served with sour cream. There's also Green Borsch (Зелений борщ, *Zelenyy Borshch*) that's made with sorrel (or any other leafy green) onions, potatoes, herbs, heavy cream and sometimes topped with chopped boiled eggs.

Salat Olivieh (Салат Олів'є): "Salad" made with potatoes, pickles, boiled eggs, chicken (or ham), onions and carrots, all of which have been cooked and small diced. These ingredients are then held together by a ton of mayonnaise.

Salat Vinaigrette (Салат "Вінегрет"): This popular, purple salad is made with cooked small diced carrots, beets, pickles and potatoes that is mixed with minced onions and peas then tossed with oil (usually sunflower). Very healthy and delicious, it's generally served as a side.

Pampushky (пампушки): Balls of dough that have been deep fried. These can then be tossed in melted butter with garlic (*pampushky z chasnykom*), in cinnamon sugar, or made with poppy seeds. Usually served with borsch.

Varenyky (Вареники): Small dumplings made with unleavened dough and filled with mashed potatoes, cheese, or cabbage. These are usually boiled and then tossed in butter and served with sour cream. A dessert black cherry Verenyky is also made.

Pelmini (Пельмені): Resembling tortellini, these small, paper thin dumplings are generally filled with a mixture of meat (generally pork or chicken, or a combination of both) and spices. They can be served in a chicken broth like soup, or pan fried with onions and served with sour cream.

Holubtsi (Голубці): Steamed cabbage rolls that have been filled with a mixture of meat, rice and spices, rolled up and stewed in tomato sauce. Very popular in the winter time; they are served with sour cream.

Salo (сало): Salo is raw, unrendered pork fat. Ukrainians eat it on black bread with onions or just straight up with raw cloves of garlic. They also eat it while drinking to coat the stomach and use it as a base for cooking instead of oil. They love the stuff and its existence is very much a source of national pride.

Deruny (Деруни): Potato pancakes that are fried and served with sour cream. The Ukrainian version is generally thinner than most Westerners are used to. If you find *deruny* on a menu, order it. You won't be disappointed.

Kutia (Кутя): The origins of this dish dates back five thousand years when the Ukrainian people first began to cultivate wheat. Served as the first dish during Christmas dinner, this dessert is made with honey, ground poppy seeds and whole wheat. Everyone must eat at least a spoonful for a good year.

Torte (торт): Torte is the catchall word for a variety of cakes. Unlike Western cakes, Ukrainians generally make theirs without flour, using ground walnuts or almonds instead. Because of this, Ukrainian cakes generally crunch when cut into and have a consistency resembling meringue.

Kholodets (холодець): Aspics never went out style in Ukraine. Kholodets is bits of meat or fish in cold gelatin. Ukrainians generally mix it in with their mashed potatoes or eat it with amazingly potent, bright pink horseradish (хрін, khrin). Not for everyone.

Condiment Nation

Condiment connoisseurs rejoice! Ukrainians' love affair with all things ketchup and mayonnaise has resulted in an amazing array of choices. The condiment aisle in a Ukrainian supermarket rivals the cereal aisle of the Western world. From ketchup made especially for *shashlik*, to mayonnaise that boasts "the highest" fat content, for condiment lovers it's heaven. For the rest of us, it's a little overwhelming.

DRINK

Drinking is a huge part of Ukrainian culture. However, in January 2010, Ukraine passed a law that prohibits the sale of "low-alcohol" products such a beer to anyone under 18. Also, in February 2010, a new law came into effect that bans drinking on public streets, parks, transport and sports grounds (anyone that's ever ridden a train in Eastern Europe knows how common this was). Ukrainians are still adapting to the change with many simply slipping their beer into a paper sack and calling it even. While safe to drink in restaurants or private residences, one should exercise caution at local bars as these places are prone to fights, violence and uncomfortable (story worthy) encounters with alcoholics. Furthermore, the recent ban on public drinking has made seedy bars even more crowded. Look for well-lighted bars in bigger cities that are, granted, a little more expensive as they won't attract the riffraff. In smaller villages and towns, they're best avoided altogether.

Popular Ukrainian Beverages

Beer (пиво, *pivo*): Domestic beers brewed in Ukraine are quite fabulous and are gaining popularity throughout Europe. The most popular Ukrainian beers are Obolon, Lvivske, Chernihivske, and Slavutich

Wine (вино, *vyno*): Ukrainian wine generally comes from the Crimean region,

---

Toasting

When Drinking with Ukrainians, you will generally be asked to give a toast. If you want to look like you know what you're doing, do as the Ukrainians do. The first toast is generally a thanks to the guest, the second toast is given by the guest to the host, and the third toast is always to Ukrainian women. Ukrainians and Russians alike believe only problem drinkers drink without toasting. So get ready for endless rounds and lots of dedications.

Popular toasts:

To You: За тебя, *za tebe*

For Love: за любов, *za lubove*

To Health: на здоров'я, *Na zda-ró-vye*

To the Women (third toast): За жінок, *za zhinok*

To Meeting: до зустрічі, *doe zustrichi*

On the Horses (always the last toast, because by then you're so drunk only the horses know the way home): на конях, *na konyakh* but varieties from Uzhhorod are also gaining popularity. Bottles can cost anywhere from US$2 to US$50. It's best to avoid cheaper bottles and watch out for bottles marked напівсолодке (*napivsolodke*) as these can be very sweet by Western standards. Look for bottles marked "сухе" (*sukhe*) if you like dry wine.

Samahon (самогон): Samahon is Ukrainian moonshine and generally found only in Ukrainian's homes. Recipes vary and can be amazingly potent. Exercise caution if you are given a sample. One is generally enough.

Horilka (горілка): Horilka is Ukrainian vodka. Horilka with red pepper and honey is a popular drink and is also used as a cure for colds. Horilka infused with fruit is also popular.

Kvas (квас): Kvas is a fermented alcohol drink made with honey, water and yeast – it tastes like you're drinking bread. Sold on the streets from big barrels in the summertime, this is a popular, refreshing drink.

Why Ukrainians Tap Their Necks When They Want a Drink

Sometimes you'll see Ukrainians tap the upper part of their neck, just below their jaw, as a sign that they want another drink. Here is the story that is often given as a reason for this habit:

In the early nineteenth century, there was a fisherman in Odessa. As he was working one day in the harbor, he saw in the distance one of the vessels of the Russian fleet beginning to sink. Dismayed, he rushed over in his small boat, reaching the despairing sailors just in time and saved every last one of them.

Extremely grateful, these sailors told their tale of woe to the Tsar. The Tsar, impressed by the man's good deed, invited the fisherman to his palace. He told the fisherman he could have anything that was within his power to grant. The man thought for awhile, and decided that he would like to be able to drink for free anywhere in the Russian Empire. The Tsar obliged him by giving him a certified letter which said something like: "Dear Russian patriot, the man before you is the savior of twenty-three Russian lives. Please grant him any drink he requests, as a favor to your royal majesty." And so, the man was relatively happy. His greatest expense would thereafter be subsidized by the Father of the Slavs.

But the man got fantastically drunk five to six nights a week. Inevitably he lost the letter, and found himself sheepishly trucking back to the capital to request another note. This happened several times before eventually the Tsar yelled, "Enough! Lord knows I'm gonna be doing this exact same thing next month, so how the hell are we going to get you to hang on to the damned note!?" Resplendent in his wisdom, he eventually came up with an idea: a small tattoo of his signature, branded onto the man's throat.

And so, whenever any old man walks into a store in Ukraine, he taps his upper throat three times, as a joke, in the hopes that maybe, just maybe, he'll find a shopkeeper stupid enough to think a tattoo's there.

- Nick Brown

WATER

It's probably best for Westerners to drink water only from bottles. Even water in buildings that is "filtered" can pose a problem for Western stomachs. If using water to make tea or coffee from a building, ensure that you properly boil the water before use. Beer and other alcoholic beverages are safe to drink. In supermarkets or from kiosks you can buy sparkling water (вода з газом, *voda z hazom*) or flat water (вода без газу, *voda bez hazu*) for around US$1 a pint.

Money & Costs

Outside of major cities, Ukraine is generally a cheap place to travel. Museum entrances, theatre tickets, and transport are inexpensive. In larger cities, food can be outrageously expensive with an average meal in a posh restaurant in Kyiv costing about US$40 per person (without drinks). If you choose to eat at cafeteria style restaurants, Ukrainian fast food chains, or smaller cafés where the locals dine, this cost can be cut down to around US$5 per person.

Clothing is also overpriced by Western standards. A pair of ordinary jeans will easily run 350UAH (US$43) and if it's a name brand expect to pay a lot more. Although name brand stores pack the main strip of Kyiv, inflation has caused their prices to soar. If you do go shopping, it's best to go to the *bazaars* as this is where the locals shop and where you'll find the best prices.

Public transport within cities generally costs anywhere from .75 kopecks (10 cents) to 5UAH (75 cents). Taxi prices generally sky-rocket the second an accent is spotted, but shouldn't be more than 2.50UAH (30 cents) per kilometer. Negotiate the price prior to leaving. Long-distance travel has recently gotten more expensive, but it's still relatively affordable. A bus ticket from Kyiv to other major cities (like Odessa or Lviv) will generally cost around 100 to 175UAH (US$12 to US$22) depending on the bus. A second class train ticket will cost around 150 to 200UAH (US$19 to US$25).

Hotels, overall, are exorbitantly priced throughout the country. In Kyiv, a decent room will set you back US$100 a night, with Western chains charging US$270 a night. In smaller cities and the country side, a comfortable room will set you back around US$40 a night. Renting an apartment is a better deal. You'll get more comfort

---

Bread and Salt

When Ukrainians are expecting an important or particularly admired guest, this guest will generally present them with bread and salt upon arrival. The bread is usually an elaborately decorated loaf that is presented upon a *rushnyk* (embroidered towel). Bread in Ukraine is the most respected food, whereas salt represents long friendships.

Salt used to be heavily taxed and very expensive which could explain its inclusion in this ceremony. Honored guests when presented with the bread and salt should tear a piece of the bread off, dip it in the salt and eat it.

and privacy for around US$80 a night, regardless of the amount of people staying in it. Hostels are also gaining popularity throughout the country. It's possible to find a bed in larger cities for around US$20 a night. If you're willing to forgo some comfort, and share a bathroom, you can find a suitable room in Soviet-style accommodations for around US$20 a night.

CURRENCY

In Ukraine, coin change is called *kopecks*. There are 100 kopecks to a hryvnia. Kopecks come in increments worth 1, 5, 10, 25 and 50 kopecks. There are also coins worth 1 hryvnia. Bills are available in 1, 5, 10, 20, 50, 100, 200 and 500 hryvnia.

> Upon seeing your first Ukrainian hryvnia, you may find yourself remarking that it looks a lot like Monopóly money.

While laws have been passed that stipulate that only UAH may be used when buying goods in Ukraine, that hasn't stopped the U.S. dollar from being accepted by hotels and businesses. Many hotels all over Ukraine used to list their prices exclusively in dollar form. However, due to the recent constant fluctuations in the exchange rate, you're more likely to see UAH prices only. It's still possible to pay some travel agencies and tour guides in U.S. dollars instead of hryvnia.

Correct Change

Even though change exists, that doesn't always mean you will receive it. Ukraine is seemingly always on the verge of running out of change completely. And you will likely be asked if you have the correct change repeatedly from grumpy cashiers with low amounts of coinage. Don't be surprised if you're told no change is available and you're simply handed back whatever bills are owed to you along with a piece of gum or a plastic sack in lieu of change.

Currency Exchange

Because U.S. dollars and Euros are so readily accepted by Ukrainian businesses, currency exchanges are everywhere. Currency exchanges (обмін валюти, *obmin valyuty*) can be found all over Ukraine in supermarkets, hotel lobbies, and transportation hubs. Generally the ones located by bus and train stations are best avoided as these have the worst exchange rates. Currency should be in good condition and not torn or marked on to be accepted. Between 2006 and 2008, the UAH to U.S. dollar conversion held tight at 5UAH to US$1. But in 2009, the UAH rapidly declined in value rendering the current exchange hovering around 8UAH to US$1. This could easily change.

ATMS

ATMs (Банкомат, bankomat) are located everywhere except the tiniest of villages. Most screens have English available as a language selection. At some, it's also possible to choose to receive U.S. dollars instead of hryvnias. Most ATMs will charge a slight usage fee (generally 1 percent of your total transaction) or your home bank may charge a fee for using ATMs overseas. Cirrus, Plus, Visa, MasterCard, and EuroCard are generally the most accepted forms of ATM cards in Ukraine.

CREDIT CARDS

In larger cities, it's possible to pay for a hotel room or your bill at a restaurant with a credit or debit card. MasterCard, EuroCard, and Visa are the most readily accepted. In smaller cities, at train and bus stations, and in most supermarkets and stores, you will need to pay in cash.

It's important to contact your bank and credit card companies if you're planning on using their cards when in Ukraine. The country has a somewhat justifiable reputation for fraud rendering many banks to cut off cards the instant a card is used in Ukraine. Therefore, make sure your bank knows you are planning on using your debit and/or credit cards here to avoid this problematic situation.

TRAVELERS CHECKS

Cashing a travelers check can be a headache (if you can even find a bank that will exchange them). These are best avoided as they are usually cashed with a high commission rate. Furthermore, banks only cash them during certain hours. It's simply best to rely on credit and debit cards.

Festivals & Holidays

For expats, or those staying in Ukraine for an extended period, the number of Ukrainian holidays can be dizzying. Seemingly every fortnight is perforated with some sort of mild to extravagant celebration. It's true, Ukrainians love a reason to have a good time; perhaps that's why holidays are so popular and plentiful.

MAIN HOLIDAYS

New Year's Day

By far the most beloved holiday in Ukraine is New Year's Day (January 1st). Ukrainians celebrate this holiday with many holiday parties and gatherings. National television stations will play cherished Soviet films and the President addresses the nation a few minutes before midnight. It is during this time that the New Year's Tree is decorated. Ukrainian children believe that Father Frost (Дід Мороз, *Did Moroz*), comes on New Year's Eve to deliver presents to children that have been good that year. The tradition was moved to New Year's, rather than Christmas, during Soviet times because of Soviet atheism. Now it serves as a great way Santa can make all his deliveries, as he does in the former Soviet countries a week later!

Orthodox Christmas

The Orthodox Church uses the Julian calendar, which is thirteen days behind the Gregorian calendar used in many parts of Europe and North America. Therefore Orthodox Christmas is celebrated on January 7th. This holiday wasn't recognized under the Soviet rule, and only became publicly resurrected in Ukraine during the 1990s. Ukrainians celebrate this important holiday with a twelve-course Christmas Eve meal that represents Christ's twelve apostles. The traditional meal includes *kutia*, borsch, a variety of fish, *varenyky* and *holubtsi*. It's also not unheard of for children to appear at your door, throw rice, and then sing traditional songs in hopes of receiving candy or small change.

Orthodox Easter

Orthodox Easter is usually celebrated two weeks after Catholic Easter. The holiday is often observed by attending a midnight mass the Saturday before and having *kulichi* (traditional Easter bread) and *pysanky* (painted Easter eggs) blessed by the priest. On Easter Day, everyone greets each other on the streets and at home with *Khrystos voskres!* (Christ has risen!) to which you are expected to reply *voistynu voskres!* (Indeed. Christ has risen!).

Victory Day

May 9th is Victory Day in Ukraine. It's hard not to find a family that wasn't affected by World War II or "The Great Patriotic War" as it's referred to in Ukraine. On this day, large military parades are held. Veterans don their uniforms and wreaths are placed on the graves of soldiers and civilians who died during the war.

Independence Day

Independence Day is celebrated on August 24th with massive parades held all over Ukraine. If you are in the country during this time, try to make it to Kyiv for their parade which takes place on *Maydan Nezalezhnosti* (Майдан Незалежності, Independence Square).

Ukrainian Birthdays

Ukrainians celebrate their birthdays in the opposite fashion than most Westerners. In Ukraine it's the birthday boy/girl who's responsible for planning their birthday bash. It's not uncommon for the birthday person to spend all day in the kitchen preparing food for their party. If they work, they will also bring torte, chocolate, or alcohol to work to celebrate their day with their coworkers.

UNIQUE UKRAINIAN HOLIDAYS

Holy Trinity Day

Observed fifty days after Easter, this holiday is celebrated in observance of the descent of the Holy Spirit onto Jesus' apostles fifty days after his resurrection.

Old New Year's

On January 14th, Ukrainians celebrate the day New Year's fell on their old calendar (which was changed in 1917). One of the strangest holidays in Ukraine, this holiday is celebrated much like New Year's Day. Needless to say, January isn't a very productive month.

The Last Bell

On the last day of class, schools across Ukraine hold special ceremonies. Generally, these involve lengthy speeches by the faculty and staff. Graduating students dress up elaborately, similar to the Western notion of prom, and often perform specially choreographed dances for the event which parents and community members alike attend. If you're walking around town on this day, it's not uncommon to see kids in ball gowns heading to school.

Day of Knowledge

Taking place on September 1st (the first day of the school year), this is a very special holiday for secondary schools. Students, parents and community members attend this event. At the end of the ceremony, a girl from the first form is carried on the shoulder of an eleventh form boy (symbolism my friends) up to the front of the crowd to ring the first bell of the new year.

Women's Day

Ukrainians like to refer to this holiday as "International" Women's Day, although many Westerners have never heard of it. This very popular holiday takes place on March 8th. On this day husbands, sons and brothers will present the girls in their family with small gifts and do all the work around the house.

> There is also Men's Day (February 23rd) for good measure.

Name Days

Besides the traditional birthday celebration, Ukrainians also celebrate Name Days (іменини, *imenyny*). These days are often as important as birthdays to Ukrainians with many receiving flowers, candy, or small gifts on the day that's been designated as their name day. Name day origins date back to when people were named after saints, thus they would celebrate their name day on their Saint's day. However, the tradition has evolved to involve names that aren't taken from Saints.

> There's also a holiday for every profession (Mechanics Day, Journalist Day, Day of Medical Workers, etc) and a holiday in which every city is celebrated (the last Sunday in May is Kyiv Day). There's also Youth Day (June 24th) which shouldn't be confused with Student's Day (January 25th).

Accommodation

From sprawling apartments and private homes, to hotels with shared restrooms, and the burgeoning popularity of hostels; Ukraine gives its visitors plenty of options. The choices are of course dependent on the amount of money you're interested in spending, and the level of comfort you desire.

HOTELS

Hotels in most cities are overpriced and in Kyiv they can be ridiculously expensive. It's unlikely to find a room for less that US$50 anywhere in the country. Furthermore, in most establishments you pay by the person staying in the room and it's not uncommon for cheaper hotels to have shared restrooms and showers on each floor. Air conditioning in the summertime can also be an issue. In Ukraine, you definitely get what you pay for. If you're willing to pay a premium, there are Western-style hotels in most major cities and resort areas.

APARTMENT RENTALS

If you're traveling to Ukraine with a partner or a group of people, then renting apartments is the best way to go. You're guaranteed privacy and generally apartments are quite nice when compared to hotels. Hot water in certain build-

Apartment Rental Websites
www.uaapartments.com
www.kievapts.com
www.kievrent.net

ings can be an issue, but most apartments have their own gas powered water heaters (*kolonkas*) that provide hot water (see side bar). Larger cities have plenty of apartments to choose from in all price ranges. In Kyiv, depending on the location and the size, apartments can range from US$60 to US$300 a night, regardless of the amount of people staying in them.

Kolonka

Perhaps nothing is as frightening as the Ukrainian *kolonka,* or gas powered water heater. A standard fixture in most modern apartments, these ominous metal boxes are usually located in the kitchen. Luckily, most of the newer ones are automatic and do not require the stealthy bravery which those that live with the older models must employ.

ROOMS

In front of most train stations and some bus stations you'll see *babushkas* holding signs that say "кімната" (*kimnata)* meaning "room." These *babushkas* often rent out rooms in their private homes or apartments, or are hired by people interested in renting a room. These rooms can vary from private "mother-in-law suites" that have their own entrances, to a room located off of the public living quarters that simply has a door to section it off. While they don't guarantee much privacy, they do afford visitors a chance to see how Ukrainians live. These can vary in price, and no doubt it's affected by how much money they think you have. It can be hard to negotiate with these women (they are invariably always women) if you don't speak the language, but generally they'll bear with you in the hopes of making a sale. If you decide to stay with them, you usually leave with them immediately and follow them to the home which is always "close by," (even if "close by" means a twenty-minute bus ride). Ask how far it is in kilometers before accepting and be prepared for an adventure. This is usually a very safe and respected form of accommodation, with many Ukrainians opting for this type of travel-stay.

HOSTELS

Hostels are a recent development in Ukraine. Now existing in almost every major city in Ukraine they make a great budget conscience place to stay. Like in Europe, hostel rooms in Ukraine can vary from private double bed rooms (if you want the room, you have to pay for both beds) to a spot in an eight or twelve bed dorm. It's important to bring a lock for your suitcase as many hostels don't yet have private lockers (and those that do, don't have locks) and book in advance. Most Ukrainian hostels are run out of apartments that have been hastily converted, so space and bathrooms are limited. Generally hostel staff in Ukraine is very friendly as they are the ones that own the place.

SANATORIUMS

Ukrainians living in villages seldom travel outside of their Oblast and when they do, they likely stay at *sanatorii* (санаторії). Cast aside the Western definition of sanatoriums as a place where the chronically ill go to recuperate, in Ukraine they can be compared to Western wellness retreat lodges. Generally they are located just outside major cities, or in resort areas, with many boasting restaurants, sauna and spa facilities, along with fitness centers. When rooms are booked at sanatoriums they are usually purchased along with packages that include meals at the onsite restaurant and access to all amenities.

Information and booking regarding the country's largest sanatoriums can be made through most travel agencies. These are definitely unique places to stay, but the odd services offered like "digestive and urinary tract cleaning" may not be for everyone.

Health

Visitors to Ukraine should ensure that their immunizations are up-to-date for diphtheria, polio, tetanus, measles, hepatitis A, and typhoid. Foreigners should only drink bottled water and be conscious of where they buy food, as refrigeration is often an issue. In larger cities this isn't so much a problem and the street food overall is relatively safe since much of it is simply different variations of bread. Do exercise caution if buying street food made with meat.

Stray dogs are a big problem in Ukraine, especially in smaller towns and villages. Often times these dogs are unfriendly and will bite, so it's best not to attempt to engage them. It's also wise not to run or jog in smaller towns because of this. If you plan on hiking extensively, you might consider getting immunized against tick-borne encephalitis and rabies before you travel.

A big problem throughout Ukraine is the prevalence of uncovered manholes. In smaller towns and villages, these covers are often stolen and sold for scrap resulting in deep, open holes just ripe for falling in to. Many residents know exactly where the manholes are located, making navigating the unlit streets at night a possibility. Visitors should exercise caution when walking in smaller towns to ensure they don't accidentally fall into one of these beauties.

It's a good idea to bring a small supply of any medication you think you might need during our stay such as Tylenol, Pepto-Bismol, antacids, etc. Though pharmacies (аптека, *apteka*) are located throughout the country, it's better to already have medication on you as the brands you like might not be available.

Safety & Security

Ukraine is generally a safe and welcoming country. Anti-American and anti-EU protests are generally organized by small political groups. While rallies can occur in larger cities, these demonstrations are usually peaceful and no cause for alarm. They are, of course, best avoided.

> A list of foreign embassies in Ukraine and their addresses and telephone numbers are available at the Ukrainian Ministry of Foreign Affairs website: www.mfa.gov.ua

The most common problem foreigners experience is, of course, petty theft. Foreigners are easy to spot and targeted for pick pocketing and scams. Do your best to try and blend-in and don't draw attention to yourself. Even though it's very fashionable in larger cities to display signs of wealth, it's best not to join in. Keep your money in separate places while traveling, keep copies of your passport and visa in separate bags and always mind your belongings; especially on trains and in the metro.

If you experience a crime you should contact your embassy in Kyiv as well as local authorities. This includes theft and loss of passport. Embassy personnel can

From Those in the Know - Ukrainian Restrooms

The one thing that took the most getting used to in Ukraine was the lack of easily accessible, clean, free public restrooms. In most cases, the best you can hope for is a public toilet that charges between 50 kopecs and 1UAH. During long trips on public transportation like marshutkas, buses or trains, I got really used to just "holding it" for twelve or so hours at a stretch. Train bathrooms are often filthy and rest stop facilities are usually no more than a hole in the ground and a series of waist-high concrete stalls with no doors or lighting whatsoever. Oh, and if you don't bring your own toilet paper, you're really asking for trouble — I carried a roll with me in my backpack on all overnight trips. A good rule with Ukrainian bathrooms is to not assume anything: don't assume there will be a usable toilet, don't assume it will be free, and don't assume there will be toilet paper or that you can flush toilet paper. McDonald's provides the one glorious exception to the lack of quality bathrooms. With numerous locations throughout the country's major cities, McDonald's restroom facilities are clean, free, and possess an abundance of flushable toilet paper. I did not find nicer public bathrooms anywhere in the country, so I highly recommend making a pit stop there before beginning any type of long-distance travel.

- Thomas McCloskey

help you find health facilities (if needed), contact family members back home, as well help you understand the procedures involved in filing a police report in Ukraine. Pressing charges however, is the responsibility of the victim.

There is no local equivalent to the "911" emergency phone number in Ukraine. Ambulatory services are generally only available in larger cities. In rural parts of the country, emergency health services can take hours to arrive. Filing a police report can also be a laborious process and police can take a while to report to the scene of a crime. These are the numbers to call in the case of an emergency in Ukraine:

Fire: 101

Police: 102

Ambulance: 103

Gas Leaks: 104…You may think you'll never need this number, but you never know with those damn *kolonkas* (see page 58)

ONLINE SCAMS

Ukrainian women generally like Ukraine and don't want to leave their country. Keep this in mind if you are "talking" to a Ukrainian woman online. Generally foreigners have misconceptions about life in Ukraine and certain individuals will work this to their advantage. There are many fraudulent "Ukrainian dating services" that convince men through emails into sending money for "plane tickets," and "visas" for women to come and visit them. Generally these emails are fraudulent and are not written by the women the men think they are talking to. Furthermore, you're likely to discover that once you send the money, they ask for more money and when you protest, they stop talking to you altogether.

Communication

TELEPHONE

For Calls to Ukraine from Abroad
Dial the international access code in your country, then dial 38 (the international code of Ukraine) + city code + city number

For Calls within Ukraine
If calling within the city, you are in simply dial the telephone number, which is usually five to seven digits.

If calling out of the city or region you are in, you will dial 8, wait for the tone, and then dial the city code and telephone number (this combination is always ten digits).

For Calls from Ukraine to Abroad
Dial 8 (intercity access code), then wait for the dial tone, then dial 10 (international access code) + country code + area code (if required) + telephone number.

Basics

Be aware that international calls from Ukraine are expensive (calls to Western Europe are 60 cents a minute and calls to the U.S. are upwards of 40 cents a minute). At hotels, these prices can be three times as much. Because of the high cost of international calls, IP-telephone calling cards are becoming more popular, though the quality of the connection is worse than a standard connection. Calling cards can be bought at computer stores and street kiosks.

CELL PHONES

Most Ukrainians have cell phones and places that sell them are plentiful. If your cell phone is GSM compatible, or GSM 900 or GSM 1800, it might be possible to use your cell phone in Ukraine. You might also be able to get your phone "unlocked" so that you can use it abroad. Check with your cell phone provider.

Because of the high cost of roaming fees, it's best to buy a new SIM card when you arrive and switch out your SIM card in your phone. In Ukraine, the major providers are:

UMC: National operator of cellular connection. Standard: GSM 900

Kyivstar GSM: National operator of cellular connection. Standard: GSM 900/GSM 1800 (personally found to provide the best coverage)

DCC: Covers Kyiv, Odessa, Crimea, Donetsk, Kharkiv, Dnipropetrivsk, Zaporizhzhya and some other regions of Ukraine. Standard: D-AMPS

Beeline: Covers some Ukrainian regions. Standard: GSM

Life: Covers some Ukrainian regions. Standard: GSM

You may purchase a SIM card (SIM-карти, SIM karti) at any news stall and kiosk in Ukraine. You can also purchase vouchers for minutes from these stalls. These are sold in denominations of 25, 50, 100 and 200UAH. They resemble scratch off cards that you scratch off and text the number that is revealed to you cell phone provider. The amount of your purchase is then added to your cell phone account.

If you don't have a cell phone that is GSM compatible, it's best to leave it at home and buy a new cell upon your arrival. Basic cell phones can run as low as US$40 and nicer ones can be as much as US$200. Or go online and purchase an unlocked GSM 900/GSM 1800 compatible phone. But beware! These can be marked wrong and not work in Ukraine. Your safest bet is waiting to buy one in-county.

INTERNET

Internet cafés are plentiful in Ukraine, but be warned that they can be quite noisy and filled with teenagers playing incredibly annoying video games. The price, however, can't be beat at around US$1 to US$2 an hour (in Kyiv the price can be five times as high).

Some hotels and restaurants offer wireless internet connections. Others require the use of an ethernet to access the internet. If you're planning on using a laptop while in Ukraine, it's best to pack an ethernet cable with an RJ-45 connector.

Cellular phone providers can also provide internet access as well with GRPS and EDGE. The cost is generally US$1 per MB and requires a GSM 900 or GSM 1800 phone with a built-in modem and the purchase of a connector cable that hooks up to the laptop. The connection can be slow, but worth it if you're on the road a lot. Bring your computer to a cellular phone shop for assistance.

MAIL

Delivery within Ukraine is of the "snail mail" variety and can take upwards of seven days. For parcels to arrive in Ukraine from foreign countries, deliveries can take up to five weeks, depending on how isolated the destination may be. Parcels entering Ukraine also have to pass through customs, which means that delivering certain items is prohibited. Furthermore, packages are often opened and items have been known to be stolen. Conceal all valuables if shipping them to Ukraine, and mark all packages as "school supplies," "books", or something not that interesting. The best thing is not to ship anything of extreme value through regular mail.

Courier services are available and better if you need to deliver/receive something fast. The most popular one within Ukraine is DHL (www.dhl.com.ua) and from out of country Meest (www.meest.net). People have also been known to pay a train steward a few dollars to hold a package on a train that is traveling to another city where the receiving person will meet it at the train station.

Giving Back

WORKING IN UKRAINE

In the past, before the Orange Revolution, foreigners in Ukraine generally worked solely at the embassies and in various governmental organizations. Now the presence of Westerners working as TEFL/CELTA teachers and in universities is quite common. The process for obtaining a work visa in Ukraine can be a laborious one, but far from impossible.

Online Resources for Jobs in Ukraine

www.job.ukr.net

www.europeanjob.info

For TEFL/CELTA certification in Kyiv see www.ih.kiev.ua

For TEFL/CELTA certification in Kharkiv see: www.ih.kharkiv.com

Generally companies who hire TEFL/CELTA teachers help them in obtaining visas. For better paying jobs and locations in more comfortable cities, it is best to be certified.

If you're hoping to get a job in Ukraine that pays a Western salary, be prepared for a long wait. Generally these jobs are filled internally, and not posted. Submit resumes to Western companies that have businesses in Ukraine expressing your qualifications. In order for these companies to hire a foreigner to work in Ukraine, they must demonstrate that the job they are doing could not have been filled by a Ukrainian.

VOLUNTEER

The idea of volunteerism used to be a completely foreign concept to Ukrainians who would generally ask "Why?" when someone told them they were here "working as a volunteer." This has to do with the lingering effects of communist thinking and the premise that you do the work that's expected of you and nothing more. Not to say volunteerism isn't appreciated, it's just a new concept in Ukraine. That being said, there has been a massive influx of volunteers to the region. After dissolving from the Soviet Union, the United States Peace Corps began working in Ukraine. Over the past thirteen years, 1,800 Peace Corps Volunteers have served in Ukraine making it the largest recipient of Peace Corps Volunteers in the world. Generally volunteers work in small towns and villages, teaching English in rural schools, and organizing youth training initiatives. For more information see www.pcukraine.org

Short-term volunteer efforts are possible in Ukraine through humanitarian organizations such as Volunteers for Peace (www.vfp.org) and the Ukrainian Humanitarian Initiative (www.hope.ck.ua). In the former, volunteers generally stay in

---

From Those in the Know – Volunteering in Odessa

During my short time in Ukraine working as a volunteer at "The Way Home" (www.wayhome.org.ua), I learned more than I could have possibly imagined. I came to the organization with the assumption that I was going to walk into a classroom and simply teach English to the street kids living at our center in Odessa. Instead, I found myself handing out food to the homeless, writing press releases and grant proposals for the UN, analyzing statistics, contacting friends and family to help me spread the word about our organization through social media, attending art and dance classes, teaching an English conversation module, updating their blog, and even washing a few dishes in the kitchen. My work at "The Way Home" could not have been more varied and well rounded.

During my stay, I worked closely with Even Jahr, Manager of International Relations and Fundraising. Together, we spread the word about the foundation's work via Facebook; after a few weeks, we had already quadrupled our membership. We also created models for upcoming projects that will cater to two underrepresented groups of people in the Odessa region: homeless and/or abused women and HIV positive street children. Unfortunately, the State does very little for these two groups of individuals, so our organization is devoted to helping them by creating a safe place for them to come get shelter, medical help and legal assistance.

My work at the foundation was colorful, varied, and always a challenge. I highly recommend this organization to all interested in making a small difference in a part of the world that really does have the capacity for change. I know that the organization will only continue to flourish and make a meaningful impact in the lives of the street children as the years go by. The best of luck to all the wonderful people who donate time and money to this stupendous cause.

- Erica Batres

dormitories and youth hostels and work on archeological sites and city restoration projects. In the latter, volunteers stay with host-families and are utilized in summer schools, youth camps, and orphanages.

Religious organizations are also prevalent, especially in the East. If you're a Westerner and traveling in rural areas, do not be surprised if someone mistakes you for a missionary as it's quite common for a mission group to enter the area to open a church. Generally they are welcomed, but a little misunderstood. Locals, who are mostly Eastern Orthodox, are often confused as to why a group is trying to convert them to another form of Christianity.

ECO-TOURS & GREEN TOURISM

Ukrainians have warmed up to the notion that if they label something as "eco-tourism" or "green tourism" (зелений туризм, *zelenyy turyzm*), they can make more money. Because of this, it is wise to heavily investigate sites that are promoting themselves as such. Most genuine green tourism takes place in the Carpathians and Crimea, as well as in the Odessa region. Generally, they promote homestays which allow visitors to garner unique insights into the lives of Ukrainians.

Some good places to check out are ruraltourism.com.ua and zeleniyturizm.com.ua. Also check out the Union for the Promotion of Rural Green Tourism Development in Ukraine (www.greentour.com.ua) which works with many nonprofits to develop green tourism in Ukraine and promote rural tours that are environmentally conscious and economically supportive of local communities. Lviv Eco Tour (www.lvivecotour.com) also organizes trips to the Carpathians that emphasize environmental awareness.

Basics

Kyiv

Introduction

Entering the capital of Ukraine is an odd mix of the overtly familiar and the sublimely foreign. Massive avenues open into giant squares, punctured with classic Soviet monuments and oppressive building façades. French haute-couture lines have shops along the city's main drag nestled next to *"gastronome"* that sell sausage by the hundred grams. Old men smoke and play chess in the park, next to young college kids that make out with abandon. New sushi restaurants are opening up daily, the clubs rage until the wee hours of the morning and, in the winter, *babushkas* sell hot coffee from thermoses to men in two thousand dollar business suits.

Completely modern, but the city has yet to shake off the residue of its previous lives. The electric current that shot through Kyiv and powered the country's nationalistic vibe during the Orange Revolution has yet to fizzle, but it's dwindling. Now the city feels like a chaotic wonderland of bustling creatures in a hurry to go, go, go! And in this city, there sure is enough to keep you moving.

HISTORY

Ask any Ukrainian schoolchild about the history of their country and undoubtedly they'll start by telling you how Kyiv was founded – and for good reason. Kyiv has arguably been in existence, one way or another, for over fourteen hundred years. To tell the history of Eastern Europe without telling the history of Kyiv is simply impossible.

Of course, like all historical accounts in this country, the history of Kyiv begins with a legend:

> One day as three brothers, named Ky, Shechek and Koriv and their sister Lybid, sailed down the Dnipro River, they came across a span of land that raised high above all others. So beautiful was the area, and so plentiful were the valleys surrounding it with fauna, that they just had to settle a city here. They named it Kyiv, after the Eldest brother, and history was born.

Though some historians tend to argue with this viewpoint, it's the one that stuck. Other historians theorize that Kyiv was in-fact settled by the Khazars (which were

Turkic peoples) or the Hungarians. They theorize that the name "Kyiv" comes from the Turkic name for riverbank: *Küi*.

One thing is for certain; that the city didn't really start to take off until 879 AD, when Scandinavian King Oleh sent two attachés, Askold and Dir, to the city to set ties with Kyiv's ruling leaders. According to the official nationalistic stance, a few years later King Oleh himself came down to Kyiv to settle disputes between warring tribes, and ended up taking over as a compromise leader. Now serving as Kyiv's (some would argue "self-proclaimed") ruler (this will be a recurring theme) this was beginning of Kievan Rus. Soon the river was crowded with vessels transporting goods throughout the vast empire and a relationship with Constantinople based on trade, was founded.

So, for a short time, seemed that Kyiv was a settlement of pagan-loving, festival digging, wealthy hippies. But newly minted Kievan ruler Volodymyr was apt to change that. Being what you might call a connoisseur of religions, Volodymyr sent out envoys and consulted theologians about various belief systems, you know, in between raiding entire countrysides. Evidently Islam was dismissed because "drinking is the joy of the Russes" and Volodymyr could not foresee an existence without that pleasure. Judaism was also contemplated, even while Volodymyr himself practiced Paganism. It was Orthodox Christianity that won out when his boys reported back on the majestic beauty of the Hagia Sophia in Constantinople, reportedly saying: "We knew not whether we were in heaven or on earth. For on earth there is no such splendor or such beauty, and we are at a loss how to describe it."

Either that, or the whole "we can make a killing if we align with the Byzantine Empire" thing got to him.

Volodymyr adopted Christianity, married the Emperor's daughter, rounded up all of Kyiv for a mass baptism in the Dnipro River and voila! Kievan Rus was now a Christian City and one of the East's most important strongholds. By the eleventh

It was during this time that Volodymyr's son, Prince Yaroslav the Wise, constructed Golden Gate (see page 80).

Kyiv or Kiev?

Kiev is the Russian transliteration of the city's name, which has been used for centuries: back to the times of Kievan Rus. Yes, even revered Ukrainian nationalist Taras Shevchenko said "Kiev."

But times, they are a' changing, and when Ukraine became independent, there was a large movement to recognize "Kyiv" – the Ukrainian transliteration – as the proper spelling since it symbolized the country's departure from all things Russian. Kyiv is the spelling now used in all the country's official documents and recognized as the correct spelling by the United Nations and the U.S. Government as the country's capital.

In everyday life the spellings are used interchangeably, and noticeably differ in popularity depending on the part of the country you are visiting.

century, the glory-age of Kievan Rus was in full force with over four hundred churches, eight markets, and fifty thousand inhabitants living within its perimeters. At the time it was the largest city in Europe and its center of culture.

But all good things must end and soon men were arguing over who was to lead the country. Like Argentina in the 1940s (*Evita*, anyone? Anyone?), every day there seemed to be a new ruler who took the city by force. When the Mongols invaded in 1240 AD, the city's defenses were so weakened that it was leveled in no time.

After that, the city was bounced around from country to country. Being a part of the Grand Duchy of Lithuania for some time, it really didn't get its groove back till it was handed over to Russia in the eighteenth century. It was the sugar boom of the early twentieth century that really set the town off with mansions like the House with Chimaeras (see page 82) and the Central Synagogue (see page 84) being built by millionaires with money made from the sweet stuff.

During the Bolshevik Uprising, the city was frequented by outbursts between the Red Army and the White Ukrainian forces. Many artists depicted these events in their works, including Mikhail Bulgakov who lived on Andriyivs'kyi Uzviz, whose house still remains there today (see page 79).

During this time (1917-1918), Mykhailo Hrushevsky headed the *Tsentralna Rada*, which was the first independent Ukrainian legislation, and the precursor to the modern Verkhovna Rada. They pushed for a socialist regime, but their brief period of glory was soon washed over by the red tide of communism. At the end of it all, 822 of its deputies were declared outlaws. Most were executed, sent to gulag camps, or died mysteriously. The lucky ones emigrated to foreign lands.

In the 1930s, Kyivans began to suffer tremendously from controversial Soviet policies. Ukrainian nationalism was oppressed and all forms of art, culture, or religion that could be viewed as oppositional to Stalin's doctrines were criminalized. It was during this period that many of the region's churches were destroyed (see St. Michael's Golden Domed Monastery page 83).

Nazi Germany invaded Kyiv on September 19, 1941. Before the Red Army evacuated the city they planted ten thousand mines and bombs, controlled by wireless detonators, throughout the streets. They set them off on September 24th, completely obliterating entire roads, killing one thousand Germans, and leaving only one building standing on Kreschatyk.

This small victory did little to stop the most horrific war crime yet to be seen on Kyiv's soil. During that first month of September, over forty thousand Jewish citizens of Kyiv were rounded up and executed in Babiy Yar (see page 88). It's estimated an additional sixty thousand people lost their lives there as a result of being POWs, or being viewed as part of the resistance movement. The city wasn't retaken until November 6, 1943; but, by then, 80 percent of its inhabitants were homeless.

After the war, the intense industrialization of Kyiv led to a housing crisis. According to Soviet policies, all cities were to be redesigned using the same general development plan, which had a way of kicking urban development to the curb. Because of this, massive (very unattractive) apartment blocks were built just outside the city center to house the workers. During its makeover, Kyiv was forced to adopt its Soviet leader's architectural taste for better or for worse. Khrushchev, who evidently had a love for non-ornamental, concrete designs, declared all previous forms of architecture "excessive" and disbanded the Soviet Academy of Architecture in 1955. Unsurprisingly the style of architecture that now bears his name is also one of the most unsightly – Khrushchev is to thank for those cramped, dreary apartment blocks that suffocate the perimeter of the city.

In the 1980s the wave of Ukrainian nationalism so popular in the west of the country, began to catch on in the capital. Finally, after 57 years as the capital of the Ukrainian Soviet Socialist Republic, Kyiv became the capital of independent Ukraine in 1991. It was in Kyiv that the most famous televised images from the Orange Revolution (see page 20) were filmed. Pillars with graffiti from those famous protests still remain. Look for them framed behind plexiglass, in front of the city's Central Post Office.

> An old Russian proverb says: "If Moscow is the heart of Russia and St. Petersburg is its head, then Kyiv is its mother."

TRANSPORTATION

By Plane

Boryspil International Airport (Міжнародний Аеропорт "Бориспіль") is where international flights leave and depart from Kyiv. There is also the smaller Zhuliany Airport, but it mostly handles a few domestic flights and private charters. Boryspil Airport is located thirty-four kilometers from the city, which makes for plenty of breathless early morning dashes to reach it in time after a long night out in Kyiv.

The building itself is a little chaotic, but improving. Before recent terminal expansions, hallways were literally bulging with an over abundance of passengers. Terminal D is expected to be completed in 2011 and construction of a new runway sometime between 2012 and 2014, should vastly improve things.

Before landing in Ukraine you will be presented with a registration card. It's important to have an address of some kind to put on the card (be it your hostel, your hotel or a friend's place).

Upon disembarking your plane, you will be ushered down a hall through customs. The guards there speak English but probably won't say a word to you. Just present your completed registration card and passport (opened to the visa page if you needed one) and wait to be waved through. After grabbing your luggage, you'll pass through the customs area. You needn't declare anything unless you have ungodly amounts of cash on your person. Those with things to declare will go through the Red Line, those who don't have anything to declare may proceed through the Green Line.

From there you'll enter the main airport where throngs of people crowd the exit waiting for loved ones with flowers and chocolates. Honestly, it can be a mildly depressing scene if you're entering the country by yourself.

Two currency exchanges (обмін валют, *obmin valyut)* are located inside the airport, but it's better to wait until you are in the city center as the exchange rate is better there. At the airport, taxi drivers eagerly accept U.S. Dollars and Euros. An ATM (банкомат, *bankomat)* is also located in the airport as well as credit card accepting public telephones. If you succumb to the whispers of the taxi drivers, be prepared to shell out at least 200UAH (or US$25) for the thirty-five-minute drive into the city center (but more likely they'll start out at 250UAH). Haggle them down, or go outside the airport and take an hour-long bus ride or marshrutka ride to the Central Train Station (Центральний вокзал, *Tsentral'nyy˘ vokzal)* for 25UAH. The buses depart from in front of the airport on the right. From the train station, you can easily hop on the metro or take a (cheaper) taxi to your final destination.

By Bus

International buses arrive at Kyiv's Central Bus Station (Центральна автобусна станція, *Tsentral'na avtobusna stantsiya)*, which unfortunately makes for a depressing introduction to the city. Located at Moskovska Ploshcha (Московська пл.), the entire square is currently undergoing construction so it can feel clustered and chaotic. However, the renovations haven't affected schedules; only emotional states. A currency exchange is located in the main lobby as well as an ATM outside next to the main entrance. A taxi from the bus station into the city center will run you about 50UAH. Another option is taking trolleybus #1, #2, #4, #12 or #42 one stop to the Lybidska (Либідська) Metro Station and then jump on the metro from there.

By Train

Kyiv's Central Railway Station (Центральний вокзал, *Tsentral'nyy˘ vokzal)* is one of the most pleasant ways to enter the city. Newly refurbished and adjoined by the ultra-modern Southern Railway Station, it makes for a convenient way to enter the city. ATMs and currency exchanges are located throughout the building as well as Internet cafés and pay phones. Outside the old entrance, white buses provide transport to a variety of Ukrainian cities; look for the name of the city on the window and pay the driver. Entrance to the Vokzalna (Вокзальна) Metro Station is also easily accessible. Just walk out the old entrance, look left and you'll see the metro entrance, under the Green "M," on the far side across from the McDonald's.

By Car

Before starting this adventure, I suggest getting an awesome GPS and taking a deep breath. You'll also need your driver's license and car registration papers. When you enter the country, you'll have to sign a paper swearing that you'll take the car out of the country before a certain date (generally two months after entering the country). Automobile insurance is required in Ukraine and can be purchased at the border. However, it's easy to get swindled into buying something you don't need if you don't speak Ukrainian or Russian. You might want to look into buying short-term automobile insurance that covers Ukraine while in your home country to avoid this problem all together. Keep in mind insurance is required for a minimum of two weeks, even if your stay in-country is shorter than that.

CITY TRANSPORT

Getting around Kyiv is incredibly easy. Kyiv is equipped with trams, trolleybuses, marshrutkas (those white mini-vans you keep seeing everywhere) as well as the metro and buses. Public transportation, however, is not for the faint of heart as one could easily spend hours waiting for an un-cramped bus. You *can* fit inside any bus, or metro carriage, no matter how full it looks. Just push yourself in and get cozy with your (unsmiling) neighbor!

Trolleybuses, Trams, & Buses
Тролейбуси, трамваї і автобуси, *Troleybusy, tramvaï i avtobusy*

Surface transportation in Kyiv is not taken by those in a hurry. Traffic jams and congestion make these vehicles look like massive slugs, slowly churning away, determined to get somewhere…eventually. But hey! It's a great way to get a look around the city. Get a window seat and take your own private tour of Kyiv.

Single tickets cost 1.50UAH and can be bought from the driver, or from certain street kiosks. Thirty-day passes cost 160UAH. Once you get on the vehicle, make sure you immediately validate your ticket or you risk the chance of being targeted by the undercover inspector and fined 40UAH.

Marshrutkas
Маршрутки

These privately-owned white buses or route-taxis (the yellow ones) are smaller and therefore have an innate ability to jump curbs and swerve by pedestrians, making them infinitely faster (and scarier) than the aforementioned trolleybuses. Currently, tickets range from 2 to 3UAH, and you pay the driver as you get on. Generally they run the same routes as the city buses, except marshrutkas are marked with what stops they make on their side window and front windshield (visibility be damned).

When you're nearing your stop, yell out "next stop please" (Наступна зупинка будь ласка, *nastupna zupynka bud' laska*) with great conviction.

Funicular
Фунікулер

A ride on this baby will run you 2UAH and take you from the Podil (Поділ) District up the side of Andriyivs'kyi Uzviz (Андріївський узвіз, "Andrew's Descent") and drop you off behind St. Michael's Cathedral, or vice-versa. This ride is highly recommended after a walk down St. Andrew's Descent, as St. Andrew's Ascent leaves you too breathless to enjoy the craft booths. Opened in 1905, the Funicular transports an estimated ten to fifteen thousand commuters and camera wielding tourists a day.

The Metro
Метро

If the Cold War starts up again, I'm heading back to Kyiv and hanging out in the Metro. Half the time it takes to get to one stop from another is spent riding an escalator down into the pits of the earth, disembarking from it, walking ten feet, and getting on another descending escalator. Your ears literally pop when you're going back up; it's that deep. Perfect for the brink of apocalypse.

> **Ukraine Fun Fact #612!**
> The deepest metro station in the world is Arsenal'na Metro Station in Kyiv at 303 feet (105 meters) underground.

Recent fare hikes have caused mass grumblings; currently one metro ride is 2UAH (quite an increase considering that it was 50 kopecks up until 2008). Fifteen-day passes can be bought from the token booth at the entrance of the metro stations for 48UAH. Thirty-day passes will run you 95UAH. The metro runs from 6:00 to 24:00 with the busiest times from 8:00 to 9:00 and 17:00 to 18:00 (but it is always going to be crowded). Take extreme care to mind your belongings as close quarters are the rule. Zip your purse, take your wallet out of your back pocket, and get creative with hiding spots. Like any metro in the world, it's known for pickpockets.

When entering the metro, get your token from the booth or from the kiosks attached to the wall. Then simply put the blue token in the coin slot at the entrance gate of the metro and wait for the green light. The object is then to run through as quickly, and awkwardly, as possible in hopes that the protective gate doesn't decide to randomly close on you (which, sometimes happens). Resembling a battering ram, the black arm that catapults itself out to block its victims is a cruel design feature, undoubtedly constructed by Stalin.

Currently the metro is composed of three lines: the Red (Sviatoshynsko-Brovarska Line), the Blue (Kurenivsko-Chervonoarmiys'ka Line) and the Green (Syretsko-Pecherska Line). Yellow and Light Blue lines are currently underway. Photography is begrudgingly allowed, but filming is illegal.

Attractions by Metro Stop
Here are some sights divided by their closest metro stop. Note that you may have to take a trolleybus or marshrutka from these stops to reach them. For further instructions, see the following Sights and Attractions section (pg 78).

Arsenal'na Metro (Арсенальна): Mariinsky Palace and Park, Pechersk Lavra

Dorohozhychi Metro (Дорогожичі): Babiy Yar

Hidropark Metro (Гідропарк): Dnipro Beaches

Respubliksy Metro (Республіці): The Ukrainian Museum of Folk Architecture and Rural Life

Zoloti Vorota Metro (Золоті Ворота): Taras Shevchenko National Opera House, Golden Gate (ancient city wall of Kyiv), St. Sophia's Cathedral, St. Andrew's Cathedral

Kontraktova Ploshcha Metro (Контрактова площа): The Chernobyl Museum, Andriyivs'kyi Uzviz

Kreschatyk Metro (Хрещатик): St. Michael's Gold Domed Monastery, The House with Chimaeras (the Horodetsky House)

Maidan Nezalezhnosti Metro (Майдан Незалежності): People's Friendship Arch

Percherska Metro (Печерська): Motherland Statue (Rodina Mat) and Great Patriotic War Memorial and Museum

Poshtova Ploshcha Metro (Поштова пл.): Podil District, Funicular

Universytet Metro (Університет): St. Vladimir's Cathedral

INTERNET

Wireless internet (Wi-Fi) access is becoming increasingly accessible in the capital with the vast majority of hostels (and some hotels) offering it to guests for free. Because of this, it might be wise to bring a small laptop for easy hookup and cheap Skype calls (some internet cafés charge an absurd amount to use Skype, so it's best if you have it on your computer).

Wireless internet is also becoming a big trend in restaurants and cafés, but sometimes you will have to pay 10UAH per hour for access via prepaid cards. These cards can be bought from the hostess stand or from your waiter. Generally they are good for up to one-month from activation and can be used anywhere that charges for Wi-Fi capabilities. Free Wi-Fi in cafés is, thankfully, increasing in popularity.

Beware of "Internet Clubs"

All over the country you'll see buildings with blacked out windows and neon lit "Інтернет-клуб" (Internet Club) signs that look like they're hiding something – like gambling. A few years ago gambling was outlawed, so these places started popping up all over the country. The computers inside them are hooked up to online gambling websites (conveniently bypassing the laws) and aren't really used for writing emails. If you're looking for legit internet places look for UkrTelecom (Укртелеком) buildings throughout the country. Generally this phone company houses an internet section in all of their buildings. Or just look for Інтернет-клуб places that don't look like mini-Vegas.

Internet Cafés

Central Post Office *(Центральне пошта, Tsentral'ne poshta); Kreschatyk 22 (Хрещатик 22); Metro Stop: Maidan Nezalezhnosti (Майдан Незалежності); Tel: (+380) 44 230 08 51; From 10UAH per hour; Open 24 hrs*

Oscar Internet Center *(Оскар Інтернет-центр, Oskar Internet-tsentr); Kreschatyk 48 (Хрещатик 48); Metro Stop: Teatral'na (Театральна); From 10UAH per hour; Open 24hrs*

"Vault 13" Computer Club *Chervonoarmiys'ka 19 (Червоноармійська 19); Metro Stop: L'va Tolstoho (Льва Толстого); Internet Sunday-Thursday from 09:00-23:00 3UAH per hour, 23:00-9:00 2UAH per hour; Friday and Saturday Internet 3UAH per hour; Open 24hrs*

POST OFFICES / MAIL

Central Post Office (Центральне пошта, *Tsentral'ne poshta*) You can't miss this monolithic building located on the corner of Independence Square. Inside, it's probably home to the widest selection of Ukrainian post cards and surly counter workers. But don't worry, they're adept at understanding the intricacies of the pantomime and will eventually help you mail off a box. Make sure you check out the columns in front of the main entrance that still have leftover graffiti from the Orange Revolution spray painted upon them. *Khreschatyk 22 (Хрещатик 22); Metro Stop: Maidan Nezalezhnosti (Майдан Незалежності); Tel: +38 (044) 230 08 38; www.ukrposhta.com; Open 08:00-21:00, Sundays 09:00-19:00*

FedEx *Kikvidze 44 (Ківідзе 44); Metro Stop: Druzhby Narodiv (Дружби Народів); Tel: +38 (044) 495 20 20; www.fedex.com; Open 09:00-19:00, Closed Sat and Sun*

UPS *Mechnykova 20 (Мечникова 20); Metro stop: Klovs'ka (Кловська); Tel: +38 (044) 280 10 19; www.ups.com; Open 09:00-19:00, Closed Sat and Sun*

DHL *Vasylkivska 1 (Васильківська 1); Metro Stop: Lybidska (Либідська); Tel: +38 (044) 490 26 00; www.dhl.com.ua*

TOURS

To be fair Ukraine is best experienced by just showing up and seeing what unfolds. If, however, you don't have much time in Ukraine and want to pack it all in a week's time, tours might be your best bet. Get ready to spend more money than really necessary as credible, English-speaking tour companies in Ukraine charge a premium.

Travel agency "Terra Incognita" Offering package tours ranging from three days to twelve nights, as well as day tours throughout Ukraine, Terra Incognita is great for families or groups wishing to organize mass outings. They can also set up and arrange camping tours in the Carpathians as well as adventure tours like spelunking (including equipment). *01001, Ukraine, Kyiv; Mala Zhytomyrska 16/3 (Мала Житомирська 16/3), Office 4; Tel.: +38 (044) 504 03 43; Cell: +38 (067) 506 80 39; info@terraincognita.info; www.terraincognita.info*

Olymp Travel LTD If you have an idea of where you want to go in Ukraine, but are worried about finding hotels and booking train tickets in advance, Ukraine Destination can do all that for you. Their website provides a comprehensive list of hotels (arranged by city, cost, and quality) that you can book through them online. Also, if you email them to let them know where you want to go and when, they can arrange your preferred method of transportation. *Shovkovychna 24 (Шовковична 24); Tel: +38 (044) 253 71 08; dima@ukrainedestination.com; www.ukrainedestination.com*

Sonata-Travel Providing all types of tours throughout Kyiv and Ukraine, Sonata Travel can arrange ethnic and genealogy tours, adventure and thrill seeking tours, as well as business and historical tours. You can also book accommodations and transportation through their website. *Dmytrivska 19A (Дмитрівська 19A), Office 4; Tel: +38 (044) 507 02 30; admin@tour-ua.com; www.tour-ua.com*

City Tours of Kyiv

Mysterious Kyiv Showing off the bizarre side of Kyiv, Mysterious Kyiv offers tours of the city's caves, "secret Stalin tunnels," and day trips to Chernobyl. They offer their tours in a variety of languages along with reasonable prices. Their website is also fabulous (though sadly not in English). *Tel: +38 (044) 491 11 76; tour@interesniy.kiev.ua; www.interesniy.kiev.ua*

Kyiv City Tours If you want an English speaking tour guide to show you around Kyiv, this is the site to arrange it through. Their website lists prices for prearranged tours or you can tailor one to your liking. If you're only in Kyiv for one day and want to make sure you see everything, this is probably your best bet. *Pereulok Mikhailovskiy 7 (Провулок Михайлівський 7); Tel: +38 (067) 265 79 92; info@kievcitytours.com; www.kievcitytours.com*

Prime Excursion Bureau Specializing in nature and cultural excursions, Prime Excursion Bureau offers over twenty-five different excursions within Kyiv (Percherska Lavra, Jewish History tour) and day trips to surrounding areas like Chernihiv and Sofiyivsky Park in Uman. Individual and group tours can be arranged though their website which is available in German and English. *Schekavyts'ka 30/39 (Щекавицька 30/39), Suite 4; Tel: +38 (044) 227 77 78; info@primetour.ua; www.primetour.ua*

MEDICAL AND EMERGENCY SERVICES

In case of an emergency there is really no better city to be in than Kyiv (well, in Ukraine that is) for medical treatment. They even have hospitals that specialize in cosmetic surgery and offer botox for walk-ins. Western-style hospitals exist in the capital at a hefty price. Make sure you carry proof of your insurance with you. Buying a travel insurance plan that covers medical evacuation is also highly suggested; especially if you're traveling outside the capital.

American Medical Center (Американський медичний центр) Offers twenty-four-hour emergency visits, women's health, outpatient care and medical evacuation. They also have an English-speaking staff. *Berdychivska 1 (Бердичівська 1); Metro Stop: Luk'yanivska (Лук'янівська); Tel: +38 (044) 490 76 00; www.amcenters.com; Open 24hrs*

Dobrobut (Добробут) Offers twenty-four-hour emergency care and consultations, as well as services for adults and children. This hospital offers in-patient service as well as medical transportation within Ukraine and abroad. *Pymonenka 10 (Пимоненка 10); Metro stop: Luk'yanivska (Лук'янівська); Tel: +38 (044) 495 28 88; www.med.dobrobut.com; Open 24hrs*

PHARMACIES
АПТЕКА, *АПТЕКА*

Apteka #24 *Chervonoarmiys'ka 10 (Червоноармійська 10); Metro stop: L'va Tolstoho (Льва Толстого); Tel: (+380) 44 235 43 08; Open 24hrs*

Bosm Pharm (Босм Фарм) *Shevchenko 17 (Т. Шевченка 17); Metro stop: Universytet (Університет); Tel: +38 (044) 235 50 17; Open 24hrs*

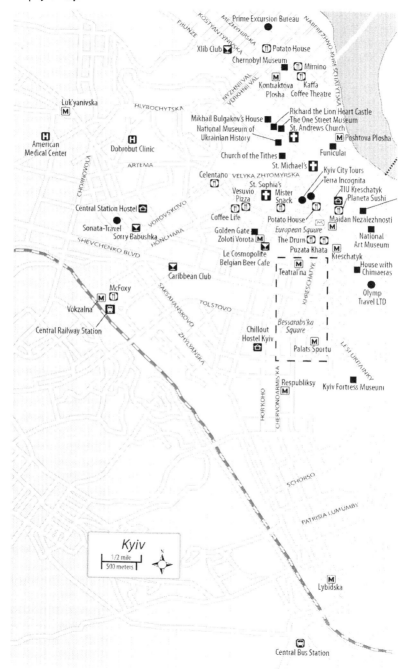

Kyiv

1/2 mile
500 meters

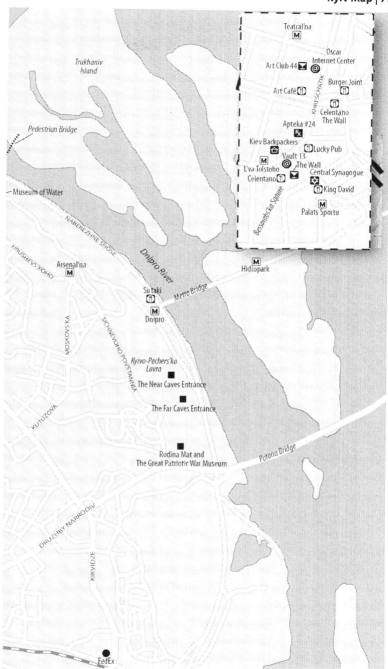

Sights & Attractions

The following sights and attractions have been organized by metro location.

AROUND METRO KONTRAKTOVA PLOSHCHA
КОНТРАКТОВА ПЛОЩА

Chernobyl Museum
Чорнобильська музей, *Chornobyl's'ka muzey*

Though there's not much information in English at the museum, the sad story of the Chernobyl disaster is explained through thousands of photographs, videos, short documentary films, and interviews. The uniforms that the firefighters wore while battling the blaze are on display here, as well as the signs from various villages around the region that no longer exist due to the tragedy. Respectfully put together, the museum shows the devastating loss of life and the effect the disaster has had on the entire region. Audio tour guides in English can be rented at the ticket booth for US$3. To operate it, simply key in the "station #" you are at into the walkie-talkie device. *Provulok Khoryvyj 1 (провулок Хоревий 1); Open 10:00-18:00, Saturday 10:00-17:00, Closed Sunday; Admission 10UAH, Children 3UAH.*

Andrew's Descent
Андріївський узвіз, *Andriyivs'kyi uzviz*

Winding its way down from the Kyiv's Upper Town to the old, commercial district of Podil, Andrew's Descent is boasted as the "Montmartre of Kyiv" by tourism agencies. Hyperbole aside, it is quite brilliant. Meandering down Zamkova Hill, it continues for 719 meters before ending near Kontraktova Ploshcha. Throughout the week, artists, street performers, and crafters set up booths to sell items varying from hand stitched table clothes to delicately painted *pysanky* and old Soviet era artifacts (which may or may not be real). Along the road there's also various booths selling knickknacks like "I (heart) Kyiv" shirts and magnets. Load up on them now because outside of Kyiv, cheesy knickknacks are hard to find (and after all, won't you regret not getting that vodka bottle magnet/bottle opener?). Andrew's Descent is best appreciated when in one of those European strolling moods, taking advantage of street cafés, of which there are plenty here. *Metro: Kontraktova Ploshcha (Контрактова площа)*

"The Castle of Richard the Lion Heart"
Замок Річарда Левове Серце, *Zamok Richarda Levove Sertse*

Originally constructed for Dymytro Orlov, between 1902 and 1904, he intended to lease out the building's apartments to tenants. However, when he died in 1911 he left his wife and five children with a whole lot of bills to pay. The house was sold off and went through so many owners, who either died or couldn't escape the place fast enough, that it was rumored to be haunted or cursed. It got its name in 1967 when a well known Kyiv-writer, Viktor Nekrasov, wrote a story for the literary magazine

Novy Mir. In the story he mentions several of the houses on Andriyivs'kyi Uzviz, one of which he called Richard's Castle; and the name stuck. A former bohemian hideaway, and a favorite with artists, it was turned into communal apartments by the communists. In 1983 plans were made to turn the building into a hotel. Since then investors and owners have changed with the seasons, and to this day it remains fenced in and empty. An eerily beautiful sight, look for the almond white building with black spires. It's easily spotted as it's the only building on the street with blacked out windows at night (creepy). *Andriyivs'kyi Uzviz 15 (Андріївський узвіз 15)*

Mikhail Bulgakov's House
Михайло Булгаков будинок, *Mykhaylo Bulhakov budynok*

During his life, Kyiv-born Russian writer Bulgakov and his family lived in two different houses. He penned *The White Guard* in which he described the plight of the Turbin family during the Russian Civil War. In the book he vibrantly describes Andrew's Descent, which in the book he called "Aleksey's Descent." A plaque marking the location of Bulgakov's home gives the "incorrect" address as "13, Aleksey Descent." *Andriyivs'kyi Uzviz 13 (Андріївський узвіз 13)*

St. Andrew's Church
Андріївська церква, *Andriivs'ka tserkva*

Located at the top of Starokyivskaya Hill, overlooking the Podil District and Andriyivs'kyi Uzviz, St. Andrew's Church is hard to miss. Built in 1747 by order of Russian Tsaress Elizabeth Petrovna (Peter the Great's daughter), it is based on a design by Italian born, but naturalized Russian architect, Bartolomeo Rastrelli. Constructed in the baroque style, it's one of the rare churches to survive Bolshevik atheism with little damage.

Since 1968, the church has been open as a museum. The museum though, cannot do justice when compared to the exterior, so perhaps it's best to appreciate the church's beauty from outside. Also be sure to take advantage of the views from the church's fantastic balustrade. *Andriyivs'kyi Uzviz (Андріївський узвіз 23); Open 10:00-18:00, Closed Wednesdays*

Why St. Andrew's Church has no Bell Tower

As you may notice, the church has no bell tower, for which two reasons are given. The first explanation offered is that the Tsaress planned to oversee the church herself and there would be no need for a bell tower to call the congregation to service. The second more whimsical story offered is that when Saint Andrew (who prophesied that Kyiv would be a great Christian City, before anything was even there) first visited the area he erected a cross on the spot where the church now stands. At the time, according to legend, there was a sea where the Dnipro River lies, but it drained away when the cross was placed and receded back into the river. A part of it though remained hidden, deep beneath the hill the church now stands on. So if church bells were to ring, the water underneath would be disturbed and rise up, flooding Kyiv and the entire left bank of the Dnipro. Hence, bells were omitted.

The One Street Museum
Музей однієї вулиці, *Muzey˘odniyeï vulytsi*

Located at the base of Andriyivs'kyi Uzviz, the small One Street Museum is a pleasantly arranged collection of artifacts, documents, clothing, antiques, postcards and furniture collected from old homes and buildings on the street. The museum seeks to tell the story of the famous road without preconceptions or biases. Though not in English, the museum and its displays are self-explanatory. Guided tours in English can be arranged for 100UAH. *Andriyivs'kyi Uzviz (Андріївський узвіз 2-В); Open: 12:00-18:00, Closed Mondays; Admission: 20UAH Adults, discounts for children; Tel: +38(044) 425 03 98; www.onestreet.kiev.ua/about-museum-eng*

AROUND METRO ZOLOTI VOROTA
ЗОЛОТІ ВОРОТА, GOLDEN GATE

Zoloti Vorota
Золоті Ворота

Included on the UNESCO World Heritage List Zoloti Vorota, literally meaning "Golden Gate," marked the entranceway to the old city of Kyiv. It was built by the Grand Prince of Kyiv (affectionately known as Yaroslav the Wise) in 1037. In 1832 what was left of the ruins were excavated and in the 1970s a pavilion was constructed with a small museum to show off the ruins. In 1982 the gate itself was reconstructed for Kyiv's fifteen hundred year anniversary. Now a museum and architectural and archeological site, Golden Gate offers visitors a glimpse of Kyiv's past and fabulous views of Volodymys'ka Street. If you don't feel like paying an ever-changing admission rate, just admire it from afar. *Zolotovorits'ka 8 (Золотоворітський 8); Tel: +38 (044) 234 70 68*

St. Sophia's Cathedral
Софійський собор, *Sofiyš'kyy˘sobor*

Constructed in 1037, St. Sophia was built to commemorate the site at which Kievan Rus was victorious over the Pechenegs, an Asian nomadic tribe. The oldest remaining church in Kyiv, it was commissioned by Prince Yaroslav the Wise, whose tomb is located inside the church. The church took its name from St. Sophia's Cathedral in Constantinople. The beautiful thirteen-cupola sanctuary adjoined Prince Yaroslav's palace. So ornate were the church's frescoes and mosaics that many foreign diplomatic meetings were held there, along with worship services for the community. The 76-meter high bell tower was completed in 1752, and the fourth story of the bell tower and gilded cupola were added in 1852. The eighteenth century refractory now works as a museum that displays models of Kyiv before it was ravaged by the Mongol Invaders of 1240. The interior of the church, which still has many of the original frescoes intact almost a millennium later, can also be viewed. *Volodymyrska 24 (Володимирська 24); Admission: Grounds 2UAH, Bell Tower: 5UAH, All Exhibits: 20UAH; Open 10:00-17:00, Wednesday 10:00-16:00*

National Museum of Ukrainian History
Національний музей української історії, *Natsional'nyy muzey ukraïns'koï istoriï*

Attempting to cram nearly "9,000" years of bloody Ukrainian history into one building, The National Museum of Ukrainian History houses all things Ukraine; from prehistoric times to modern day. Situated on a bluff behind Andriyivs'kyi Uzviz, look for the massive Stalinist building. Inside the museum displays coins and bills from ancient times, artwork, and archeological finds. While there's not much in English, it does make for an interesting stroll for history buffs, but it's not necessarily a must do. *Volodymyrska 2 (Володимирська 2); Admission: 12UAH; Open 10:00-17:00 Closed Wednesdays.*

Church of the Tithes
Десятинної церкви, *Desyatynnoï tserkvy*

The Church of the Tithes was the first stone church in Kyiv. It was built in 996 by order of (you guessed it) Prince Volodymyr to commemorate the Baptism of Kyiv Rus. The Prince set aside a tithe of his income to finance the church's construction; thus where the church got its name. It collapsed in 1240 during a Mongol raid under the weight of Kyivans who took refuge on its roof; or a fire was set to it and it burned it to the ground. Either way, the result was the same. It's been reconstructed several times (once in wood, another time in stone, oddly enough never in straw) but now it lays in ruins after it was destroyed for the final time by Soviet authorities in 1935. Fenced in, it serves as the backdrop for street vendors and makes for an oddly poignant abandoned archeological site. There have been murmurs that a church would again be built at this site, but oppositional viewpoints have come forth stating that to construct anything here would disrupt the "archeological goldmine" that lies beneath it. *Volodymyrs'ka 2 (Володимирська 2)*

AROUND METRO KHRESCHATYK
ХРЕЩАТИК

Kreschatyk Street
Хрещатик

Beginning at European Square (Європейської площі, *Yevropeys'koï ploshchi*) and ending at Bessarabs'ka Square (Бессарабської площі, *Bessarabs'koï ploshchi*), Kreschatyk is the street Kyivans proudly reference when discussing their modern city. With stores like Mango, Zara, and Adidas lining the wide boulevard, it blows to bits all the stereotypical notions people have when they hear "Kyiv, Ukraine." Before the shopping malls (one is located underneath the European Square and another massive one begins at Bessarabs'ka Square) and the TGI Friday's – which sadly have begun to infiltrate Eastern Europe – this area was nothing more than deep ravines and gorges that Kievan Rus Princes used as hunting grounds.

During World War II, the retreating Russian army booby trapped the boulevard with explosives, destroying the beauty of the street's architecture and the Germans all in one shebang. It was rebuilt with typical Soviet flare, but it's far more beautiful than you would expect upon hearing that. On weekends and holidays the street is closed to traffic and well-dressed pedestrians flood the main thoroughfare. Be a true Kyivan and take a few laps down its stretch, and be sure to keep an eye out for the man with the squirrel and the impressive line that forms to have a picture taken with it.

House with Chimaeras
Будинок з химерами, *Budynok z khymeramy*

The name of this place doesn't do this nineteenth century home justice. Though, sadly, visitors can't visit the interior (which was built complete with a wine cellar and a special room for the owner's cow). Its exterior, however, is worth the short hike alone. Frogs, mermaids, elephants, rhinos, and a myriad of other creatures created in concrete are attached to the building and serve as storm drains. Concrete was a new and expensive material in the nineteenth century, but a concrete dealer donated the material to the architect Vladislaw Horodetsky knowing that the publicity received from the house would alone be worth it.

The design of the building is an architectural wonder. Built to take advantage of Kyiv's sloping streets, it has three floors on its front side and six on the other. It's now used as a Presidential Building for diplomatic ceremonies, such as the 2006 meeting between former Russian President Vladimir Putin and then Ukrainian President Viktor Yushchenko.

To get to it, walk southwest from Khreschatyk's Metro Station towards Zankovetskoy Street (Заньковецької вул). Turn right on Zankoyvetskoy Street and continue for 180 meters, take a left at Lyuteranskaya Street (Лютеранська вул) and continue for 275 meters. Turn left at Bankova Street (Банкова вул) and the house will be up ahead on the left. *Bankova 10 (Банковій 10)*

AROUND MAIDAN NEZALEZHNOSTI
МАЙДАН НЕЗАЛЕЖНОСТІ, INDEPENDENCE SQUARE

Maidan Nezalezhnosti
Майдан Незалежності, *Independence Square*

Located on the northern end of Kreschatyk, this airy square is encircled by massive buildings and dotted by an abundance of fountains. Underneath it, tunnels lead to various shopping malls and the metro, creating an ever-rotating spring of pedestrians who pop up onto the street like prairie dogs. In 2001, a **Monument to Berehynia** was erected on the site of the former Lenin monument; it's the tall column with the statue that looks like a golden angel on top of it. Berehynia is seen in Slavic mythology as a "hearth-mother" goddess and her presence on Maidan is to serve as the guardian of the nation itself. It was built to commemorate Ukraine's tenth year of independence.

Directly behind Berehynia is a building which you'll find yourself seeing and thinking: "maybe it's a city garden?!" It is not my friends; it's just another mall – The Globus Mall. There's also other statues dedicated to the city's ancient protectors: one to the **Archangel Michael** and to **Kyi, Schek, Khoryb and Lybid**: the three legendary brothers and sister, who, according to legend, founded Kyiv (see page 66). Look for the fountain in front of The Globus Mall with the three guys and girl wielding bows and arrows and looking bad-ass.

St. Michael's Golden-Domed Cathedral
Михайловский Золотоверхий Монастир,
Mikhailskiy Zolotoverkhiy Monastyr

Located opposite the main thoroughfare leading to St. Sophia's Cathedral, and right by the Funicular, St. Michael's is an impressive working monastery whose golden domes and Easter-egg blue paint make it hard to miss. If you're thinking it's in remarkably good shape considering how old it is (the original was built 1108 by Prince Sviatopolik), you're right. The church and the surrounding monastery, which was still in fantastic condition, were demolished in 1932 by Soviet authorities who believed that it lacked "historical and artistic value" and therefore did not merit preservation. The reconstructed cathedral was completed in 2000.

As you enter the church grounds, you'll notice a somber monument to the victims of Holodomor (see page 17) to your left. Within the church grounds, the museum tells the tragic history of the monastery as well as neighboring churches that were destroyed by the Soviets. Placards and displays are explained in Ukrainian and English. *Mykhailivs'ka Ploshcha (Михайлівська площі); Church Grounds Open 08:00-19:00. Services Daily at 08:00 and 17:00, Sundays at 08:00, 10:00, and 17:00. Museum Ticket Office open Tuesday-Sunday, 10:00-17:00; Admission 5UAH*

The Accursed Prince

Prince Sviatopolik, who is responsible for building the original St. Michael's Church, was also known as The Accursed Prince because he killed his two very respected and liked half-brothers (Boris and Gleb) in order to secure the throne. Fortunately, he evidently missed one as his remaining half-brother Yaroslav (as in Yaroslav the Wise) was infinitely ticked off when he heard the news. He immediately came down the Dnipro and laid some serious smack on Sviatopolik – who was soon sold out by his own men and thus, Yaroslav prevailed.

National Art Museum
Національний художній музей, *Natsional'nyy̆ khudozhniy muzey*

Built to resemble a Greek temple in the nineteenth century, the National Art Museum boasts twenty-one galleries featuring a collection relatively unknown outside Eastern Europe. Featured collections displayed include Ukrainian iconography, sculptures, and paintings by artists such as T. Shevchenko, K. Kostandi, and M. Pymonenko. *M. Hrushevs'koho 6 (М. Грушевського 6); Admission 10UAH adults, 5UAH students; Open 10:00-17:00, Friday 12:00-19:00, Sat 11:00-18:00, Closed Monday and Tuesday.*

Museum of Water
Музей води, *Muzey̆ vody*

Okay, granted when you hear the name you may think this museum is going to be boring as hell. But give it a chance! Located in Kreschatiy Park, inside a 130 year-old water tower, the Water Museum was open in 2003 with the goal of informing visitors about the water resources of Ukraine. Luckily they somehow found a way of fulfilling that mission in an entertaining way (miracles *do* happen). Inside the museum, ancient water towers are displayed as well as aquariums, a massive toilet bowl (odd), and a contraption that makes a giant bubble *M. Hrushevs'koho 1C (M. Грушевського 1C); Admission 15UAH adults, 10UAH students and children; Open 10:00-16:00, Closed Monday and Tuesday*

AROUND PALATS SPORTU METRO
ПАЛАЦ СПОРТУ

Central Synagogue
Центральна синагога, *Tsentral'na synahoha*
Built in 1898 by philanthropist Lazar Brodsky, this stunning building served as the Jewish community's epicenter for nearly thirty years. In 1926 it was seized by the Soviet Union and turned into a puppet theatre. During the Nazi occupation it served as a stable for German soldiers' horses. The building wasn't returned to the Jewish community until the after the fall of the Soviet Union. Today it holds educational programs and traditional services. The Museum of Jewish Heritage is also housed within it. *Shota Rustavelli 13 (Шота Руставелі 13)*

Kyiv Fortress Museum
Київська фортеця музей, *Kyïvs'ka fortetsya muzey*
This "museum" is more like a collection of nineteenth century fortification buildings. These buildings, strung throughout the neighborhood of Pechersk, were built by the Soviet Army and served as barracks, ammunition and weapons storage. The *Kosyi Kaponir* (this building at the center of the "fortress") served as a prison for political inmates for twenty years until it was turned into a museum in 1920. The most interesting building is the small fortress on top of *Lysa Hora* ("Bald Mountain"). Built in 1872, it was here that political traitors and dissenters were executed. *Hospital'na 24 A (Госпітальна 24А); Admission 3UAH; Open 10:00-17:00. Closed Friday*

AROUND KYIVO-PECHERS'KA LAVRA

Kyivo-Pechers'ka Lavra
Києво-Печерська Лавра, *Kyyevo-Pechers'ka Lavra*
Catholics have Rome, Orthodox Christians have Kyiv. If you're wondering why hoards of crowded busses and pilgrims are flooding the walkways up to the Lavra, you'll soon understand why.

Set on seventy acres, and built overlooking the Dnipro, its impressive gold domed buildings seem to spill over the mountain. Its beauty continues underneath it as well, as a labyrinth of caves was carved out here. The name is derived from the Ukrainian word *pechera*, which means cave, and *lavra*, which is an Orthodox term granted to senior monasteries. It was founded in 1051 by monks Antony and Feodosiy with the intent of spreading Orthodox Christianity throughout the region.

Together they dug out the series of caves where they, and other monks, began to study, worship and live.

In the twelfth century, the Lavra served as a leading cultural and artistic place of study. It was badly damaged by the Mongolian Tatars in 1240, but was rebuilt in the eighteenth century. Around that time the **Bell Tower** was added, which still stands as Ukraine's tallest at nearly one hundred meters. In 1926, during Communist Rule, it was shut down and turned into a museum, but since then it's been partly returned to the Orthodox Church. The monastery is functioning again through the Kyiv Theological Seminary and Academy.

To enter the Lavra you will have to pay and, unfortunately, there is a different entrance price for foreigners. There are also many museums inside the Lavra (listed following) which charge an additional entrance fee. English tours can easily be arranged on the spot. Just listen out for the whispered "you want English tour?" by the older women hanging out by the entrances. *Ivana Mazepy 21 (Івана Мазепи 21); Foreign Admission Price: 16UAH adults, 8UAH children; Open 09:00-18:00*

Cave Monasteries

While the grounds are fantastic, the real reason to come is to see the Cave Monasteries. It was here that the bodies of monks were placed after they died; the dry, cool temperature naturally embalming them. This is seen by many as a miracle and pilgrims flock to pay their respects in these underground tombs; which are open for viewing. The tunnels are claustrophobically tight, and armed with only a candle for light, it can be an eerie voyage.

There are two caves that allow visitors: the Near Caves and the Far Caves. The **Near Caves** (Ближніх печерах, *blyzhnikh pecherakh*) are located inside The Church of the Raising of the Cross and were so named because of their proximity to the Dormition Cathedral. Admission is "free" but you will have to buy a candle (5UAH) before you enter. Women who plan on visiting the cave monasteries should plan their dress in advance (see sidebar). There are seventy-five burial niches within this cave, one of which holds the remains of Antoniy, the Monastery's founder (thus why this cave is sometimes referred to as "Antoniy's Cave"). Some of the tunnels are restricted to believers and pilgrims only. Monks, apt at spotting tourists, will kindly point you away from sectioned off parts. Photography is strictly prohibited and if you try and take a picture, the monks' kindness will quickly fade away. Be respectful and keep your camera in your pocket. *Admission: 5UAH (candle purchase); Open 08:30-16:30.*

The entrance to the **Far Caves** (Дальні печери, *Dal'ni pechery*) is located in the Church of the Conception of St. Anne. It's also known as the Caves of Theodosius, in honor of the Saint. This was the original cave built by Antoniy and Feodosiy. Inside there are forty-five burial niches and three churches: Rizda (Nativity), Feodosiyivska (St. Theodosius'), and the Blahovishchenska (Annunciation) Church. The former two have eighteenth century bronze iconostasis, while the latter has a wooden iconostasis built in this century. *Admission is Free (donations highly suggested); Open 08:30-16:30.*

Lavra Dress Code

If you're planning to enter the caves, make sure you dress appropriately before you visit. Women are required to wear a headscarf (which can be bought outside the lavra entrance) and a skirt or dress that extends below the knee; pants are begrudgingly allowed. Shoulders must also be covered. Men should remove their hats, and wearing shorts is forbidden.

MUSEUMS WITHIN THE LAVRA

Museum of Microminiatures
Музей мікромініатюр, *Muzey mikrominiatyur*

It's a little odd that the most popular attraction within the Lavra has nothing to do with God. The Museum of Microminiatures is one of those, "Really?! This is a museum?" moments, of which there are many in Ukraine. The exhibits here are so tiny that they must be viewed through a microscope. The queues to view things are long, but time passes quickly by people watching and seeing their faces as they gasp in appreciation at viewing "Flea outfitted with Golden Horseshoes." Seriously, all joking aside, the stuff is pretty impressive considering that it takes artist Mykola Syadristy more than a year to complete each piece. One of four microminiature museums in the world, this museum also displays the book that holds the Guinness Book of World Records for the smallest book in the world (the book is twelve pages of Shevchenko's *Kobzar* measuring a mere 0.6 mm). *Admission: 5UAH; Open 10:00-13:30, 14:30-17:00, closed Mondays.*

Museum of Historical Valuables
Музей історичних скарбів, *Muzey istorichnikh skarbiv*

The treasures found inside this building have been borrowed and displayed by many museums around the world. Jewelry containing precious stones and intricate medal works, like a Scythian Queen necklace dating back to the fourth century, are housed here. Coming in at 1.4 kilos, the piece is constructed out of pure gold. Also not to be missed is the collection of Jewish and Western European ceremonial silverware. *Admission: 12UAH, students and children 6UAH; Open 10:00-17:45, closed Monday.*

The State Museum of Ukrainian Decorative Arts
Національний музей українського народного декоративного мистецтва, *Natsional'nyy muzey ukraïns'koho narodnoho dekoratyvnoho mystetstva*

Throughout your time in Ukraine, you'll have abundant opportunities to see examples of Ukrainian crafts. Here is yet another. If you really fancy images of Ukrainian icons, painted *pysanky*, and examples of embroidery, this place is for you. If you're in a time crunch, you can easily find another museum later on that displays the same things, or just take a walk along Andrew's Descent to see newer versions, for free! *Admission: 5UAH adults, 3UAH students and children; Open 10:00-18:00, closed Tuesdays.*

State Museum of Theatre, Music and Cinema Arts of Ukraine

Державний музей театрального, музичного та кіномістецтва України,
Derzhavnyy̆ muzey̆ teatral'noho, muzychnoho ta kinomistetstva Ukraïny

The only museum of its kind in the country (which is incredible considering the number of random museums in Ukraine), this museum displays the history of Soviet films and Ukrainian theatre. Examples of eighteenth century marionettes used in "puppet theaters" throughout the country are featured, as well as costumes and instruments used by Ukrainian theatrical guilds. Created in 1923, it hoped to document Ukraine's cultural history and likely was the only reason some of this stuff survived Stalin's purge of Ukrainian nationalism in the arts. *Admission 6UAH, students and children 4UAH; Open 10:00-17:0, closed Tuesday.*

Ukrainian State Museum of Books and Printing

Державний музей книги І друкарства України,
Derzhavnyy̆ muzey̆ knyhy I drukarstva Ukraïny

For book nerds and lovers of Eastern European history, this museum is worth dropping in for. (All other travelers could probably live with the fact that they missed out on it.) The museum is located in the building that formerly housed the Lavra's eighteenth century typography center. The collections on display include manuscripts dating back to the period of Kievan Rus. First edition prints of Ivan Fedorov's (Ukraine's first printer) 1574 book *Acts and Epistles of the Apostles* are proudly shown here as well. *Admission 5UAH adults, 2UAH students and children; Open 10:00-18:00, closed Tuesday.*

Rodina Mat Statue and The Great Patriotic War Museum

Батьківщина Мати і Великої Вітчизняної війни музей,
Bat'kivshchyna Maty i Velykoï Vitchyznyanoï viy̆ny muzey̆

Located around one kilometer south of the main entrance to the Lavra, you can't miss this colossal twelve-ton statue that stands on a hill overlooking Kyiv's left bank. Resembling something that looks likes it belongs on *The Empire Strikes Back's* Death Star, the base of this structure holds the Great Patriotic War Museum. Those so inclined, can also take an elevator straight up to the top of her head.

In front of the statue is a memorial complex that holds helicopters and tanks from the communist era, an eternal flame or two, and eerie reliefs of soldiers and villagers. The music piped in throughout the complex sounds like the soundtrack to a Doomsday Film – epic to say the least.

The Great Patriotic War Museum is by far the best museum in Ukraine. Though the placards are all in Ukrainian, the thousands of relics are self-explanatory. With over fifteen thousand artifacts displayed throughout its sixteen halls, the museum concentrates on Ukrainians contributions to the "victory over Nazism" and the atrocities committed on its soil. Many foreigners don't realize how badly the entire country was impacted. This is blatantly apparent in hall #6 as a pair of gloves made out of human skin are on display.

The last hall is a crazy mish-mash of artifacts: thousands of items plastered to the walls, covering the ceiling, and stuck haphazardly on a table that runs the length of the room. Sadly though, the museum seems to gloss over the horrors suffered by Jewish communities on Ukrainian soil. *Ivan Mazepi Vulitsa 44 (Івана Мазепи 44); Admission 4UAH; Open 10:00-17:00, Closed Mondays*

JUST OUTSIDE OF KYIV

Folk Architecture and Life Museum
Музей народної архітектури та побуту,
Muzey˘narodnoï arkhitekturi ta pobutu

Have you ever been to those tourist attractions where they do historical reenactments, replete with actors dressed in period clothing? Well this museum, which takes up the entire village of Pyrohovo on the outskirts of Kyiv, brings that to a whole new level. This open-air museum is divided into "villages" with each representing different regions of Ukraine. The buildings, windmills, churches, hen houses, cow sheds, school and farm houses shown are quite literally the real deal. Taken down, shipped over, and reassembled piece by piece, or else literally picked up and moved here; it's like a Ukrainian Epcot Center.

If you have idolized views of village life, this place probably won't do much to change that. Everything in Pyrohovo looks so damn perfect. No village could be this clean. Where is all the chicken crap and evil geese?

Kyivans come to Pyrohovo to "appreciate the nature," while Westerners are more inclined to rent bikes and ride horses here. In the summertime, actors dress up in traditional garb and reenact village life (how lovely everyone looked while milking cows!) and vendors come out in full force selling everything from corn on the cob to *shashlik*. If you can plan it, don't miss Ivana Kupala day here held on the night of July 6th/7th. *To get to Pyrohovo, take marshrutkas #3 or #156 from the Lybidska Metro Station. Admission 15UAH. English tour guides available for hire on site; Open 10:00-17:00.*

Babiy Yar
Бабин Яр, *Babyn Yar*

On September 29, 1941, Nazi soldiers gathered Kyiv's entire Jewish population (33,771 civilians), marched them out to this ravine on the outskirts of town, and executed them over the course of two days. Ukrainian nationalists, Soviet prisoners of war, communists and Gypsies would later face the same horrific fate, bringing the total estimated number of lives lost here between 100,000 and 150,000. Because of Soviet policies, the horrific history of Babiy Yar was slow to be acknowledged. Even in 1961, Russian poet Yevgeny Yevtushenko opened his seminal work with the line "No monument stands over Babiy Yar."

The Soviets never admitted the atrocities committed against Jews here. Even when the Soviets did erect a memorial at the site in 1976, they did so in true Soviet form; making no mention of the Jews. Even now, the tragedy that occurred here seems like it's brushed over and not completely acknowledged. Very little information is displayed outside the memorials: one dedicated to the children that died here and another depicting a menorah that was placed here in 1991.

It can be overwhelmingly sad to think of such a small ravine stacked up with over 34,000 bodies, but it's the sight of teenagers and grown adults sunbathing and playing frisbee here, like this is any other park, which might truly move you to tears. To reach the ravine, get off at Dorohozhychi Metro and head south from the exit. Go through the underpass, to the other side of the road, and head south again. Follow this road through the park and you'll see the main Soviet Monument ahead.

Eat & Drink

Kyiv can be an incredibly expensive place to eat out with plenty of places to splurge in the city. But if you know where to go, it is possible to eat out, have a good time, and wake up with money in your pocket.

Budget

Puzata Khata (Пузата Хата, The Paunchy House) If you're traveling throughout Ukraine, this chain of restaurants will become your lifeline. You will literally find yourself asking if the city you are in has one, and you will become devastated if it does not. Why? Because if you don't know anything about Ukrainian food it's possible to come here and try it all, and not break your bank. Laid out cafeteria style, you can simply point to a dish, put it on your tray and move on. Loading up with enough food to make you paunchy will only cost around 50UAH, and the food is quite good. They even have beer on tap. With three locations throughout Kyiv and an abundance throughout Ukraine, this is a budget traveler's dream find. *Located on Khreschatyk 15 A (Хрещатик 15 А, Khreschatyk Metro Stop) as well as Sahaidachnoho 24 (Сагайдачного 24, Kontraktova Ploshcha Metro Stop);+38 (044) 391 46 99; Open daily 08:00-23:00; Sides 7-10UAH, Entrées 12-22UAH; www.puzatahata.com.ua*

 Potato House (Картопляна хата) So when you told people you were visiting Ukraine, no doubt they told you, "hope you're ready to eat lots of potatoes! HA! HA!" Oh the originality. Indulge their sense of spot-on-humor and eat here, at the Potato House; except don't get the stuffed potatoes, get a Ukrainian Burrito. Trust me, it's amazing. They also have draught beer and an odd Che Guevara and Native American fetish going on in this chain of restaurants. It's possible to come here and load up for a night out and still have beer money left over. Go crazy. *Zhitomirskaya 6-5 (Житомирська 6-5, Zoloti Vorota Metro), Nizhniy Val 37/20 (Нижній Вал 37/20, Kontraktova Ploshcha Metro); +38 (044) 229 21 53; Open Daily 9:00-23:00; Meals 30-50UAH; drinks 5-14UAH; www.potatohouse.biz*

Mister Snack (Мистер Снек) I love when Ukraine transliterates English names into Cyrillic, and "Mister Snack" is by far one of my favorites. All right, so if you're in a hurry – or don't have that much money – and don't mind eating what basically amounts to fast food, this place will do. They offer Ukraine's take on a panini (mostly it's just a warmed chicken and cheese sandwich) and "salads" that amazingly contain no vegetables. It's not a bad place, especially for cash-strapped individuals, as it is easy to stop by and get out for under 30UAH. *Volodymyrska 29 (Владимирская 29, Zoloti Vorota Metro); +38 (044) 229 79 04; Open 8:00-23:00; Meals 20-35UAH; Drinks 5-12UAH*

Celentano (Челентано) This is another one of those massive chains that you'll find yourself frequently visiting while in Ukraine. The food, a descent take on quick pizza, is reliably good. If you stick to pizzas and salads (and stay away from the "lasagna") the prices can't be beat. A whole pizza will feed a dainty woman for one day, and make a grown man feel somewhat satisfied. Add whatever toppings you like (note: the Cyrillic word that sounds like "pepperoni" isn't what you're thinking, it's peppers) and get a draught beer for the ten-minute wait. *Yaroslaviv 37 (Ярославів 37, Zoloti Vorota Metro) Chervonoarmiys'ka 23-B(Червоноармійська 23-B, Lva Tolstoho Metro) Bessarabs'ka Square 2-C (Бессарабської площі 2-C, Kreshatyk Metro); +38 (044) 235 66 87; Open Daily 09:00-23:00; Meals 40-65UAH; Drinks 6-14UAH; www.pizza-celentano.com*

Verona Pizza (Верона піци) This place delivers, which is incredible. Even more incredible is your pizza is still hot when it arrives. They also do dine-in and take-out pizza by the slice. A little bit more expensive than the all-over-the-place Celentano, Verona Pizza is worth the splurge if you're a person of refined tastes. *Lva Tolstoho 1A, (Льва Толстого 1A, Lva Tolstoho Metro Stop) 10:00-23:00; +38 (044) 379 10 10; Open Daily 10:00-23:00; Meals 12-60UAH, drinks 5-14UAH; www.veronapizza.ua/en*

"That Burger Joint" No one actually knows the name to this place, which is nothing more than a plexiglass covered stall located on the street right before TGI Friday's. Its proximity to the restaurant everyone knows, but no one will admit going to, is probably the reason why it's so popular. It offers street fare, like a Ukrainian take on a burger. It's incredibly cheap and tried out enough by the expat community to vouch for its quality. *We're going to say it's located on: 3A Bessarabs'ka Square (Бессарабської площі, Teatral'na Metro), Open Daily 11:00-22:00*

McHuh?

You have to go the McDonald's by the train station. Don't judge me. It's for nothing other than getting what is perhaps the grandest photo opportunity you will come across. Right next to the McDonald's (we're talking a fry-toss away) is a brilliant example of just how lax creative copyright laws are in Ukraine as a "McFoxy" opened here in 2010. It looks just like McDonald's; from the slightly arched yellow sign, to the generic McDonald's-like menu. Except it's mildly cheaper. Everything looks the same, yet it's somehow different, right? From experience, I can tell you the best camera angle to get both signs in the picture is from the old entrance of the Central Train Station.

Splurge (a little)

If you're looking for a good place to sit down and enjoy a meal, these are the places to go to. While other (more expensive) restaurants can be found, the ones listed below do a good job of not leaving you with buyer's remorse when the bill comes.

Planeta Sushi (Планета Суші) Yes, they have Sushi in Eastern Europe – the whole Asian food scene exploded into the region about five years ago. It can be quite decent, but terribly expensive which makes it hard to appreciate. Planet Sushi does a good job of killing your craving, without ruining your budget. Along with sushi, their menu features nigiri, yakitori, salads, and a variety of hot dishes like noodle bowls and pot stickers. *Khreschatyk 12 (Хрещатик 12, Maidan Nezalezhnosti Metro); +38 (044) 462 49 94; Open Daily 11:00-02:00; Meals 40-100UAH; Drinks 10-25UAH; www.planet-sushi.rosinter.com*

Sirtaki (Сіртакі) Named after the traditional Greek dance, I've heard (but have never seen) that sometimes rowdy guests take to dancing on the wooden tables and start busting plates. Perhaps that only happens on Fridays and Saturdays (when it's best to book in advance). Order a hookah, get a beer and watch as your homemade bread or grill plate is cooked in the open kitchen. They also offer dolmades, souvlaki, and an assortment of goods covered with feta cheese. Expect truly bizarre, impromptu laser shows to happen on Saturday. *Naberezhne Shose, Stairs #5 (Набережне шосе, Dnipro Metro); +38 (044) 428 88 54; Open: 12:00-last guest; Meals 45-100UAH, Drinks 12-60UAH; Reservations Recommended*

 Vesuvio Pizza (Піца Везувій) When you want real pizza head here. These people don't mess around. Vesuvio's Pizza has been open for seventeen years and it's amazing! Get the "Pizza Diablo," a fiery concoction of pepperoni, red chili flakes, and onions (gasp! A Ukrainian pizza place that puts onions on their pizza). With pies big enough to share and a decent beer selection, this place is a winner. Sadly, their more central Kyiv location closed, but the food is still worth the short hike to its present location. *Reytarska 25 (Рейтарська 25, Zoloti Vorota Metro);+38 (044) 278 30 28; Open: 10:00-22:00; Meals 35-120UAH, drinks 8-14UAH; www.vesuvio.ua*

King David (Король Девід) This restaurant is owned by the Central Synagogue with all proceeds going to their various charities. The menu is divided between Kosher and European fare, but all of it is delicious. It offers falafel, pitas, and hamburgers for a decent price in a nice setting. *Esplanadna 24 (Еспланадна 24, Palats Sportu Metro) Open: 11:00-23:00, Closed during Shabat; Meals 45-95UAH, drinks 6-10UAH*

Mimino (Міміно) Kyiv has many Georgian food places, but the best one is located in the Podil District. Named after the mustached Georgian pilot from an old Soviet Film, this place is an excessively decorated maze of halls. Be prepared for a bit of sticker shock when you see the wine list prices (a halfway decent Georgian wine was listed for 500UAH, what?!) but the food is basically comparable to prices in Western restaurants. The selection of khachapuri is amazing, the ajika sauce spicy, the lavash hot and fresh and the service is fantastic. If you can find someone with a "karta chain loyalty card," you can get 20 percent off. *Spas'ka 10A(Спаська 10A, Kontraktova Ploshcha); +38 (044) 417 35 45; Open: 11:00-23:00; Meals 99-190UAH, drinks 8-62UAH; www.karta.ua*

Pubs with Grub

The Wall (стіна) Located under the market in Bessarabs'ka Square, The Wall is one of the oldest continually running restaurants/bars in Kyiv. Every inch of this place is open to be carved upon and after ten years it seems like everyone is Kyiv has their name somewhere in here. The food is decent and the beer selection plentiful. Great for catching a sport match, a relaxed lunch, or a rowdy night out. *Bessarabs'ka Square, 2 (Бессарабської площі 2, Teatral'na Metro); +38 (044) 235 33 88; Open Daily 11:00-02:00; Meals 25-70UAH, drinks 8-35UAH; Reservation Recommended*

Le Cosmopolite Belgian Beer Café (Ле Космополіт) If you're sick of drinking Ukrainian beers (for shame!) and are longing for something different, then Le Cosmopolite has got you covered. The food is overpriced and the atmosphere is a little uppity, but they have Chimay, De Koninck, Leffe, and Steenbruge White Beer. *Volodymyrska 47 (Володимирська 47, Zoloti Vorota Metro Stop); +38 (044) 278 72 78;Open Monday-Thursday 10:00-23:00, Saturday 11:00-02:00, Friday 10:00-02:00, Sunday 11:00-11:00; Meals 40-120UAH, drinks 14-60UAH; www.belgianbeercafe.com*

Lucky Pub (Лакі Паб) Though it hasn't been open long, praises for Lucky Pub are being sung in hostels throughout Ukraine. It's been touted as having "the best service in Ukraine," as well as being the best place to watch sport matches. Come in any night of the week and it's like a mini United Nations. With reasonably priced pub fare, a good beer selection, and an amazing atmosphere, this place needs to be on your "to do" list while you're in Kyiv. *Chervonoarmiys'ka 13 (Червоноармійська;13, L'va Tolstoho Metro); +38 (044) 499 13 13; Open Daily11:00-01:00; Meals 35-70UAH, drinks 10-40UAH*

The Drum (Барабан) To find this place is a bit of challenge, but those that do are rewarded with an awesome atmosphere, moderately priced food, and the bragging rights that accompany getting here. The Ukrainian food they serve is delicious, but their burger with fries is what keeps people coming back. Decent beer and wine selection, and jazz music on the weekends only adds to its appeal. To find it, turn down Prorizna Street from Khreschatyk and look for an archway on your right, barely a block up. Go through the archway, into the courtyard (looks like a parking lot), and look to your left. You'll see the restaurant tucked into the basement floor, with stairs leading down to it. *Prorizna 4 (Прорізна 4, Khreschatyk Metro); +38 (044) 279 23 55; Open 11:00-23:00; Meals 45-100UAH, drinks 10-40UAH*

Doctor's Bar (Доктор Бар) Don't expect to find this place listed online, hell the entrance to this place doesn't even have a sign. I've heard of locals trying to take tourists here only to have them freak out and run away because they thought they were being taken into an alleyway to get robbed. "Doctor's Bar" as it's now been christened – because the servers dress up like nurses and sometimes shoot shots into your mouth from plastic "syringes" – is a hidden gem. To get here, take a taxi to the address listed and walk through the apartment building's interior hallway to the exit on the opposite end. Now you're in a dark courtyard and sort of worried. Look to your right and you'll see stairs leading down to an unmarked door and smokers hanging out; you're here! With the cheapest beer in Kyiv and inexpensive good steaks with all the sides, this place cannot be beat. *Vorovs'koho 31a (Воровського 31A, Zoloti Vorota Metro); Open Daily 13:00-last guest; Meals 40-80UAH, drinks 5-25UAH*

Cafés

While Lviv is regarded as the coffee capital of Ukraine (for good reason), Kyiv is doing its best to catch up. These are the places to kill that caffeine headache you've had going on for a while. And all of them brew "real" coffee; no instant stuff here!

Kaffa Coffee Theatre (Каффа кави театру) Get a seat on the terrace and watch the world stroll by while sipping your cup of Yemen Mokka Matar (ohh la la), or head inside and listen to what amounts to Eastern European yuppie culture. They get a little crazy with all the spiced coffee they offer, but stick to the basics and you'll be buzzed and happy in no time. A little bit more expensive than other coffee places, it's worth it if you're a coffee snob and in desperate need to get the taste of instant coffee out of your mouth. *Skovorody 2 (Сковороди 2, Kontraktova Ploshcha Metro); Open Daily 09:00-21:00; Coffee 17.50-35UAH; www.kaffa.ua*

Coffee Life If you like Starbucks, you will be disappointed to find out that there is not one in Ukraine. But Coffee Life desperately wants to fill that void. From the font they use, to the color schemes, the layout of their shops, and their coffee cups, you can tell what they are going for: unapologetic plagiarism. But hey, you're not here to judge, you're here to get a cup of coffee. Just take a moment to enjoy their slogan before you run off with your drink: "coffee as lifestyle." Awe bliss. *Yaroslaviv 26 (Ярославів 26, Zoloti Vorota); Open Daily 08:00-22:00; Coffee 20-31UAH; www.coffeelife.com.ua*

Art Café Located right next to the St. Petersburg Hotel, this funky, chic café is where it's at. Coffee lovers lounge for hours in the smoke-filled upper room, while the lower (smoke free) room is popular with the business crowd and health conscious. The (sometimes) English speaking staff is amazingly friendly and energetic from endless shots of espresso. Downstairs there's a small bookshop. It's like an honest-to-God café. *T. Shevchenko 2/4 (Т. Шевченка 2/4, Teatral'na Metro Stop); Coffee 21-35UAH*

Nightlife

Art Club 44 Located though the archway on 44 Kreschatyk, down the alleyway on the left, and through the unmarked door, this is one of those places that everyone in town below fifty years of age knows about....and frequents. Known for live music, Art Club 44 is popular with locals and foreigners alike. Unfortunately, their popularity has started to go to their heads and recently they've started charging crazy admission rates. *Kreschatyk 44 (Хрещатик 44, Teatral'na Metro); +38 (096) 288 84 24; Open 10:00-02:00; Cover 40-70UAH*

Caribbean Club (Карибський клуб**)** Of all the stories I've heard about people getting ripped off or scammed in Kyiv, they all seem to start out with "I was at Caribbean Club..." Sure they have a cool salsa night, and yes it can be great fun to hear Latin music in Ukraine, but you might want to double-chock your tab on the way out. However, this hasn't affected its popularity by any means and it still remains one of the city's most popular night spots. *Cominterny 4 Комінтерну 4, (Universytet Metro); +38 (044) 288 12 90; Open 20:00-06:00; Drinks 10-45UAH;*

Sorry Babushka A go-to place for Kyiv's club lovers, Sorry Babushka is a three-story mega-club. The ground floor has karaoke, the second floor does eighties and nineties music, and on the top floor is your average disco music. On Wednesdays, they have karaoke competitions in which the winner receives various electronics as prizes. Awesome. *Dmitrievskaya 18/24 (Дмитриевская18/ 24, Universitet Metro); +38 (044) 486 03 00; Open Wednesday-Saturday 18:00-06:00; Drinks 15-45UAH; www.sorrybabushka.com.ua*

Xlib Club (Xlib) Taking its name from the most simplistic of foods (bread), Xlib Club is tucked away in the Podil District. The lack of excessive decoration is a breath of fresh air in Kyiv, and the design is modest to say the least. With one room made for jamming out, and the other for lounging and recovering, this is the place for people who like to party but who don't take it too seriously. *Frunze 12 (Фрунзе 12, Kontraktova Ploshcha Metro); Open Thursday and Sunday 20:00-02:00 Friday and Saturday 23:00-06:00; Drinks 15-45UAH*

Accommodations

HOTELS & HOSTELS

Finding affordable places to stay in Kyiv can be a nightmare. Luckily, the concept of hostels has arrived thanks in large part to a bevy of foreigners who decided to stay here...and open some hostels. Because the hostel scene is new and developing, be sure to check out www.hostelworld.com for the most-to-date info on the hostel you choose and whether it's open for the season or not.

Chillout Hostel Kyiv Run by two Polish girls, this hostel has a definite bohemian vibe going on. The hallways are painted with funky murals that a past guest did in exchange for a cheaper room rate. The beds are decent, the common room always full of laughing people, and the (albeit small) kitchen bustles in the late afternoon as people crawl out bed to make their first pot of coffee. This is not the place to stay if you're hoping for peace and quiet, but it is not a crazy party hostel either. It's just...chill. Located near L'va Tolstoho Metro, it's in a safe location and its no sex-tourism policy keeps out the creepers. The private room, while quite bare, has the largest, most comfortable bed I've slept on in Ukraine. *Horkoho 22B, apt 35, (Горького 22B, Lva Tolstoho Metro) Bunks from US$15, Double Private US$22/pp; chillouthostel@gmail.com*

Central Station A favorite with expats, Central Station is a fifteen-minute walk from the train station…and then a walk up five flights of stairs. However, the owners are amazingly friendly and the atmosphere is quite laid back. It's also one of the cleanest I've ever seen. While a little far from the center, it's hard to beat the comfort level this place offers. No lock-out, free Wi-Fi, comfortable beds, and tea and coffee all day. Their private room is also top-notch. *Gogolivska 25, Apt 15 (Гоголівська 25, Zoloti Vorota Metro);Bunks from US$15, Double Privates from US$27/pp; info@tiuhostels.com*

TIU Kreschatyk After sleeping here a few nights I needed my back popped; yeah the beds are kind of rough. But for the price and the location, TIU Kreschatyk is hard to beat. Free Wi-Fi, hot water that lasts enough for everyone to grab a shower in the morning, and a kitchen large enough to cook for you and your friends are reasons enough to stay here. But the fact that you can literally walk out its front door and be on the main drag of Kyiv is what seals the deal. *Kreschatyk 8b, Apartment 11 (Хрещатик 8B, Maidan Nezalezhnosti Metro); Bunks from US$12, Double Private from US$27/pp; info@tiuhostel.com*

Kiev Backpackers If you've come to the capital of Ukraine to party, then this is the place for you. Replete with a sauna and owners who love to take guests out on rowdy mass trips to Lucky Pub and Vodka Bar, they'll ensure you have a good time. When you wake up from your stupor, you can enjoy real drip coffee or espresso, and of course they have free Wi-Fi and all the regular goodies. This place also offers shuttle service to their other hostel down in Odessa during the summer months. *Chervonoarmiys'ka 18, Apt 15, (Червоноармійська 18, L'va Tolstoho Metro); Bunks from US$15, Privates US$20/pp; info@tiuhostels.com*

APARTMENT RENTALS

If you're coming to Ukraine in a group larger than two, it makes economical sense to just rent an apartment. More comfortable and less expensive than renting hotel rooms, the places listed below can get you on your way.

Absolut Apartment With apartments that will be sure to satisfy your needs while abroad, Absolut has apartments throughout Kyiv, but they mostly focus on acquiring those in the center or near historical points of interest. You can also request a specific area. Most apartments include TV, internet, and equipped kitchens. You can also specially request ones that include luxuries such as indoor saunas or jacuzzis. *Baseina 7 (Басейна 7, L'va Tolstoho Metro); +38 (044) 540 13 10; One room: US$40-100, Two rooms: US$50-125, Three rooms: US$85-210, Luxury US$275-400; www.hotelservice.kiev.ua*

Apartments in Kyiv Okay, so the website is a testament to Google Translate in action, but you have to give them credit for listing everything in six languages. Offering centrally located apartments that can be rented from short- to long-term (and they won't even sigh if you tell them you just want one for one day), they offer a variety of apartments to fit any budget. Check out their website for pictures and details of all twenty-six of their Kyiv apartments. *Baseina 9, office 5. (Басейна 9, Maidan Nezalezhnosti Metro); +38 (044) 229 35 35; "Standard" apartments: US$40-70, "Business" Apartments: US$60-100, "VIP": US$90-130; info@apartment.com.ua; www.apartment.com.ua*

Apartments Rent Kyiv Offering "deluxe" apartments, Apartments Rent Kyiv offers decked out rooms with air conditioning and a full-service concierge service that can handle all your needs; from airport transfers, to interpreter or tour-guide services, they can handle anything you throw at them. Great if you are here for business and don't mind spending a little more on the company's dime. Check out their continually updated information online. *T. Shevchenko 1B, office 11 (Т. Шевченка 1В, Kreschatyk Metro); +38 (044) 561 05 63; One-room Apartments: US$45-95, Two-room: US$65-140, Three-room: US$110-300, VIP: US$270-400; info@rentkiev.net; www.rentkiev.net*

Chernobyl (Чорнобиль)

A few days after the Chernobyl Disaster, citizens of Kyiv watched as their children participated in the annual May Day Parade. To cancel the event would have provoked panic throughout the country, so the Soviet Authorities enforced its continuation. On May 1, 1986, the same day the (now abandoned) amusement park in Prypiat was set to open, parents watched their children parade down the center of Kreschatyk. In the meantime, eighty miles north, children that lived within the area of the explosion were hurriedly shipped off to family or friends (farther south and within the city of Kyiv, housing was being created for the displaced residents of Chernobyl). But even as these communities were being rushed out, the full horror of the incident wasn't being talked about. Government officials waited days before admitting something happened. That "something" being the release of over four hundred times the nuclear material than that of the atomic bombing of Hiroshima.

So it might seem a bit odd to think that there are tours heading towards a city in which your natural inclination should be to run away. Though they are relatively safe (the radiation you're exposed to is supposedly the same as you would be on a transatlantic flight), you still have to sign some paperwork and wear "approved clothing": no shorts, no open toe shoes, no short sleeve tops.

Most of the tours leave from Kyiv early in the morning and get to Chernobyl by 11:00. After showing your passport at the checkpoint, you're driven to the center of Chernobyl where a "briefing" takes place. Maps are shown of the area and the radiation levels within. Resembling a map that's been attacked with a red paint balloon it's interesting to see the intensity of the radiation fizzle out in spots, expanding from its center in tiny almost iridescent strips. Your guide will explain to you how the 350 residents within Chernobyl heed to this map, careful to stay away from the highly contaminated zones, which may exist only a few feet away from completely clean areas.

You're then huddled back into the car and the infamous Geiger Meters are passed out: already beeping. You drive past a field of abandoned tanks and to a now deserted fishing camp. From there it's over to the Nuclear Reactor #4, which is currently being covered by a massive sarcophagus.

It can be an odd feeling watching people snap photos and pose in a place which caused such great sorrow for so many people. The mixed feelings experienced here are often compared to those felt while visiting Auschwitz. Seeing the massive House of Culture and the decomposing four-story school building of Prypiat is an oppressive sight. It can be easy to forget the somber feelings associated with Chernobyl when you are with a group of foreigners (locals couldn't afford to go on such an expensive trip, and probably wouldn't want to if they could). During my tour, a girl in our group asked our guide to smile "for once" in his picture and he snapped back "I will not smile here. This is not a happy place." And that sentiment is never more obvious than when you see the abandoned amusement park that never had its opening.

Tours to Chernobyl are costly, at least USD$110 per person for groups and rocket up in price if you want a private tour. A number of reliable tour companies offer them in a variety of languages. You should register in advance. Same day reservations are not allowed.

Chernobyl Tour Companies

Hostels and hotels in Kyiv generally have businesses they recommend for Chernobyl tours. The following businesses can book individual or group tours, or can put you with a group; thus making your trip cheaper.

Solo East Travel (This is the company I used) *office@tourkiev.com; tourkiev.com; +38(044) 406-3500*

Tour2Chernobyl *info@tour2chernobyl.com; tour2chernobyl.com; Tel: +38 (093) 239 77 67*

Ukrainian Web *ukrainianweb@yahoo.com; ukrainianweb.com' Tel: +1 416 763 4256*

Berdychiv (Бердичів)

A sleepy little town about two and a half hours west of Kyiv, Berdychiv has a rich and mournful history. Though the city might lack charm, locals here make up for it. Being one of the friendliest towns I've come across, it is also one of the only predominately Russian-speaking cities I've encountered west of Kyiv.

The history of this town is irrevocably interwoven with Jewish history. In the 1789 census, Jews constituted 75 percent of the population and at one time the city boasted over eighty synagogues. By 1861, it was the second largest Jewish community in the Russian Empire.

It is easy to imagine, as you walk along the outskirts of town, Tevye, from "Fiddler on the Roof," rolling his milk cart along the dirt roads and singing through his sorrow here. Shoelem Aleichem, author of the book *Tevye and his Daughters* which "Fiddler on the Roof" was based upon, was born about three hours east of here. But he based the village of Anatevka on Jewish villages throughout Ukraine, and being Ukraine's largest, it's easy to see how this city might have influenced him.

The sorrowful fate for the Jews of Berdychiv began long before 1940s. In the 1920s, Soviet forces invaded and destroyed most of the synagogues. In the 1930s, Yiddish, which had previously been recognized, was outlawed as well as all Jewish cultural events and programs. When the Nazis began invading Ukraine in June of 1941, many Ukrainians were unprepared. Berdychiv's relative close proximity to the border meant many residents didn't have enough time to escape. And by July 1941 an "extermination" unit and Jewish ghetto was established within the city. They didn't leave until October, after they had killed all thirty thousand Jewish residents of the town.

These days, the town of Berdychiv is an important pilgrimage for many faiths. With a Carmelite Monastery and a Chabad Synagogue, it's not uncommon to see

Catholic and Jewish pilgrims disembarking from the crowded summertime marshrutkas arriving from Kyiv.

The sights below are well worth seeing but it's important to try a Berdychivske Beer during your stay here. Brewed within the town and having a whopping ABV rate of 11 percent, it's not to be missed.

TRANSPORTATION

Berdychiv makes an easy (albeit long) day trip from Kyiv. For those headed further west, it also makes a convenient overnight stay as it's only about forty-five minutes from Zhytomir and one hundred kilometers away from Vinnytsia. Buses to both those cities run throughout the day from Berdychiv's central bus and train station. From Kyiv, it's a two and a half hour marshrutka ride. To catch the marshrutka, take the Red Line to the Zhytomyrska (Житомирська) metro stop. When you get off the subway, take a right and then a left after the turnstiles. Then walk all the way down the underground walkway and take the right exit. You'll see the white marshrutkas marked Berdychiv (Бердичів) lined up on the left. They leave whenever they get full.

SIGHTS

There are two synagogues within Berdychiv. The **Shabad Synagogue** is located on Yanova 9 (Янова 9) and they can arrange Jewish tours of the city as well as their building. Call +38 (041) 432 02 35 to arrange one. The other synagogue is located on Soborna 9 (Соборна 9). It's not always open and visitors wishing to view it should arrange a tour by calling +38 (041)432 20 62.

In 1630, John Tyszkiewicz the Voivode of Kyiv founded **The Monastery of the Displaced Carmelite Father** as thanks to God for having been freed from captivity by the Tatars. During this time, Ukraine was under Lithuanian and Polish rule. Thus, a Catholic monastery was naturally built. Resembling more of a fortress, or castle, than a place of spiritual worship, it is worth a visit. Currently the exterior of the monastery within the courtyard is under construction, but the main church is open to visitors (10:00-17:00, closed Monday, admission 5UAH) and the **Museum of Berdychiv** in the interior of the courtyard is free.

St. Barbara Church is where Honore de Balzac made his love an honest woman. She was the Polish Countess Evelina Hanksa and the two had started a fifteen-year correspondence after they met in 1832. Unfortunately, she was married at the time, so after her husband finally died, Balzac, being the romantic that he was, travelled to Russia to try and win her over. Beating out Hungarian composer Franz Liszt and fighting with the Tsar for permission, he finally wed her in 1850. He would die five months later. A plaque commemorating their wedding is affixed outside the church on Karalipnika Street.

The **Jewish Cemetery** is located about three miles from the city center. To reach it, take marshrutka #1 from the central bus and train station; the cemetery will be on your right. Depending on the time of year, the cemetery might be overgrown (they tend to let it go in the winter when the tourists are lower in number), but look for a white cement fence across the street from a gas station. It is here that Rabbi Levi Yitzchok, the revered Hasidic leader, is buried.

WHERE TO EAT

Café Amsterdam (meals 35-60UAH, drinks 5-15UAH) has good pizza and great Ukrainian style salads at a decent price in a funky setting. To reach it, take any marshrutka from the central station and get off at the Central Market (Центральний ринок, Tsentral′nyy̆ rynok). Café Amsterdam is directly across the street from the market.

It may seem odd, but this Jewish town has got its own **Sushi Bar** (meals 50-80UAH, drinks 5-15UAH). The people that run it evidently sent their chef to Japan for training and so it's always fresh, well made, and (comparatively) cheap. They also serve the infamous Berdychivske Beer! To reach it take any marshrutka from the central station and ask to be left off at the "*Univermag*". When it stops, walk in the direction the bus is headed and turn left at the next block. Sushi Bar will be ten meters ahead on the left.

If you feel like grabbing something on your own, there's a **Kvartel Supermarket** located across from the Central Market.

WHERE TO SLEEP

There's only one hotel in Berdychiv so your choice is an easy one.

Hotel Mirabella This hotel has clean rooms and all your basics. Internet service is available but goes on and off randomly. Beds are comfortable and the water is always hot. You could do far worse. The small café attached is a little overpriced, but the quality and convenience factor might be worth it. Basic rooms start at US$40 with suites hovering around US$55. *Lenina 20 (Леніна 20); +(38) 041 434 09 70*

Uman (Умань)

HISTORY

First mentioned in 1616, Uman was initially a fort that protected against Tatar raids and housed a substantial Cossack regiment. In 1768, the Massacre of Uman occurred after Cossack rebels raided the area during an anti-Polish uprising. Polish nobles and Jews from the surrounding areas fled to the city of Uman for protection during the raids, but the military commander betrayed their trust and let the Cossacks in when they promised to spare the others. Over the course of three days, twenty thousand Jews and Poles would be massacred.

Uman would later become part of the Russian Empire and a number of aristocrats would take up residency there. For more information on Uman's expansive history, check out www.uman.info.

TRANSPORTATION

Uman, while lovely, doesn't have much that draws overnight visitors; it's best done as a day trip. From Odessa (4 hours), marshrutkas run often from the Central Bus Station. From Kyiv, it is 210 kilometers (2.5 hours) and buses leave to Uman regularly from in front of the Central Train Station. Look for the white private marshrutka vans marked "Уман" which park in front of the McDonald's.

SIGHTS & ACTIVITIES

Rosh Hashanah Kibbutz

Every year on the Jewish New Year, thousands of Breslover Hasidim pilgrims flock to the city of Uman. Rabbi Nachman of Breslov, who encouraged his followers to be together on this holy day, is the central figure in these gatherings. The Rabbi was revered for his teachings and considered to be a very holy man. When he died in 1810 his closest disciple, Nathan of Breslov, organized a pilgrimage to his gravesite in Uman. This annual pilgrimage grew from a few hundred participants to several thousand devout Hasidic Jews from all around Europe who continue to honor the memory and teachings of Rabbi Nachman.

The annual pilgrimages were brought to a standstill in 1917 when the Bolshevik Revolution closed off Russia to foreigners. Still, devout followers would find a way in, risking their lives to celebrate this holy day clandestinely. In 1934 the Soviets begrudgingly allowed twenty-eight Hasidim permission to travel to Uman for Rosh Hashanah. However, this was a mere ploy as authorities conspired to murder sixteen of them while they were still in Uman. Of the others, twelve were banished to Siberia and only four escaped.

In 1989, the fall of communism brought one thousand followers. Nowadays the numbers reach about twenty-five thousand, bringing pilgrims from all over the world. Coordinators of the Rosh Hashanah event import specially catered kosher meals, set up temporary housing sites and bring in emergency medical technicians from Israel for this massive gathering.

As the popularity of this annual pilgrimage continues to swell, so does the attention it draws; not all of it is good. In September 2010, five pilgrims were deported from Ukraine and banned for five years for causing bodily harm to citizens. Uman is a small town and this annual pilgrimage no doubt draws upon its every resource. One also has to keep in mind the mindset of locals here: given its history, it's perhaps not the most accommodating place for such a gathering. Still, other locals support the annual tradition as it injects a much needed yearly economic boost.

Believers are allowed to visit the tomb of Rabbi Nachman on the corner of Belinskovo and Pushkina (Бєлінського і Пушкіна).

Sofiyivsky Park

Sofiyivsky Park is to Ukraine what Central Park is to New York. It was founded in 1796 by Count Stanislaw Szczesny (Felix) Potocki as a birthday present to his wife, Sofia Wett, and is one of the "Seven Wonders of Ukraine" (see page 118).

Count Felix bought Sofia from her (then) husband, married her himself, and constructed a 150-hectare outdoor pleasure palace for her. With waterfalls, grottos, lakes, fountains, five hundred species of trees, and an abundance of flowers that bloom year round, it really is a sight to behold. Like all popular parks constructed around that time (Versailles, Vatican Gardens), Greco-Roman myths were incorporated into the design and busts of Socrates and Plato abound. Supposedly, the trees were laid out in such a way that they spell out "София" (Sofia) when viewed from above.

Keep in mind that this park is simply that, a park. If "enjoying the nature" isn't quite your thing, then it's probably not worth a special trip down here to see.

To enter the park from the city center, head down Sadova (Садова) Street. A tourist center is located at the entrance as well as a hotel and restaurant. Open from May 1 to November 15, from 9:00-18:00; Admission: 8UAH Adults, 5UAH children; Excursion with guide in English 300UAH (up to five people); www.sofiyivka.org.ua/en.

EAT/DRINK

Espresso Bar There's nothing scarier for a caffeine addict than nothing but the sight of instant coffee for weeks. Luckily, Uman has a relatively new coffee place that offers up the real thing (much to the delight of foreigners who make a pilgrimage here before the park). *19 Tyschyka (19 Тищика, next to the store "дц"); Coffee from 20UAH; Open 09:00-23:00*

Kadubok (Кадубок) Decked out to look like the interior of a Ukrainian house from ye' olde times, this place is energetic and lively most of the time. While the menu is your standard Ukrainian fare – nothing original here – it is tasty and the amount of sour cream and butter in the dishes is sure to fatten you up for the Ukrainian winters. *7 Radyans'ka (7 Радянська); Live music from 19:00-23:00; Entrées from 23UAH; Open 12:00-01:00*

Café Hunter (Хантер) Is there anything better than walking into a place and thinking "What the hell?" Because Café Hunter does that and so much more! The walls here are plastered with the carcasses of many a mammal and the tables are covered in their hides. Resembling a hunting lodge, or someone who hates PETA, the waiters here all wear tiny "traditional" Ukrainian outfits and the food is decent enough. But you're here for the atmosphere – the strange, slightly cool, atmosphere. *Entrées from 25UAH; 16 Lenina (16 Леніна); + (38) 047 443 69 85*

SLEEP

Hotel Fortetsya (Готель фортеці) Right in the center of Uman, this hotel is within walking distance of everything. The beds are comfortable and rooms come with air conditioning and satellite TV. Some also have Wi-Fi if you're lucky enough to get one near the router. Full bar and restaurant next to the lobby. Breakfast included. *54 Chapayeva (54 Чапаєва); Double-Standard: 219UAH; Double-Suite: 280UAH; Luxe: 600UAH; (38) 047 445 00 41; uman.info/fortecya-room.htm*

Hotel Sofiyska (Готель Софіївська) Located next to the entrance of the park, this hotel is also known as Hotel Muzey, or amusingly "Hotel House of Creativity of Scientists." But don't let the names or the lack of renovations scare you off. With comfortable rooms, a bar, sauna, and café downstairs – and steps from the park in Uman – there's nothing better. *Double Standard: 200UAH, Double-Suite: 280UAH, Double Luxe: 350UAH 53 Sadova (53 Садовій); +(38) 047 443 3527*

Chernihiv (Чернігів)

At one time the second most important city in the Kievan Rus Empire, by importance and wealth, Chernihiv's golden age lasted until 1239 when it was ravaged by Batu Khan's legions. Now a sleepy town, nestled into the Northern part of the country, Chernihiv draws adventure seekers and the occasional solace-seeking tourist, rather than bellicose Princes.

SIGHTS

Dytynets (Citadel)

Remnants of the town's old life as a political stronghold remain here and around the "val" (rampart) next to the riverbank. What used to be a strategic, naturally raised fortress, is now a bustling park area sprinkled with eighteenth century cannons and the remnants of a twelfth century fortress. Domed churches line the street next to it and locals eating ice cream sit on benches contemplating the Desna River. Be sure to check out the Shevchenko statue on the eastern side of the Dytynets overlooking the river. Yes, it's another Shevchenko statue but this one depicts him as a young man and shows him (gasp!) without a mustache. Something the locals are (and should be) proud of.

Cathedral of Boris and Gleb

Собор Бориса і Гліба, *Sobor Borysa i Hliba*

Named after the two brothers – who later became Ukraine's first canonized saints – of Yaroslav the Wise who were murdered by their eldest brother, this ubiquitous-styled white church, not far from the Dytynets, is worth checking out. A bragging point with the locals is that Russian Tsar Nikolay II once came here, evidently to check out the cathedral's stunning silver Royal Doors. The doors were commissioned by Cossack leader Ivan Mazepa and were supposedly created from the melting down of one single pagan idol that was found near the church in the seventieth century. Now the church acts as a museum containing relics from the times of Kievan Rus. *Admission 5UAH; Open 10:00-17:00.*

Cathedral of the Transfiguration

Спасо-Преображенський, *Spaso-Preobrazhensky*

One of the oldest churches in Ukraine, this church was founded in 1033 by Mstislav, Chernihiv's first known prince. Known for its unique mix of Romanesque and Byzantine architecture, it has an odd look about it. Inside, centuries of wax and smoke have taken a toll on the frescoes and make for a moody ambience – perhaps that's why locals tell stories of secret passageways that lead to the Desna River that exist below the church. What does exist here are the tombs of Prince Yaroslav the Wise's son and Prince Mstislav, although neither are open to viewing for the public. *Pidvalna, Підвальний*

St. Pareskevy Church
Санкт-Параскеви Церкви

Located in Chervona Ploshcha, this red brick church, founded in the twelfth century, is hard to miss. The church takes its name from St. Paraskeva who was considered to be the patron saint of traders – a large outdoor market took place in this location before to the construction of the church. During World War II, two-thirds of the church was destroyed, but it was later rebuilt. Locals believe that an original stone in the wall bears good luck to those who rub it. Be sure to try and locate it (people watching comes in handy for this one) and make a wish! *Chervona Ploshcha, Червона площа*

Troitsky Monastery
Троїцький монастир

If you're walking here from town, you'll cross over Boldyna Hora ("Oak Hill") at the top of which you can see this monastery. Underneath this mound is Antoniy's Caves which is accessible by the Ilyinska Church; the little white and green church with the golden domes.

Antoniy's Caves

One of a few subterranean monasteries in Europe, the compound was founded in 1069 by Antoniy Pechersky (yep, the same one who founded the Kyiv-Perchersk Lavra). The caves form a series of 350-meter long passageways that contain chapels, the "largest underground church on the left bank of Ukraine," and the bones of monks (it's too damp here for their corpses to have mummified). Eerie sounds, flickering candles, and lack of people make for a creepy experience. *Admission: 6 UAH; Open 10:00-17:30, Closed Monday.*

Continuing uphill along Ilyinska Church, you'll come to the namesake of the area: the Troitsky Monastery. One of the best preserved religious structures in the country, relics of Saint Feodosiy are housed here making it a popular stop with Orthodox pilgrims. The Trinity Cathedral houses rare eighteenth century murals and is often flooded with candle-wielding tourists. Across from it you'll see the entrance to the bell tower. Climbing the 172 steps is worth it for a birds-eye view of the cathedral and the surrounding area. *To get here from the city center, take Trolleybus #8. Otherwise it's a 2km walk from the center. Open: 09:00-17:00; Admission: 2UAH*

ACTIVITIES

Kayak and Rafting on the Desna River

Many tour operators offer overnight two-, three-, or seven-day kayaking tours that can cover up to one hundred kilometers. Overnight rafting trips, replete with camping and beachside bonfires, run during the spring and summer as well.

Kayaking: **Lyubarets Jaroslav** *Operates: May - September; +(38) 050 313 50 69; baydarka@gmail.com; www.recreation.in.ua*

Rafting: **PSV Tours** (Provozin Sergei Vladimirovich Tours) *Operates from March; +(38) 067 656 89 32; www.desnatravel.com/en*

ACCOMMODATIONS

Pridesnyansky Hotel (Придеснянський Готель) Located on the banks of the Desna River in the eastern part of town, is this quiet hotel. Even though it's branded as a "tourist complex," which just reeks of Soviet infrastructure, it's been recently remodeled and isn't sticking to its roots. Doesn't the zebra patterned suite attest to this?! With a café, Wi-Fi, comfortable beds, and breakfast included, I've seen far more charged for less. *Single Standard: 210UAH, Single Premium: 250UAH, Double Standard: 330UAH; 99a Shevchenko (99a Шевченка); +(38 046 295 48 02; www.chernigivhotel.com.ua*

Hotel Ukraina (Готель Україна) The most centrally located hotel in the Chernihiv, this hotel offers comfortable, if somewhat small, rooms. The decor ranges from drab to reminiscent to tacky, but, such is life. *Single: 295/310UAH No/With Air Conditioning, Half-Suite: 490UAH, Full Suite: 580UAH; 33 Myru (33 Миру); +(38) 046 269 83 67; www.hotel-ukraina.com.ua*

Western Ukraine

Lviv

HISTORY

Lviv has existed as a settlement for over a millennium, and as a city for over seven hundred years. The city was founded by King Danylo in 1256 and named in honor of his son, Lev. Thus its Latin name Leopolis, or Leo's City.

However, Lviv has a chameleon-like history and as its ruler's changed, so did its name. The city became known as Lwów when it was a part of the Polish Lithuanian-Commonwealth around the fourteenth century. In German it's known as Lemburg; as it was referred to when it was incorporated into the Austro-Hungarian Empire in the late 1700s. During World War II when the area surrounding Lviv was invaded by Soviet and Nazi troops the nearby territories were divided between the two armies and "Lviv" became a city in the Ukrainian Soviet Socialist Republic. In 1991, it became a part of independent Ukraine and in 2006 the city celebrated its 750th year.

The city is now known as Lviv (Львів) in Ukrainian and Lvov (Львов) in Russian. But to visitors, it's known simply as one of the loveliest, if slightly unknown cities, in Eastern Europe.

TRANSPORTATION

Fly

Lviv has an international airport (LWO, www.airport.lviv.ua) located about seven kilometers from the city center. It's possible to fly directly from Kyiv as well as other nearby European cities (Frankfort, Vienna, Warsaw). A taxi from the airport to the city center runs around 50UAH (negotiate before you get in the car) or you can take Marshrutka #95 from in front of the airport to the city center, or Trolleybus #9, for 2.50UAH.

Train

Boasting one of the oldest train stations in the country (the first train arrived from Vienna on November 4th, 1861), arriving in Lviv by train is perhaps the best introduction to the city. The whole thing just screams "you're in Eastern Europe!"

Unfortunately the joyous introduction is short lived once you exit the front of the building. But don't worry, you're not in the historic center yet.

To get to the city center you can take a taxi (around 35UAH is acceptable) or take the twenty-minute tram ride. Head outside the front entrance of the station and make your way through the taxi drivers and the clusters of food stalls. You'll see the trolley tracks – take trolleybus #1. Tickets can be bought from the driver and be sure to validate them right away!

TRAVEL AGENCIES

Adventure Carpathians Adventure Carpathians, part of the "In Lviv" travel agency, is a reputable company that can arrange private genealogy tours, trekking tours of the Carpathians, day trips from Lviv and private drivers. They also do monthly group tours, which individuals can join. With English speaking guides and a staff that quickly replies to all your questions, this is the easiest agency to deal with in town. *+(38) 032 2357630; contact@adventurecarpathians.com; www.adventurecarpathians.com*

Wyr Mandriv Offering group and private tours of Lviv and the surrounding area, Wyr Mandriv is an affordable tour operator. Their website is available in Ukrainian and Russian only, but they do try to accommodate English speakers on their tours. *info@wyr.com.ua; www.wyr.com.ua; (032) 243-74-44*

SIGHTS & ACTIVITIES

AROUND MARKET SQUARE

Market Square
площа ринок, *ploshcha rynok*

Recognized, along with the city center of Lviv, as a UNESCO World Heritage Site, Lviv's Market Square is probably the reason Prague is alluded to so much when trying to describe this town. Originally designed in the Gothic style, the square was rebuilt in the Renaissance fashion when much of the city burned down in 1527.

Ratusha
Ратуша, Town Hall

Located in the center of Market Square, you can't miss this eighteenth century building with fountains of Greek gods on either side. The view from the top of its sixty-five-meter high neo-Renaissance tower provides the best views of the city. If the 306 steps that lead to the top do not leave you breathless, the view certainly will. Looking out over Lviv from this viewpoint, it's easy to see why Lviv is often called the "Florence of the East."

The town's original Ratusha was built of wood in the fourteenth century but it burnt down shortly after. It was rebuilt in the fifteenth century. Its tower, however, was demolished and rebuilt in the nineteenth century after it was deemed unsafe. The replica that replaced it does little to pacify the nerves; it's still a dizzying climb. *Admission 3UAH; Open 11:00-17:00*

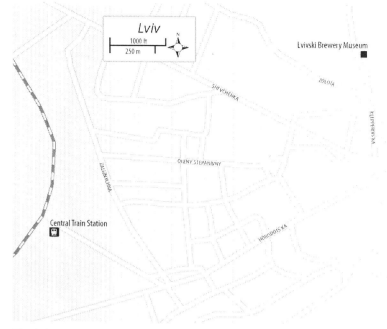

Black Stone House
Чорна кам'яниця, *Chorna kam'yanytsya*

It's hard to miss this imposing black building in what's otherwise a candy-necklace colored square. Opinions vary why this amazing example of sixteenth century architecture is black. Some say it's simply a result of the sandstone absorbing the dust, dirt, and smoke that has filled the square over the years (coal was used here for heating until the mid-1900s). Others say it's a result of the white lead, which coats its polychrome, oxidizing. The more interesting theories involve ghosts, witches and curses.

In the past it was known as the Kyiv House, because its first owner was from Kyiv. Then it became known as the Doctor's House after Dr. Anczewski, who had the house decorated with the sculpture of St. Martin. Look for it on the front of the house – it's the one of the man cutting his cloak in half to share it with a beggar. *Pl. Rynok 4 (пл. Ринок 4)*

AROUND THE CITY CENTER

Pharmacy Museum
Аптека-музей, *Apteka-muzeў*

Ukrainians cannot get enough of pharmacies, so it's rather fitting that they would immortalize one and turn it into a museum. The front of house is still in operation,

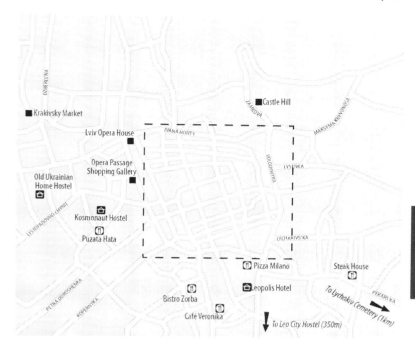

working as a compounding pharmacy and mixing up their iron wine that "cures anemia" and tastes like hell. Skip that experience and go straight for the main attraction: the back of the house which opened in 1735 as a military pharmacy.

Tickets are available from the front counter. After purchasing, visitors are ushered underneath the service railing and through a curtain, into the bowels of the building. The museum spans three floors and houses antique measuring tools, massive scales and over three thousand instruments that tell the history of this building and its residents. More fun than one could ever imagine a pharmacy museum being; it's a do-not-miss experience. *2 Drukars'ka (Друкарська 2); Admission 3UAH, Students and Seniors 2UAH; Open 10:00-17:00; (+38) 032 272 00 41*

The Weapon (Arsenal) Museum
Арсенал музей, *Arsenal muzey*

Housed inside the top two floors of the arsenal, this museum is worth a walk through as it chronologically displays swords, daggers, lances, and axes made (and most likely used) in Lviv. At one time, Lviv was regarded as the best location for manufacturers of weaponry in all of Europe, so the intricate designs and crafting on the weapons displayed are remarkable.

The building itself dates back to the fourteenth century. It took two hundred years to finish it, but no time at all for it to be ruined – it was burned to the ground

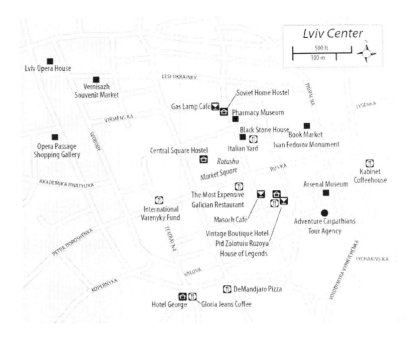

sixteen years after it was completed. The building you see now is a reconstruction based on the original. *Pidval'na 5 (Підвальна 5); Open 10:00-17:30, Closed Wednesday; Admission 8UAH, Students and Seniors 3UAH; (+38) 032 235 86 61*

Lvivski Brewery Museum
Музей пива Львівської Пивоварні, *Muzey̆ pyva L'vivs'koï Pyvovarni*

Opened in 2005 to celebrate the 290th anniversary of its brewery, this museum boasts a fine collection of beer memorabilia and production machinery; but its staff take a while to warm up to you. Tours are given in Russian and Ukrainian, but English descriptions are given under every item on exhibition. Admission times are 10:30 to 18:00, but you must go on a guided tour. When you get to the museum, pick up the phone and let the guide know you're there. The bristly welcome may be a bit off-putting, but the final film and generous pours of Lvivski beer (including one that's unavailable in stores) at the end more than make up for it. *Kleparivs'ka 18 (Клепарівська, 18); Open 10:30-18:00, Closed Tuesday; Admission 15UAH; Tours at 10:30, 12:00, 13:30, 15:00, 16:30, 17:30; +(38) 032 294 80 65*

Opera House
Оперний театр, *Opernyy̆ teatr*

In 1895 Lviv was a blossoming European cultural center and in desperate need of a theatre in which to show off. There was only one problem: the city center was already densely crowded so many proposals had placed the theatre on the outskirts of town – a European no-no. When the city held an architectural competition, one Polish architect, Zygmunt Gorgolewski, proposed that they build it in the center anyway and enclose the Poltava River to do so. Construction began in 1897 and continued for the next three years, with the building being the first in Europe to use a concrete foundation.

Shortly after it was finished, the building began to sink. Eventually it would settle, but not before stories began circulating that Gorgolewski — horrified by his "failure" – had committed suicide. In actuality, he died of heart disease shortly after finishing the project and is buried in Lychakiv Cemetery.

Originally called the Grand Theatre, the building was renamed by the Soviets. It now hosts symphonies, theatre performances and ballets. It's not sinking anymore, but potholes around its base are an ongoing problem. However, from all the tourists and brides covering the pavement in front of it, you'd never know. *Svobody 45 (Свободи 45); Matinees at 11:00 and Evening Performances at 18:00; lvivopera.org; (+38) 032 272 88 60*

ON THE OUTSKIRTS

Castle Hill
Замкова гора, *Zamkova hora*

A breathless climb here is inescapable during a trip to Lviv. Castle Hill is located just outside the historic center of Lviv at the highest point in the city – 413 meters.

Taking its name from the High Castle that used to stand here during from the thirteenth century to the nineteenth century, Castle Hill is now a hotspot for artists who do portraits for passing tourists.

The first structure to be built here was a wooden fortress constructed around the thirteenth century. Like everything in Lviv, it was destroyed and rebuilt many times — first by the Lithuanians, then by the Poles and later the Cossacks. Seemingly, every army that passed through here decided to destroy it. In the nineteenth century, they gave up trying to rebuild the fortress, clearing out the rubble and turning it into a park which remains to this day. At the summit of the hill is the Union of Lublin Mound, placed there in 1869 in celebration of its 300th anniversary.

Lychakiv Cemetery
Личаківський цвинтар, *Lychakivs'kyy'tsvyntar*

Like Recoleta Cemetery in Buenos Aires, Lychakiv's expansive grounds and grand monuments dedicated to its four hundred thousand "inhabitants" should not be missed. The tombstones and memorials written in a broad spectrum of languages (Ukrainian, Russian, Polish, German, Armenian, and Latin) tell this city's history in a poignant and heartfelt way. Originally constructed in 1787, it takes its name from the borough the cemetery used to reside in. After World War I, the cemetery went through a brutal period of destruction and neglect during which many of its monuments were destroyed. However, this stopped in 1975 when it was declared a historical site. Much of the grounds have been restored to their former glory and now it resembles more a park for the living, than a place for the dead.

Some notable tombs include that of nationally revered poet Ivan Franko, but by far the most photographed is that of "Sleeping Beauty," Józefa Markowska. Markowska was a Polish actress who died in 1877. The story behind her demise has become twisted with time. Some say she poisoned herself when she discovered her lover was cheating, while others claim that her grave is empty. The poignancy of the sculpture above her tomb (which depicts the young star in a timeless slumber) is unquestionable.

SHOPPING & MARKETS

A day in Lviv can easily be spent simply meandering through its plentiful markets. The ones below are especially interesting.

Vernisazh Souvenir Market

сувенірного ринку "Вернісаж", *suvenirnoho rynku "Vernisazh"*

Year round, this craft market bustles with bohemian artists and *babushkas* selling everything from wire wrapped jewelry and hand embroidered tablecloths, to beer steins and smoking pipes. Though expensive when compared to those in smaller towns, it's one of the only places in Ukraine where it's possible to find such gems as a "Thank God I'm Not a Moscovite" shirt and "Here we speak Ukrainian!" stickers. The selection of true, artisan crafts as well as your typical, gotta-have tourist items make this a one of the most unique markets in the county. *Located just off the main*

Masochism was Founded Here!
(or...The Ad Campaign Lviv Turned Down)

Leopold von Sacher-Masoch is perhaps best known as the man from whom the term "masochism" is derived. Born in Lviv (then Lemberg) in 1836, he worked as a professor in the city, but soon retired from teaching to become a full-time writer. Most of his stories revolved around Galician life. However, the romantic tales he penned that upheld humanistic ideals would not be the ones he'd be remembered for. When he penned "Venus of Furs," part of a collection of stories from *Legacy of Cain* in 1869, the parallels from the story to his private life were hard to dismiss as merely fiction.

You see, that same year Masoch signed a contract with his mistress, Baroness Fanny Pistor, that essentially made him her slave for six months – but only if she wore furs while playing master to keep the mood festive. So elaborate was Masoch's degradation fantasies that he had them take a train to Italy, where no one knew them, so they could role-play in the streets without being judged. She road in first-class, while he road in third —just like in the story.

When Masoch got married in 1873 to his first wife Aurora von Rumelin, he proposi-tioned her into doing the same —would she be the S to his M? She refused and they later divorced, Masoch finding married life unappealing and boring.

In 1886, an Austrian psychiatrist would pen the term *masochism* for the book *Psychopathia Sexualis* because "the author Sacher-Masoch frequently made this perversion, which up to his time was quite unknown to the scientific world as such, the substratum of his writings."

drag near the Opera House on the corner of Lesi Ukrainky and Teatralna, вул Лесі Українки та вул Театральна

Book Market

Книжковий ринок, *Knyzhkovyy̆rynok*

The Book Market takes place every day in front of the Ivan Fedorov monument (see "Literature" on page 34). Vendors set up a startling collection of Soviet books and memorabilia here daily. I think, however, it's just an excuse for these men to get out of the house to smoke and talk with one another. Once in a blue moon someone finds something of value here on the cheap, but generally it's just fun to rummage through everything. For those who fancy the written word, this open-air market is one of kind.

Krakivsky Market

Краківський Ринок, *Krakivs'kiy̆Rynok*

This bustling outdoor market is where most of Lviv's residents come to buy their fresh produce. The market is also home to fresh flowers, housewares, and all things bric-a-brac. The noise, the chaos, the haggling! It's addictive. *Located on the opposite side of Svobody Prospect from the Opera House, about a fifteen-minute walk; Bazarna 1, Базарна 1; Closed on Monday.*

Opera Passage Shopping Gallery

Located on the main strip at Svobody 27 (Свободи 27) in a restored nineteenth century building, it's hard to miss this recent glitzy shopping addition. The top floor boasts one of the most expensive Italian restaurants in town (the view might make its cost worthwhile) while the lower three floors house luxury boutique stores. Surprisingly, even if you're not a fan of malls, you might find yourself coming here often, as the best grocery store in town is located in the basement.

DAY TRIPS FROM LVIV

The following day trips are best taken from Lviv by private driver or with tour groups.

Krekhiv Monastery

Located fifty kilometers north of Lviv, the village of Krekhiv is famous for its sixteenth century Basilian Monastery. This popular pilgrimage site was established by two monks from the Kyiv Pechersk Lavra who came to this area to hang out in the caves. A landowner eventually took pity on them and offered them land in which to construct a monastery. In the seventeenth century the monastery was fortified to defend it from the Tatars and in the eighteenth century the wooden structures were removed and replaced with stone. It was the Soviets who did the most damage to the place: in 1949 it was closed and the monks who lived there either fled or were sent to Soviet prisons. It reopened in August of 1990.

"The Golden Horseshoe"

Much better than it sounds, the Golden Horseshoe is three castles spread out nearby Lviv.

Located about seventy-five kilometers from Lviv, **Olesko Castle** was built in the fourteenth century as a defense fortress, but was later transformed into a residence for aristocracy and remodeled in the Italian Renaissance style. The most interesting of the three, it now holds a museum that's regarded as having the richest collection of Polish treasures outside of Poland.

The most melancholically beautiful of the group, **Pidhirtsi Castle** (80km east of Lviv) was built in the seventeenth century into the gentle slope of a hill overlooking the Styr River. Originally surrounded by vineyards (it also had a mill and a private zoo), it boasted an expansive interior with private living quarters and halls decked out for imperial guests. Over the centuries, wars, fires, and neglect have taken its toll on the palace and now it's in a gloomy state of disrepair. The Lviv Art Gallery currently owns the building and is desperately trying to return it to its former glory. For now, it serves as an art gallery while guests may also tour the expansive grounds.

> Soviet film lovers might also recognize the castle as playing the Louvre in the 1979 film *D'Artagnan and Three Musketeers.*

Used as a residence by the Sobieski noble family, **Zolochiv Castle** was built in the seventieth century by enslaved Tatars. Constructed in two parts, the "Grand Palace" is fashioned on the then-modern Dutch style, with the "Chinese Palace" –a small church-like building– being added later as a present to Jan III's wife. In the nineteenth century it was used as a hospital, army barracks and, later, a prison. Now owned by the Lviv Art Gallery, it is under restoration, but open to visitors. On display are European coat of arms as well as jewelry and art. It is located about seventy kilometers east of Lviv.

EAT

Lviv has a fantastic number of restaurants and the highest number of cafés in the country. Pastries and coffee for everyone!

Cheap Eats

Pizza Milano (Піца Мілано) Located in a basement, this quant restaurant is another representative of that ever-present trend in Ukrainian gastronomy: the beer and pizza café. A step-up from Celentano's, it offers all of your standard fare (you order a personal pizza and pick the toppings), in a nicer setting without a drastic change in price. Order at the bar. *Soborna 12 (Соборна 12); Open Daily 10:00-23:00; Pizza 12UAH + toppings; Beer 8UAH*

Puzata Hata (Пузата хата) Incredibly busy during all times of the day, and super-popular with an ever-present onslaught of tourist-filled buses, this place is always packed. Be thankful for the crowds – it keeps the food rotating, the kitchen working, and the self-serve meals hot. *Sichovykh Striltsiv 12 (Січових Стрільців 12); Open Daily 08:00-2300; (+38) 032 244 87 28; Sides 7-10UAH, Entrées 12-22UAH; www.puzatahata.com.ua*

DeMandjaro Situated on one of Lviv's most beautiful and romantic streets, the patio seating here goes quickly. The menu is your typical fast-food fare (burgers, sandwiches, pizza) but it's cheap, decent, and you can't beat the price in this area. Popular with students and backpackers it can be a bit rowdy inside, but outside the blissful views have a way of calming down even the most frazzled of nerves. *Halyts'ka 10 (Галицька 10); Open Daily 09:00-22:00; (+38) 032 297 01 71; Entrées start at 12UAH, Drinks from 8UAH; www.demandjaro.com*

Steak House (Стейк Хаус) Come to Steak House for a different take on your traditional counter-fare. They offer fresh a la carte salads and sides, accompanied by the grilled meat of your choice. They do not, however, speak English – but don't let that stop you! Last time I was there I heard a "moo," "quack," and "oink" from foreigners placing orders. Hey, whatever gets your point across. *Pekarska 31 (Пекарська 31); Open Daily 11:00-23:00; Entrées start at 16UAH, Drinks from 6UAH; (+38) 032 276 67 06*

Splurge (a little)

Bistro Zorba (Бістро "Зорба") Tucked away off a side street, across from Café Veronica's, Bistro Zorba is a hell of a find. As close to an authentic Greek restaurant as you can get in Ukraine, the staff is patient with foreigners and their portions are generous. Be prepared to not receive a menu; patrons are simply asked if they would like "cow, pig, chicken." Try the *"Rym Steyk"* which is veal marinated in Greek spices and served with all the fixings for 55UAH. *Shevchenka 14 (Шевченка 14); Open M-Sat 10:00-23:00; Entrées start at 40UAH, Drinks from 10UAH*

International Varenyky Fund (МВФ) Located in a kitschy building, this restaurant is the place to go sample all the varieties of Ukrainian's beloved *varenyky* (little dumplings stuffed with veggies or meat, then boiled and doused with butter...lots of butter). They sell them by the pop here, one dumpling goes for 1.42UAH, so it's possible to literally try the gamut. Order some house flavored vodka to wash it all down with and feel your Ukrainian roots ignite! Entrées are priced per 100 gram and menus in English are available upon request. *3 Katedral'na (Катедральна 3); Open Daily 11:00-23:00; Varenyky 1.42UAH, Entrées Start at 16UAH, Drinks from 8-16UAH; (+38) 032 272 60 96*

Pid Zolotuiu Rozoyu (Під " Золотою Розою ") This Jewish restaurant (translated to Under the Golden Rose) plays up every Jewish stereotype you can think of. It's hard to decide if it's offensive or hilariously inappropriate. There are no prices on the menu because you have to haggle with your waiter (of course) and if you pay off someone, they'll smuggle in a pork dish for you – even though they're "kosher." This spot is also known for their fresh breads and their fruit-infused vodkas. *Across from # 48 on Staroyevreis'ka (Староєврейська); Open 11:00-02:00; Entrées start at 45UAH; Drinks from 10UAH; (+38) 050 370 38 63*

Splurge (a lot)

The Most Expensive Galician Restaurant (Найдорожча ресторація Галичини, *Nayďorozhcha Restoratsiya Halychyny*) Well, the name should tell you everything you need to know about this place, that is, if you can find it. Located on the second-floor of an apartment building, right above Kryjivka, this restaurant is well hidden. When you knock, the second floor apartment's doorman, dressed in Masonic garb, opens and asks "What are you doing here?!" When you answer that you're there to eat, you are quickly ushered through his "apartment," pushed through a back door, and into the most gorgeous (yet odd) restaurant one can imagine.

The interior is a dimly lit homage to the freemasons, with portraits of rumored members hanging throughout. Don't get sticker shock; often times the waiters will give tourists a "ten times cheaper" card (because if you don't have one, prices are crazy). Well worth the splurge, this place is like nothing else. Live music Friday to Sunday 20:00-23:00. *14 Ploshcha Rynok (пл. Ринок 14); Open 11:00-23:00; Entrées starting at 600UAH (without the discount card), Drinks from 200UAH (without the discount); (+38) 050 430 87 83*

CAFÉS

In the winter, it's hard to tell if you're shaking in Lviv from the cold, or from the caffeine pumping through your body. Walk a block and you'll see five cafés. The ones below, however, are worth seeking out.

Veronika (Вероніка) Veronika has a restaurant, but head downstairs for their pastries. Their breakfast croissants, omelets, flaky pastries (their Napoleon is top-notch), and freshly baked bread draw a crowd any time of day, so be prepared for a worthwhile wait. *21 Shevchenka (21 Шевченка); Open 10:00-23:00; Pastries 7-25UAH, Coffee 20-35UAH; (+38) 032 261 44 56; veronika.lviv.ua*

Kabinet (Кабінет) Perhaps like no other place still in existence (wow – bold statement), Kabinet embodies the feeling of an old-world coffee house. Sitting here in a leather chair, surrounded by books and patrons casually smoking, it's easy to see how coffee houses used to be *the* place for intellectual discourse – and alas, fiery debates still occur here. In the back there's a pool table that somehow doesn't detract from the mood. Bring your laptop and stay awhile while indulging in their signature cognac laced espresso. *Located across from the Arsenal Museum. 12 Vynnychenka (12 Винниченка); Open 10:00-23:00; Coffee 12-25UAH; (+38) 032 272 05 12*

Gloria Jeans Coffee (Глорія Джинс Кава) Recently opened, Gloria Jeans (an Australian coffee chain) resembles a posh New York City jazz club with mirrors on the ceiling and oversized red lamps. Comfy chairs, free Wi-Fi, and a staff that speaks English push this place over the edge. If you're craving the familiar, with a side of elitism, this is the place. With all your (expensive) familiar favorites, and one of the only places that serves an iced coffee, it's popular with the ex-pat crowd as well. *1/2 Shevchenka (1/2 Шевченка), right next to the Hotel George; Open 9:00-24:00; Coffee 20/25/30UAH depending on size; (+38) 032 297 02 97; www.gloriajeanscoffees.com.ua*

Italiys'kiy Dvir (Італійський двір, Italian Yard) If you're in Lviv in the summertime, come and see this lovely courtyard café, secluded from the (mild) hustle of the city outside. Located within Kornjakt Palace, just off of Market Square, this courtyard has been in "countless" Soviet films that no one can remember the names of. In the winter, it's a sad sight and devoid of coffee which can make for an anticlimactic experience – especially after paying the 1UAH admission fee. But in the spring, it's worth a visit. *6 Rynok Ploshcha (6 площа ринок); Open 10:00-20:00; Coffee 9-25UAH, Admission 1UAH; (+38) 032 297 53 66*

BARS & NIGHTLIFE

A few years ago the bar scene in Lviv was dead and the town shut down soon after sunset. Now the city is bursting at the seams with the country's most unique places to grab a cold one.

House of Legends (Дім легенд, *Dim Lehend)* The manager proudly exclaimed to me: "We hire dwarfs!" That's when I knew I was definitely somewhere new. Located inside a four-story apartment building that looks like it could fall over any second, this bar is a winding mass of fairy-tale themed paraphernalia. The servers dress like characters from Disney movies; there are also grandfather clocks everywhere and a dragon leers over the entrance. This place could be oh so tacky if it weren't so damn cool. Upstairs, on their fifth-floor, open-air balcony, you'll find one of the best views of the city. *48 Staroyevreis'ka (48 Староєврейська); Open 10:00-11:00; Beer 10-14UAH; (+38) 050 430 29 24*

Gas Lamp Café (гасова лампа, *Hasova Lampa*) The interior of this place resembles a dark fortress at first; a dimly lit maze of kerosene lamps. When you reach the lit world again (word to the wise: don't drink too much here or you'll never make it out), it opens up into a massive wooden loft. Sit up top to enjoy the great view of the city and the bar.

To find its slightly hidden entrance, look for the statue of a man sitting next to a lamp on the street. This man was Ignacy Lokasiewicz, a Polishman who invented the kerosene lamp and was exiled to Lviv by Austrian authorities for his evolvement with a certain revolutionary organization. Now he has a bar in his honor! *20 Virmens'ka (20 Вірменська); Open 11:00-02:00; Beer 10-14UAH; (+38) 050 371 09 08; www.gasovalampa.lviv.ua*

Kryjivka (Криївка) You'll find yourself practicing *"heroyam slava"* as you walk here; the code phrase that lets you through the door. When you knock on the wooden gate that guards this bar a slot opens and an imposing man yells "Slava Ukraini" (Glory to Ukraine) to which you reply "Glory to its heroes!" This is then often followed by "Do you have a reservation?" because this speak-easy restaurant is always packed. The interior is designed to look like the forest-sheltered bunkers that the Ukrainian Insurgent Army (UIA) hid out in during their guerilla war on the Nazis, Poles, and Soviet Union from 1943 to 1949. It's worth a tour even you're not eating –that is, if you can get past the bouncer at the door. It's also one of the only bars in Lviv open twenty-four hours. *14 Ploshcha Rynok (14 площа ринок), bottom floor; 24hrs; Entrées from 20-46UAH, Drinks from 10UAH; (+38) 032 254 61 18; www.kryjivka.com.ua*

 Masoch Café (Мазох Кафе) Resembling a bordello inside, on the outside the Masoch Café looks like any other building. Look for the bronze statue of its namesake, Leopold Van Masoch (see "Masochism" box on pg 110) in front of the building. Inside, it's much like one would expect a café that reveres masochism to look like – all red lights, whips, and chains. Perhaps the best part of this café is its patron's laissez-faire attitude. Men in business suits sip cappuccino in the daytime while dildos hang from the ceiling. At night, most come for their mixed (and rather expensive) cocktails and maybe a slap or two. *7 Serbk'ka (7 Сербська); Open 11:00-01:00; Coffee 13-35UAH, Drinks from 10UAH; (+38) 032 272 18 72; www.masoch-café.com.ua*

SLEEP

Lviv has quite a good selection of places to stay. Hotels in the city center are expensive (but worth it) and the hostels offer a fantastic bang for your buck (not to mention an ever-changing array of people to go out with).

Hostels

 Old Ukrainian Home Hostel Decorated to look like a Ukrainian village, this hostel feels more like a Ukrainian grandmother's house: cozy, inviting, and warm. It has multiple showers (which is still a novel sight in Ukraine's hostels), free breakfast, Wi-Fi, lockers, and a private room that has its own key. The guys running it, the two Igors, are also some of the friendliest locals you'll ever meet. *12 Lepkoho (12 Лепкого); Bunks from US$10, Private from US$20/pp; oldua@homehostels.com.ua; www.homehostels.com.ua*

Soviet Home Hostel Owned by the same guys who run the Old Ukrainian Home Hostel, this one is fashioned to look like the Soviets still run the place. Huge posters of Stalin and a communist flag or two add character to this lofty space that's situated right off the main square. A central location makes up for the five-floor walk-up. Showers, Wi-Fi, lockers, and breakfast. *3 Drukarska str. (3Друкарська); Bunks from US$10, Privates from US$20/pp; oldua@homehostels.com.ua; www.homehostels.com.ua*

Western Ukraine

Leo City More of a party hostel than perhaps any other hostel in the city, Leo City's backpackers are often seen traveling in herds as they hit the city's nightspots (which are conveniently close to the hostel). Centrally located and equipped with everything one needs, this is the place to stay if you're in the mood to go out. *15/7 Konopnitskot (15/7 Кононницької); Bunks from US$12, Privates from US$17/ pp; hostel.leocity@gmail.com; www.leocityhostel.com*

Central Square Hostel This ten-bed hostel is more of a shared apartment set-up than a hostel, but it's good for budget minded travelers who like to avoid the crowds. Situated right off Market Square, it offers an intimate stay in a fantastic location. Email the owners ahead to let them know you're arrival time and to arrange a no lock-out curfew (the one downfall of staying here is someone is not "on-call" twenty-four hours). Wi-Fi, free breakfast, multiple showers and laundry service available. *5 Rynok Square (5 площа ринок); Bunks from US$12, Privates from US$21 /pp; cshostel@gmail.com; www.cshostel.com*

The Kosmonaut Hostel The Kosmonaut was not only the first hostel in Lviv, but also in Ukraine (it seems every traveler has stayed here at one time or another). With cheap rates, a roomy kitchen, nice seating areas, and a friendly staff, it set the bar for the all those who followed. Though it can be noisy, it's a good place to stay if you like to meet people. They are also fantastic about organizing group outings. *8 Sichovykh Stritsiv (8 Січових Стрільців); Bunks from $7, Privates from $14 pp; info@thekosmonaut.com; www.thekosmonaut.com*

Hotels

Hotels in Lviv are plentiful and expensive. The ones listed below are worth the price.

Leopolis Hotel (Готель Леополіс) If you want to indulge yourself, stay at Leopolis. Located in a newly renovated eighteenth century building just steps away from Market Square, this hotel offers all of the city's old world charms with modern touches. Every room is uniquely decorated and includes special touches like heated tiles in the bathrooms, speaker systems throughout the room (even in the shower), Wi-Fi, and sound-blocking windows. Their staff is the most attentive in Ukraine and their breakfast is legendary (and included in the room price). *16 Teatralna (16 Театральна); Superior Room 195 Euros, Deluxe 215 Euros, Suite 350 Euros; reservations@leopolishotel.com; www.leopolishotel.com; (+38) 032 295 95 00*

Vintage Boutique Hotel (Вінтаж Бутік Готель) This hotel is on the smaller side; from the room size, to the lobby, to the "business center" (a computer with internet access). But the staff is friendly and attentive, the location is fabulous, and the hotel itself attractively decorated and cared for. The recently renovated rooms all come with air conditioning, satellite TV, Wi-Fi, slippers, and private bathrooms. The rate includes complimentary breakfast. *25/27 Staroyevreis'ka (25/27 Староєврейська); Single room 750UAH, Double 950UAH, Suite 1150UAH; info@vinatgehotel.com.ua; vintagehotel.com.ua; (+39) 032 235 68 34*

Hotel George (Готель Джорж) Hotel George is located in the heart of the city center on the lovely Svobody Avenue, making it an amazing deal for the price. For the price-conscious traveler, rooms with shared bathrooms are available, but rooms with private baths are also an option. The building itself was designed by renowned Viennese architects Ferdinand Fellmer and Hermann Helmer in the neo-rennaisance style, but it's probably more famous for the fact that Ewan McGregor parked his motorcycle in the hallway here in his documentary *Long Way Round*. *1 Mitskevycha (1 Міцкевича); Tourist Class (shared bathroom) 350UAH, Standard 600UAH, Superior 650UAH, Suites from 750UAH; info@georgehotel.com.ua; georgehotel.com.ua; (+38) 032 297 11 44*

Apartments

When booking an apartment in Lviv, make sure you request one in the city center and double check that it has running water twenty-four hours a day and a hot water heater. Generally the apartments are old but full of charm, and they make a great choice for those traveling in a group.

 InLviv Apartment Rentals InLviv has a slew of apartments: from budget minded one bedrooms, to grandiose lofts with all the comforts of a four-star hotel. The staff is very friendly, informed, and speak English. They can also arrange extras like tours, but they're not pushy. *One bedroom apartments from 310UAH, two bedroom from 375UAH, three bedrooms from 475UAH; contact@inlviv.info; www.inlviv.info/apartments; (+38) 032 235 76 30*

Kamyanets Podilsky

Out west in Ukraine things get competitive as far as the best place to visit. Lviv, Chernivtsi, and the small isolated villages in the mountains all put up a grand fight. But there's something about KP, and when you see it, you'll know why.

TRANSPORTATION

Train

A recent addition of an express train that runs daily to Kyiv (6 hours) has made KP a worthy destination for those who planned on just hanging out in the capital for a few days. The overnight slow train still runs daily (12 hours). Unfortunately, the isolated train station runs to few cities in the West other than Khmelnytskyi. The train station is eleven kilometers north of the city center on Pryvokzalna (Привокзальна). To get to the city center, take bus #1 from the train station.

Bus

The main bus station is located close to the city center (2 blocks), with buses running continuously to Chernivtsi (2.5 hours), Khmelnytskyi (2 hours), and Khotyn (45 minutes).

HISTORY

Kamyanets Podilsky is named after the rock formations upon which it is built. The city was founded around the eleventh century as a settlement of Kievan Rus'. The Old Town of Kamyanets Podilsky is built on the "island" – an isolated dot of land that's a result of the severe pin-curl the Smotrych River makes.

During the fifteenth century, nearly twelve hundred Armenian Families resided in Kamyanets Podilsky. Though the beginnings of the city were heavily influenced by Armenian culture, much of what remains today is the result of Polish influences that began around the fifteenth century when Poland made the city the capital of Podole Voivodship.

In the sixteenth century it was conquered by the Ottoman Turks (hence why the Cathedral of SS Peter and Paul has a minaret on top of it) then returned to Polish rule. The Russians conquered the city in 1793 and used the fortress as a prison for

Ukrainian nationalists. It was during this time that the city became mostly inhabited by Jews who were forced here under a Russian resettlement policy that did not allow them to live in major cities.

Later, in 1919, the Ukrainian National Republic declared Kamyanets Podilsky its short-lived capital. Shortly thereafter, the city was used by the Germans as a Jewish ghetto during World War II. Some 85,000 people died here during the war and nearly 70 percent of the old town was destroyed.

SIGHTS & ACTIVITIES

To get to the Old Town, cross the New Bridge over the Smotrych River to the island. As you cross the bridge you'll notice a lookout tower rising from the steep slope of the canyon. Called **"Potter's Tower,"** this structure was constructed in 1583 and garnered its name by the town's potters who looked after it. On the opposite side of the crossing you'll also notice some treacherous stairs leading down to the banks of the river.

Upon entering the old town, follow the road to the left and you'll enter the **Polish Market Square**; the heart of the Polish Quarter. Under a German town law (the Magdeburg Rights) the city was sectioned off into four ethnic enclaves: Poles, Ukrainians, Armenians, and Jews. The fourteenth century **House of the Polish Magistrate** (*Ratusha*) is located here and now houses a museum (which could be passed over without regret). In front of the *Ratusha,* you'll see the **Armenian Well** which was constructed in 1638.

If you continue on, you'll see to your right the **Cathedral of SS Peter and Paul.** In 1674, when the Turks took over, they started converting all the city's churches into mosques. Thus, that's why there's a minaret on top of this cathedral. When the city

---

Seven Wonders of Ukraine

People love lists. It creates a mission and inspires them to spend money and travel to places. No doubt this is why people visit the Great Pyramid of Giza, right? Because of that "Seven Wonders of the Ancient World" thing? Well, a Ukrainian politician thought so and boldly set off on a mission to comprise the ultimate list: The Seven Wonders of Ukraine. If you think Ukraine doesn't have enough "wonders" to fill a list of seven, then you haven't been looking in the right places. But what is surprising is that the first list comprised over a thousand candidates. Yes, for a brief time everything was worthy of being declared a "wonder." Luckily the list was whittled down by an objective group of historians to just twenty-one candidates. These finalists were then voted for online to make the final list. The only thing Ukrainians are more proud of than Verka Serduchka, is the following seven places:

Sofiyivsky Park (Uman)
Kyiv Pechersk Lavra (Kyiv)
Kamyanets Podilsky Historical Complex and Fortress (Kamyanets Podilsky)
Island of Khortytsya (Zaporizhia)
Chersones: "Ukrainian Pompeii"(Sevastopol)
Saint Sophia Cathedral (Kyiv)
Khotyn Fortress (Khotyn)

was given back to the Poles, the Turks imposed an agreement stating that the minaret could not be removed nor destroyed. The Poles naturally agreed to this article, and did not disobey it, but they did place a 3.5-meter tall golden statue of the Virgin Mary on top of it. It remains the only minaret in the world that's topped with a Christian image. The minaret is open to visitors if you feel so inclined to climb the 145 steps to its top.

Across from the Armenian Square is the newly renovated eighteenth century **Greek Catholic Church – St. Jehoshaphat's**. Continuing down Starobulvarna, you'll eventually come to the eleventh century **Turkish Bridge**, named after the Turks that fortified it.

The reason people come to the island is to see **The Fortress** (Admission: 10UAH, 09:00-18:30, 09:00-16:30 Monday). During the summer, people cook *shashlik* around its grassy knolls, and in the winter bundled-up brides take pictures before it, smiling through the cold. The fortress itself is breathtaking. Still remarkably beautiful after the beatings it has taken (built of wood in the tenth century, destroyed by the Mongols in 1240, and rebuilt by Italian engineers in the sixteenth century). It's a little worse for wear, but looks like every kid's dream castle. The castle walls that connect the nine unique towers are free to be climbed upon and in the center there's the **main courtyard**. To the north of this is **"Debtor's Hole,"** where those who couldn't pay their bills were placed. During times of great financial crisis, many perished here: the small tower becoming so packed with prisoners that many suffocated.

The Karmalyuk Tower is the most famous as it was used as a prison. Built in 1503, it takes its name from a former prisoner – **Ustym Karmalyuk** – who was said to be so sexy that women would throw down locks of hair to him. Eventually he had amassed enough that he was able to make a rope with it all to escape! It's like Rapunzel, in reverse.

Festivals

Twice a year the masses are drawn away from the fortress and to the city center for its festivals. In May the city celebrates **Kamyanets Podilsky Day** which features a hot air balloon festival. During this time it's possible to rent out a balloon tour for 120 Euros for up to six people. In September an **International Tournament of Knights** is held, which anywhere else would look extremely lame, but in Kamyanets Podilsky men in knight costumes holding lances just seem natural.

SLEEP

Kamyanets Podilsky is still getting its footing as far as its recent boom in tourism goes. Luckily some Western-style hostels have opened here over the past year, which makes staying here and getting around extremely easy.

TIU Kamyanets Podilsky Western-owned with English speaking staff, this little hostel in a mere fifteen-minute walk from the old town, and a five-minute stroll from the bus station. Offering free Wi-Fi, tea, coffee and all that jazz, it's the best

Western Ukraine

hostel in the area (even if the beds are rather hard). *69 Harharina (69 Гагаріна), Apt. 4; info@tiuhostels.com; +(38) 098 669 47 83; Bunks: US$17, Privates: US$19/ pp*

Hotel 7 Days Located in one of those oh so popular monolithic Soviet hotel blocks, Hotel 7 Days has 223 rooms. Even though its façade may be less than welcoming, its staff makes up for it and the rooms are well cared for. Comfortable beds, Wi-Fi, satellite TV, and a viewing platform on the twelfth floor make it worth the splurge. In the lobby, there's a European and Oriental restaurant. *4 Soborna Street (4 Соборна); Standard Single: 325UAH, Standard Double: 440UAH, Semi-Luxe: 710UAH; sevendays@kp.rel.com.ua*

Hotel Gala A bit more removed than the other hotels (a fifteen-minute walk to old town), Hotel Gala has a coffee shop, bar and bowling alley in its lobby, which makes it a popular night-spot in the sleepy town of KP. The rooms are clean, if a little small, and the staff is friendly. Check out their travel agency for tours of nearby Khotyn. *84 Lesya Ukrainka (84 Лесі Українки); +(38) 038 493 83 70 Standard Twin: 295UAH, Triple: 360UAH; Deluxe Apartment: 580UAH; gala-hotel.com*

EAT

London Steakhouse (Лондон Стейкхаус) Unlike other "steak houses" in Ukraine, people come here to get their red meat cravings filled. With beer, top notch (if sometimes slow) service, and a decked out lobby that actually does resemble something British, London Steakhouse is a good choice. They also have free Wi-Fi. *11 Knyaziv Koriatovichiv (11 Князів Коріатовичів); Open 10:00-23:00; Steaks 22-48UAH; Sides 9-14UAH; Beer 6UAH; www.gala-hotel.com*

Griffin Bar (Гріффін Бар) Don't be put off by the drab appearance when you first walk through the door of this bar. Head upstairs and watch the mood drastically change. With a good selection of beer, great (if somewhat typical) Ukrainian fare, and friendly service, this cheap spot is a great find. *25 Hrushevs'koho (25 Грушевського); Open 11:00-22:00; + (38) 067 795 51 84*

MakSmak (МакСмак) The only twenty-four hour pizza and beer café in KP, this place comes alive after the discos close. If you're a glutton for punishment, you can bring your own vodka because they don't sell it – which makes for the best (and worst) idea ever. *6 Ural's'ka (6 Уральська); +(38) 038 492 25 33*

Celentano When you're not in the mood for surprises, head to this popular pizza chain. *9 Kn. Koriatovychiv (9 Кн. Кориатовичей); Open 10:00-22:00; (0-3849) 3-67-90*

NIGHTLIFE

KP is in essence a village, so it's a little surprising how much they love to party here.

Playboy Club For a clubbing experience that can only be brought to you by Eastern Europe, head to the Playboy Club. While there are no naked go-go dancers, there is an eclectic mélange of people: from the University kids home for the weekend, to the village doctor who just needs to dance off the stress, this is perhaps the most epic of village discos. *31 Hrushevs'koho (31 Грушевського); 20UAH entrance fee, 50UAH bottle of Vodka.*

Zhara (Жара) If you're feeling sexy enough to get past the face control, swagger over to this fun disco that boasts the largest bar in the city (village?). Though the place sometimes takes itself too seriously, the music is good, the energy level is always high, and the people are there to have fun. *15 Hrushevs'koho (15 Грушевського); +(38) 077 475 45 99*

Khotyn

Built in the fifteenth century, Khotyn Fortress (Open 10:00-18:00; Admission 8UAH) is located on the banks of the Dniester River. The original fort, a rudimentary wooden structure on a pile of dirt, was constructed on this site in the tenth century because of its prime location within the trade route from the Varangians to the Greeks.

Over the years the fortress was rebuilt and added onto until eventually the fortress walls were six meters thick and up to forty meters high in some parts. In 1621 the structure was put to the test when the Poles teamed up with forty thousand Cossacks to defend the structure against 250,000 invading Turks. And, like a scene out of the movie *300*, somehow they pulled it off. Thus the reason a statue of Cossack leader Petro Sahaydachny greets you as you enter the fortress. For a brief moment he ruled, but his victory was short lived as the Turks took over in 1711.

Now tourists clamber all over it, scaling the walls and picnicking upon its high points. One of the Seven Wonders of Ukraine (see page 118), it has posed as various French and English castles in a number of Soviet films.

Khotyn's Castle Legend

A castle isn't interesting without its legends, and looking at the side wall of the Khotyn Fortress you can still see evidence of Khotyn Fortress' greatest one. The large dark spot on its wall is believed to have been created by the tears of the Khotyn rebels that were killed by the Ottoman Turks inside the fortress. Another depressing explanation is that the wet spot was created by the tears of Oksana, a young girl who the Turks buried alive behind the wall.

GETTING THERE

The easiest way to get here is a quick, thirty-five-minute direct marshrutka ride from Kamyanets Podilsky (20km). Also, every Kamyanets Podilsky to Chernivtsi bus stops enroute. To get to the fortress from the bus station, turn right and head back in the direction that the bus was coming from. Follow the signs that say "фортеця." For those who aren't so much into walking, you can also grab a cab across the road from the bus station for around 12UAH.

Chernivtsi

Chernivtsi carries the weight of its cultural reputation around like a burden. How can a city possibly live up to expectations when phrases like "the streets are swept with roses," and "the chickens write poetry in the dirt in Chernivtsi" are uttered? Talk about pressure.

It's hard to describe Chernivtsi. Sometimes it feels like you interrupted the city in the middle of it getting ready; given more time, surely it would have been splendid looking. Other times it feels like a joyous college town, all laughter and youthful exuberance.

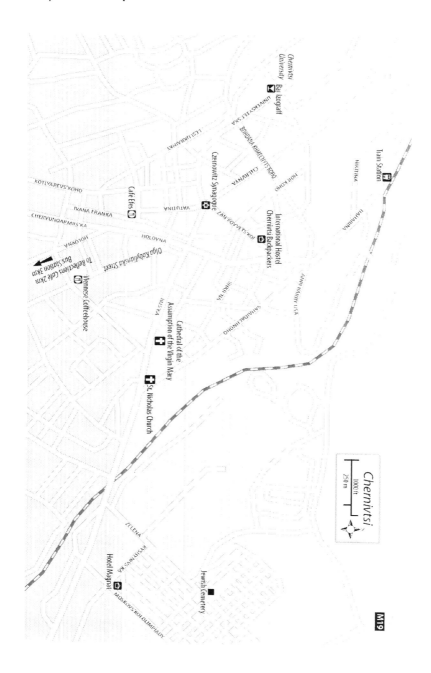

Chernivtsi
University

Balzographf

UNIVERSITY SKA

BOHDANA KHMELNYTSKOHO

HOR KOHO

Train Station

NIKITINA

Czernowitz Synagogue

CHERVANA

VATUTINA

KOTLYAREVS'KOHO

Cafe Eles

IVANA FRANKA

CHERVONOARMIIS'KA

HOLOVNA

MAHARINA

International Hostel
Chernivtsi Backpackers

JOS. ZADOVEYTS'KA

Olga Kobylianska Street

HOLOVNA

SIMIL'NA

RUS'KA

SKM. KATA USA

SALHANOHO

To Reflections Cafe 2km
Bus Station 3km

Viennese Coffeehouse

Cathedral of the
Assumption of the Virgin Mary

St. Nicholas Church

Chernivtsi

1000 ft
250 m

M19

ZELENA

SK. SAMUSAN

Hotel Magnat

MOSKOVS'KOI OLIMPIADY

Jewish Cemetery

If it is possible to feel like the past is whispering to you through buildings, then that is here. Walking around Chernivtsi's streets you can see the influences of various cultures in every façade. Yet, more often than not, it's a culture that no longer exists within the city.

TRANSPORTATION

Train

The train station is located one and a half kilometers north of the center. Train tickets can also be bought at the Train Ticket Office at 128 Holovna (128 Головна, Open 09:00-18:00). Trains run daily to Kyiv (15 hours), Lviv (5.5 hours), and further routes like Moscow. It's also possible to go to Bulgaria from here on the Moscow-Sofia train (12 hours). A taxi from the train station to the city center will run about 9UAH. *The train station address is 38 Gagarina (38 Гагаріна).*

Bus

Hourly shuttles run to Khotyn (2 hours) and Kamyanets-Podilsky (2.5 hours) from the bus station. Two buses head to Lviv daily (7 hours) and four buses leave daily for Ivano-Frankivsk (4 hours). For the crazies, there is also a bus to Kyiv (9 hours) and one to Odessa (13 hours). In the summer, a bus leaves to Bucharest every morning; or once every-other-day in the winter. *The bus station address is 219 Holovna (219 Головна).*

HISTORY

Chernivtsi is second only to Lviv as far as cultural schizophrenia goes. The first settlement in this area was located on the left shore of the Prut River. Mongols destroyed that settlement in 1259. From then on, settlements would be concentrated on the right side of the river. From 1359 to 1775 the city and the surrounding area were a part of the Principality of Moldavia (now Moldova). In 1775 the city, and some surrounding areas, were annexed to the Austrian Empire and became known as Bukovyna (the land of beech trees), with Chernivtsi as the capital. In the nineteenth century it was a part of the Habsburg Empire. It was during this time that much of the city's architectural gems were constructed. For a brief time after the First World War it became a part of Romania. In 1944 the city was reincorporated into the Ukrainian SSR becoming, for the first time, a predominately Ukrainian city. Still regarded as the capital of the unofficial Bykovynian region, Polish, Armenian, and Jewish influences can be seen all of over the city.

SIGHTS & ACTIVITIES

Chernivtsi's main sights can be seen in the breadth of a day since these attractions exist mostly around Tsentralna Square (центральна площа). Trolleybuses #3 and #5 run between the city's southern bus station and the northern train station, making stops in the center along the way.

Jewish Cemetery

About fifty thousand Chernivtsi citizens are buried in this cemetery that was established in 1866. Among them are the first Jewish mayor of the city, Eduard Reiss, as well as Yiddish poet Eliezer Steinburg, and many of the city's chief Rabbis. The cemetery also contains four mass graves that hold Jewish soldiers from the Austrian army of World War I, Turkish soldiers, Romanian citizens who died between 1941 and 1942, and Jewish civilians who perished during the Holocaust. The cemetery's current state is an overgrown mess, which only adds to the melancholic effect this place has on people. Inscriptions on the tombstones are in Hebrew, German, and Russian, and many of the stones from the Soviet era have pictures of the departed on them — most of them incredibly young. To get here, follow Ruska Street across the bridge and take the first left at Zeleny (Зелені) Street. The cemetery is about a half mile down the road.

Jewish History

In 1940 Chernivtsi became occupied by the Red Army and the city's large Romanian intelligentsia fled to Romania, while its Bukovyna German population was repatriated by the Soviet-Nazi agreement. When Romania switched its loyalty from France and Britain to that of Nazi Germany in July 1941, Romania retook Chernivtsi as part of "Operation Barbarossa" (the code name for Nazi Germany's invasion of the Soviet Union). It was during this time that Romanian military dictator Ion Antonescu (whose policies were immediately responsible for the deaths of over four hundred thousand people) ordered the creation of a Jewish ghetto in the low lying level of the city. Fifty thousand Bukovina Jews were crammed there, many of whom perished or were deported to Transnistria. In 1944 when the city was reincorporated into the Ukrainian SSR, many of the cities remaining Jews left to Israel.

Czernowitz Synagogue

The former synagogue was built in 1873 when the city, then known as Czernowitz, was a part of the Austria-Hungarian Empire. The synagogue used to be famous for its Moorish Revival style with its distinct North African feel. In 1940 the synagogue was closed by the Soviets when they took control of the city from Romania. And in 1941 it was badly burned by German and Romanian soldiers when Romania (an ally to the Nazi regime) reclaimed the city. In 1959 the building was turned into a movie theatre and remains so to this day. Painted Easter egg blue and missing its once fantastic dome, it no longer resembles anything related to its former life. *Located on the corner of Zan'kovets'koï (Заньковецької) and Universytetska (Університетська) Street.*

Monument to Paul Celan

Paul Celan (1920-70) was born in Chernivtsi in 1920 when it belonged to Romania. His parents were German-speaking Jews who lived at 5 Saksahanskoho (5 Саксаганського) Street. During World War II, his parents were two of the thousands who were sent to concentration camps. Celan himself survived a horrific stay at the Old, Kingdom labor camp. After the war, Celan expressed immense guilt over the death of his parents, whom he tried to persuade to go into hiding with him. In 1948 he wrote his most famous poem "Todesfuge" (Death Fugue) and since then he has been regarded as one of the most important German language post World War II poets. He would later commit suicide by drowning himself in Paris' River Seine. When the monument was erected to him on Holovna (Головна) Street in 1992, it was the first non-Soviet monument in the city.

St. Nicholas Cathedral

Looking at this Cathedral for too long can make you dizzy. Referred to by locals as the "drunken church," the cupolas on this church are surrounded by four spiraling turrets-giving it the appearance of being twisted. Built in 1939, it is a replica of the fourteenth century Romanian temple Curtea de Arges, which can be found on the Romanian one leu banknote. *Located at 35 Ruska Street (35 Руська).*

Cathedral of the Assumption of the Virgin Mary

Right down the street from St. Nicholas Cathedral, lays the city's first stone temple. Constructed in 1820, this Greek Catholic church's interior was badly destroyed and used as a warehouse during the Soviet Era. It has since been restored. *Located at 28 Ruska Street (28 Руська).*

Olfa Kobylianska Street (Кобилянська)

According to legend, this pedestrian avenue was so prized by the city's citizens when it was constructed in the late eighteenth century that it was scrubbed with soap at daybreak and a policeman with a stick would beat anyone who dared walk upon it with dirty feet. Nowadays, it's not so posh, but the beauty is still there with dainty three-story buildings gracing its sides and plenty of benches to sit upon and people watch. Buildings to seek out are the Polish People's House (36 Kobylianska) and the German People's House (53 Kobylianska).

Art?

Just off Olga Kobylianska (Ольга Кобилянська) Street is Theatre Square. Be sure to find the statue of four men: three looking up, and one looking down holding his…manhood. Why? If you look across from where the men are staring you'll notice a statue of a topless woman.

Chernivtsi University

The central building in this horse shoe shaped university is the former **Residence of Orthodox Metropolitans of Bukovyna and Dalmatia** and is rightly regarded as the architectural symbol of Chernivtsi. Built in 1882 by Czech architect Josef Hlavka, the building's design was heavily influenced by Moorish and Byzantine architecture. With its red bricks, curved walls, and colored tiles — not to mention its expansive, jaw-dropping interior and perfectly manicured lawns — it's no wonder there's more tourists here daily than students. To the left of the Residence you'll see the **Seminarska Church** which is now used for concerts and ceremonies. *2 Kotsubinskoho Str. (2 Коцюбинського); www.chnu.cv.ua*

EAT

Reflections With a diverse menu and dearly missed culinary gems like pesto pasta, lentil soup, teriyaki steak, and fried shrimp, Reflections attracts gastro-pilgrims from all over. They even serve breakfast items and they open early enough to enjoy it! *66 Holovna Street (66 Головна); +(38) 037 252 6682; Open 09:00-21:00; Entrées 28-80UAH, Drinks from 6UAH*

Viennese Coffeehouse You would think with its history that coffee houses would be all the rage in this part of the world. Sadly, you're moving into the instant coffee belt of Ukraine. But do not fear! Chernivtsi still has the diehards, and Viennese Coffeehouse may be one of its best. A little more expensive than an average cup of joe, you're paying for the real stuff here. Pastries can be bought at the counter, or ordered at the table (they have an English menu). Try the Napoleon, you won't be disappointed. *49 Kobylianska Street (49 Кобилянська); Open 10:00-21:00; Desserts 12-21UAH; Coffee or Tea 12-24UAH*

Café Efes As you can guess by the name, this is a Turkish Restaurant, and it gets all things right. With English menus, cheap beer, and food that is spiced just right, this place is popular with the tourist crowd that knows what's up and students who can't get enough. *13 Franka (13 Франка); +38 (0372) 517677; Open 11:00-22:00; Entrées 20-45UAH, Drinks from 5UAH*

NIGHTLIFE

Bar Izograff (Бар "Ізограф") The most popular bar in the city, this place is open till 04:00. It's your typical, "Shut up, I just want to dance" disco, and nobody is complaining. Book a table for large groups and don't expect the party to relocate; it's not uncommon to walkout and see the sunrise here. Located across from the cinema. *7a Universytets'ska (7а Університетська); +38 (0372) 524372; Admission 20UAH; Bottle of Vodka 50UAH; Beer 7UAH*

SLEEP

Eventually, you're going to have to go to bed in this fun loving town. These are some places to crash.

International Hostel Chernivtsi Backpackers Conveniently located in a quiet square, not too far from the train station, Chernivtsi Backpackers Hostel offers everything you could want in a hostel in Ukraine — even if the beds are a bit rough. But toughen up! If the hostel staff has their way, you won't be in your bed that long anyways. Book in advance on www.Hostelworld.com and let them know your arrival time; the hostel is not staffed 24/7. *25 Zankovetska Street (25 Заньковецької); Bunks from US$17; info@tiuhostels.com*

Hotel Magnat One of the newest hotels in town, Hotel Magnat is centrally located. With only nine rooms (one room is a single), the place is quiet and the service is polite. Though they don't offer all the jazz of the bigger hotels, they don't have the attitudes either. Luxury rooms come with a pull-out couch and a plush jacuzzi tub. *16 a Tolstoho (16а Толстого); Semi-Luxe room: 320UAH, Luxury Room 420UAH; +38 (0372) 526 420*

Carpathians

Ivano-Frankivsk

Ivano-Frankivsk is typically used as a breezeway; nothing more than an attractive gateway to the Carpathians. However, the Necco Wafer colored neoclassical buildings and the long stretches of pedestrian boulevards that open into breezy squares demand more of your time. Ivano-Frankivsk begs to be used for a night or two of relaxation; especially before you head off into the rugged mountains. Rest up for your next big adventure here.

HISTORY

The city was originally founded as Stanisławów, after the Polish Hetman, in 1650. It remained so until 1950 when it was renamed after the revered Ukrainian author and poet Ivan Franko.

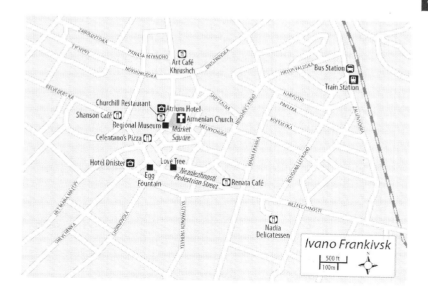

TRANSPORT

Ivano is most commonly used as a launching pad to the rest of the Carpathians. Arriving from Kyiv (12 hours) by train is an easy overnight ride. From Lviv it's a three hour marshrutka ride or a seven hour train ride. From its bus station – which is located in front of its train station – one can get to Yaremcha (1 hour), Kolomyia (1 hour), and Chernivtsi (4 hours).

SIGHTS & ACTIVITIES

Ivano doesn't really offer much as far as "must-see" tourist attractions, which, in all honesty, is part of this city's appeal. Spend a leisurely day strolling through its city center and check out **Market Square** (пл. ринок), which is lined with pleasant, soft hued neoclassical buildings. Just off to the side of the square, you'll see the former **Armenian Church** (1762) with its twin bell towers and blue domes. Presently, it's being used by one of the Ukrainian Orthodox Churches. The square is also home to a Greek Catholic cathedral and a Roman Catholic cathedral. Bask in the glory of it all, grab a coffee, and relax with the knowledge that you're not really missing anything by skipping out on the **Regional Museum** (4a Rynok Pl., 4 пл. Ринок).

Stretching from Ivana Franka (Івана Франка) Street to Halyts'ka (Галицька) Street, **Nezalezhnosti (Незалежності) Street** is the city's main pedestrian drag. Originally designed as a city park, it serves as the main go-to spot for political protests, holiday celebrations, parades, and festivals. It's here that the **Egg Fountain** lies, which is possibly the grandest testament to Ukrainians love for all things *pysanky*. The fountain is bowl shaped, resulting in a little hollowed walkway where you can stand "beneath" the fountain and not get wet. A popular spot with brides, the photo op line can last for hours.

Also along this stretch is Ivano-Frankivsk's version of Odessa's Mother-in-law Bridge (see page 147): the **Love Tree**. Located at 11 Nezalezhnosti (11 Незалежності), this metal tree is hard to miss as it is completely engulfed in locks and chains. A killing could be made selling locks here for 10UAH, but so far this niche market has yet to be claimed.

Continue down the square and you'll soon encounter numerous beer tents and an open park where old men play chess and kids ride around on (rented) Power Wheels.

EAT

Churchill Restaurant (Черчілль Ресторан) Located in the Atrium Hotel, Churchill is a swank, leather clad, English themed lounge and restaurant that is known for its…Italian food. Something about the interior design though makes you want to curl up with a Tennyson novel, a glass of cognac, and a cigar. *31 Halyts'ka (31 Галицька); Open: 12:00-24:00; Mains from 80UAH, Drinks from 12UAH; +(38) 034 255 78 79; www.atrium.if.ua*

Shanson Шансон Shanson is an eclectic restaurant that offers Ukrainian, European, and Georgian fare in a setting reminiscent of London's old high tea rooms. One step away from being too pretentious, the food is good – even if the service is a bit too stuffy. *17 Bel'veders'ka (17 Бельведерская); Entrées from 35UAH, Drinks from 10UAH; shanson-café.com*

Renata Café (Рената кафе) Renata Café is the place to go for coffee and desserts. The outside terrace is especially lovely in the spring and summer when the pedestrian walkway is crowded with musicians and city lovers. *30 Nezalezhnosti (30 Незалежності); Coffee 12-20UAH; Dessert: 11-24UAH; +(38) 034 275 03 19*

Art Café (Khrushch Арт-Кафе "Хрущ на Вежі") Looking like it was designed by a seventh grader with a fetish for all things Egyptian, Khrushch Café hopes to "inspire your mind to reflect on time and space." With cheap beer, breakfast specials, and good coffee, it's easy to relax here and reflect on anything (like, why is there a Buddha statue next to that pyramid?). Live music every Thursday night. *22 Halyts'ka, 6th floor (22 Галицька, 6 поверх); Open: Monday-Friday: 09:30-23:00, Weekends: 10:30-23:00; Beer from 5UAH; Breakfast (salad, toast, jam, coffee) 15UAH; +(38) 034 271 57 76; hrusch.if.ua*

Celentano's Pizza This old standard is located on 3 Halyts'ka (Галицька, 3). *+(38) 034 222 54 24; Open 10:30-22:00*

Puzata Hata (Пузата хата) For cheap food fast, head to the "Metro" supermarket where this popular cafeteria style chain serves up hot Ukrainian favorites. *225M Vovchinets'ka (225M Вовчинецька); Monday-Saturday Open 09:00-22:00, Sunday 09:00-21:00; puzatahata.com.ua*

Nadia Delicatessen (Надя Делікатеси) Located in the same building as the massive Hotel Nadia, this carry-out deli is a popular lunchtime spot with locals, as well as hotel guests looking for a quick bite. With roasted chicken sold by the 100 grams, as well a large assortment of deli-salads, pastries, and hot bites like chicken *kotleti*, this is possibly the best take-out place in Ukraine. *40 Nezalezhnosti (40 Незалежності); Open 10:00-21:00; +(38) 044 490 71 37*

SLEEP

Hotel Dnister (Готель Дністер) The building is pleasant enough if a little outdated. The rooms are typical of Soviet-style inns, but Dnister's rates are some of the cheapest in town. If you're just looking for a place to crash before heading off into the mountains, you could do far worse. *12 Sichovykh Striltsiv (12 Січових Стрільців); Standard with shared bath single/double: US$25/36, with private bath: US$35-65; +(38) 034 222 35 33*

Hotel Nadia (Готель Надія) While this may look like one of those unpleasant, mega-hotels, Hotel Nadia is an increasingly pleasant surprise. The English speaking staff is incredibly helpful and the rooms are clean and comfortable (although small). Wi-Fi is available (30UAH per 24hrs) and the delicatessen attached to the hotel is one of the most popular places in town. Their in-house tourism office can also arrange excursions throughout the Carpathians. *40 Nezalezhnosti (40 Незалежності); Standard Single/Twin: 350/540UAH; Deluxe Single/Double: 400/580UAH; +(38) 034 253 70 77; www.nadia.if.ua/en*

Yaremcha (Яремче)

Driving into Yaremcha, you'll notice the traffic on the mountain roads suddenly picks up; going from one horse-drawn carriage, to a swarm of cars, many with foreign plates. Often criticized for being "too touristy," Yaremcha is an anomaly in the Carpathians: a tourist town that's never hesitated to embrace its visitors. Recently, the Prut River bank has been cleaned up and the highway redone, so entering Yaremcha is like entering Epcot's version of Hutsul Land: sparkling and bright, with everyone smiling.

It's proximity to the ski lifts of Bukovel and Verkhovyna, as well the Dovbush hiking trails surrounding it, make it a great place to stay and explore this area. For more, check out www.yaremche.org.

TRANSPORTATION

Yaremcha is easy to reach by bus from Ivano-Frankivsk (1.5 hours) and Kolomyia (1 hour). Buses leave sporadically to Chernivtsi (3.5 hours) as well. Getting here by train is possible via the Lviv-Rahkiv, Ivano-Frankivsk-Rakhiv, or Kolomyia-Rakhiv lines.

SIGHTS & ACTIVITIES

The most famous Hutsul craft market in all of Ukraine, it is also the most expensive, the **Yaremcha Craft Market** (Open 09:00-17:00) offers everything you've already seen. But its location makes up for the redundancies. Submerged beneath the tree line and teetering slightly above the town's waterfall, the location comes in at a close second to shopping. Be sure to grab some hot *MacCoffee* and then take the stairs out front, behind the bridge, that lead down to the falls for the best photo spot.

The Dovbush Rocks are located off the main highway in Yaremcha (beside the restaurant *Hutsulshchyny*, Гуцульщини). It's boldly titled the "Outdoor Museum of Nature," but it is otherwise known as a hiking trail. The trail winds back through the forest, dotted by signs highlighting various species of flora. But the main reason people start this four-hour loop is to get to the rocks named after Ukraine's Robin Hood: Oleksa Dovbush. The hoodlum hid out here from 1738 to 1745 with his people's resistance army, *Opryshky*. The rocks themselves are an impressive sight with many caves and tight spots that bring to mind the movie *127 Hours*. Bringing a Swiss Army knife with you may not be such a bad idea.

Ukraine's Robin Hood

Oleksa Dovbush was born in the eighteenth century in the Hutsul village of Pechenizhym. He gained infamy for parading around the woods with a posse of fifty devoted followers – occasionally leaving them to rob the rich. Almost no written accounts of him exist, so the legend of him was preserved mostly in various folk songs. Though he was pursued by Polish armies, it was shagging a married women that did him in. He was shot by his girlfriend's husband and killed in 1745.

EAT

Hutsulshchyny (Гуцульщини) Designed to resemble a typical wooden Hutsul home (except, you know, ten times bigger), Hutsulshchyny is a bit touristy, but good. A vast menu with *shashlik*, soups, potato dishes of all sorts, as well as hits like Plov, make this an enjoyable stop. During the high season, traditional bands play here in the evening. Don't be embarrassed to ask your server to take your photo – they're used to it. *Svobody (Свободи); +(38) 034 343 33 78; Entrées 20-48UAH; Drinks from 6UAH*

SLEEP

Cottage Veresk (Котедж Вереск) Cute as can be, the rooms here look like something out of a children's book. The cottage is within walking distance of the falls and craft market, and the friendly staff is more than happy to arrange transportation to the nearby ski lifts. *Petrasha (Петраша); Standard Summer/Winter: 200/250UAH; Luxury Summer/Winter: 300/350UAH; +38-097-998-47-23; lili-veresk@mail.ru*

Hotel Yaremcha (Готель Яремче) This newly opened hotel was designed incorporating Hutsul styling (rugs on the walls and embroidered sheets) and "European expectations" – meaning all rooms have bathrooms, television, air conditioning, and a coffee maker. In the heart of Yaremcha, this hotel is setting the standard as they have package tours (hiking, horseback riding, kayak excursions, etc.), which guests can sign up for. Yaremcha also has unseen perks like twenty-four hour guarded parking lots and unlimited coffee in the morning. *6 Petrasha (6 Петраша); Standard Room Regular/New Year's Rate: 350/550UAH; Semi-Luxury Regular/New Year's Rate: 550/750UAH; Luxury Regular/New Year's Rate: 650/900UAH; +38-063-114-48-41; www.yaremche-club-hotel.com*

Kosiv (Косів)

Arriving at the center of Kosiv, it's easy to be underwhelmed. Its downtown area looks like you caught it at a bad moment. But don't despair, the beauty of this town lies on its outskirts. Nestled into the hills surrounding it are sprawling villas and well-maintained hiking paths. A hotspot for craft gurus, it's known for its artists who still use traditional means to make their crafts.

TRANSPORTATION

Buses leave daily to Kosiv from Ivano-Frankivsk (90km), Kolomyia (35km), Yaremcha (60km), and Chernivtsi (76km).

SIGHTS & ACTIVITIES

Let's be honest, you're here for their weekend **Craft Market** (every Saturday from 6:00 to 13:00) where you can snatch up embroidered shirts and rugs, painted Easter eggs, pottery, spoons, and leather goods – all for less than anywhere else in the region. Taking place along the main square in the city center, get there early before all the good deals are gone.

Kosiv is also quite proud of their **National Museum of Hutsulschyna Folk Art and Mode of Life Museum,** which displays wood carvings, embroidered shirts and cloths, ceramics, as well as recreations of traditional Hutsul living quarters. Only a must-see for lovers of all things Hutsul. *55 Nezalezhnosti, (55 Незалежності); Open 10:00-16:00, Closed Monday; Admission 5UAH*

SLEEP

Kosiv is probably best seen as a day trip as not much goes on here during the week. However, if you want to be there early for the Saturday market…

Carpathians

Hotel Bayka (Готель Байка, Hotel Fable) Located on the outskirts of town, with gorgeous views of the mountains, getting here on foot is nearly impossible. However, with isolation comes peace and a sense of blissful solitude. While the decor may not match the surroundings (rooms have zebra and cheetah print designs), the building itself is breathtaking. Additional charges abound as using the indoor pool, gym, or sauna will cost you extra, but petting the bears (yes, they have two four hundred pound bears) is terrifyingly free. The hotel can also arrange excursions like horseback riding, fishing, mushroom and berry picking, as well as arrange bicycle hires. The best free breakfast in Ukraine is also included. *150 Nad Hukom St. (150 Нaд Гуком); Semi-Luxury single/double: 295/330UAH, Luxury single/double: 345/380UAH; +(38) 034 782 36 58*

Slavske (Славське)

Cheaper than Bukovel, this place is non-stop during the winter tourist season, but quickly falls into hibernation the rest of the year. Its tranquil beauty brings to mind Beauty and the Beast, or Heidi, or some other pop culture reference worthy of describing it. Farm houses nestled into the mountain side welcome visitors and if the hotels (there are two good ones) are filled, it's completely acceptable to go knocking from door to door to see if they have a room available (about 100UAH per person, per night during the high season is the asking price).

TRANSPORTATION

Located on the main train line, Slavske is easily assessable via the Lviv-Uzhhorod train (2 hours) or the overnight Kyiv train (12 hours). By car it's a 140 kilometer drive from Lviv on the main highway (E471/M06) to Uzhhorod.

SIGHTS & ACTIVITIES

People come to Slavske to ski…and that's about it. It is easily the most accessible ski spot in the country, so lines for the ski lifts in the winter can be long. Furthermore, different sides of the mountains are owned by different people who can't seem to work on anything together. Therefore, different passes to different lifts must be purchased depending on what side you'd like to ski on. Furthermore, roads to the lifts will destroy most automobiles, so skiers must take Soviet-era military trucks to get to them.

Don't let all this deter you. All this commotion, in reality, makes for quite a fun experience. After all, where else can you take military-grade automobiles up a mountain in ski gear? Look for the queues that form on the roadsides to catch one (5UAH). Lift tickets begin at 100UAH per day.

Other Ski Spots

Bukovel The first "European" style ski resort in Ukraine, and the second highest in Ukraine, Bukovel is also the country's most expensive. With snow-making machines, meticulously groomed slopes, and omnipresent security personnel, Bukovel is *the* ski destination in Ukraine. Currently there are fourteen lifts and over fifty kilometers of runs, but they have plans to have 278 kilometers of runs and thirty-five lifts by 2012, which would make it one of the twenty largest ski resorts in the world. Hotel prices in high season range from 700 to 1,500UAH per night. Bukovel is located about thirty kilometers west of Yaremcha. Check www.skibukovel.com for lift ticket and hotel information.

Drahobrat Drahobrat is Ukraine's highest ski resort, with a base elevation at 1,300m. Its high elevation usually means Drahobrat is the first to open for the season and the last to close. Located within the most dramatic peaks of the Carpathians, Drahobrat offers some of the steepest (and scariest) drops in Ukraine (make sure you have health insurance). Room rates during high season run 160 to 300UAH per person. For the cheapest room rates, check out www.adventurecarpathians.com

SLEEP

Four Seasons Cottage This homestay is located in an attractive mountain lodge. With the fireplace roaring in the winter and guests sitting around drinking mulled wine, you might feel like you're in a movie. The bottom floor houses the guest-accessible kitchen, as well as bathrooms and living quarters, while its four rooms are located upstairs (each themed after one season). Transportation and equipment rentals can be arranged in-house. *105a Shevchenka (105a Шевченка); Summer/Winter Rates: 250/400UAH; +(38) 067 673 66 22; www.4seasons@slavsko.lviv.ua; www.slavsko.lviv.ua*

Pearl of the Carpathians (*Perlyna Karpat*) This enormous hotel becomes a rowdy stomping ground during the high season. Outside the pool and bar area is a popular hotspot, and inside their sauna can be rented out by the hour. The rooms are plush with most having balconies that overlook the gorgeous mountains and the hotel's sheep. The most expensive hotel in the city, expect to be a little spoiled. *43b Franka (43 Франка); Singles Spring/Autumn: 255UAH, Winter: 510UAH; Junior Suite Spring/Autumn: 390UAH, Winter: 900UAH; + (38) 032 297 15 16; www.perlyna.com*

Uzhhorod (Ужгород)

Uzhhorod, which takes its name from the Uzh River that divides it, is a chaotic and seemingly brusque mix of influences. According to the 2001 census, the city has a blend of Ukrainian, Russian, Hungarian, Slovakian, and Romanian citizens. This eclectic mix is evident everywhere one looks: from the assorted spices and pre-made salads available in the market, to the multiple script used on billboards. As the capital of Zakarpatska Oblast, Uzhhorod has a distinct feeling unlike any other town in the West. Like all true border towns, it's a little noisy, a little dirty, a little crowded, and a little better for it.

TRANSPORTATION

Uzhhorod is generally passed through the way to somewhere else. The first major town you will hit if crossing the border from Slovakia or Hungary, it is a popular place to sleep for the night, before hitting the road again.

Fly

Uzhhorod does have one tiny airport (UDJ) that seemingly only has flights from Kyiv, Moscow, and Simferopol. Check out Aerosvit's website (www.aerosvit.com) for flight information.

Train

Direct routes to Kyiv (16 hours), Odessa (21 hours), Kharkiv, and Moscow run daily to/from Uzhhorod's train station. The main train line runs north to Lviv (6 hours) and south towards Chop (30 minutes). To get to/from Slovakia and Hungary, you will need to transfer at Chop. *Uzhhorod Train Station: 5 Stantsiina (5 Станційна); +(38) 031 223 23 00*

Car

The M06 highway runs from Budapest to Kyiv and goes through Uzhhorod.

SIGHTS & ACTIVITIES

Uzhhorod Castle

Ужгородський замок, *Uzhhorods'kyy̆ zamok*

Built in the fifteenth century, Uzhhorod Castle underwent many sieges but was never taken; when you see it, you'll know why. While not spectacular looking, its sturdiness is unquestionable as its high walls and position on a hill overlooking the city served it well. Inside the grounds are immaculately cared for and small exhibitions are open within its buildings (the taxidermy exhibit on the second floor, which features "local animals," should not be missed). For a unique opportunity,

---

From Those in the Know – Ukrainian Charity

It was a cold winter day in January, and the ice-painted roads of western Ukraine were covered with a layer of melting snow. I was walking with a friend, who was visiting from New York, back to the train station, which had just come within sight. As we made our way to the entrance, we passed an old Ukrainian woman with her head wrapped in a traditional handkerchief. She was hunched over and as we passed by her she extended her hand and murmured something indecipherable in Ukrainian. I shook my head and grabbed my companions arm, bracing against the entreaty. As we passed, I turned around to see how a Ukrainian would respond to her begging and saw a middle age man stop, lean towards her, and extend his hand to help her step up onto the sidewalk.

I had just refused to give my hand to help an old woman, in the middle of winter, step onto the sidewalk.

This realization paralyzed me. Had I become so blind to not see the humanity in an individual? What was wrong with me? When did I begin judging people before giving them a chance?

It occurred to me that the people in Ukraine who have lived through so much upheaval – politically, socially, and economically – have generated a sentient presence; an insight into humanity. Many Ukrainians may not have extra money to donate, but when an old woman reaches out her hand, they will see what she is asking for before making a judgment how to respond. One lesson, out of many, I have learned from them.

- Danielle Kuczkowski

head to the castle's central **Tasting Hall,** which features a Transcarpathian wine tasting room. The tasting includes three reds and three whites from the region, including a Lemberger, Cabernet Sauvignon, Merlot, and a Riesling. *33 Kapitalna (33 Капитульная); Castle Open: 09:00-17:30, closed Monday, Museum: 10:00-17:30, closed Monday, Tasting Hall: 10:00-17:30, Closed Monday; Castle Admission: 10UAH Adults, 5UAH Students, photography/video 10UAH, Tasting Hall: 45UAH, Special Exhibits: 4UAH; +(38) 094 918 36 68; info@uzhgorodcastle.com; www.uzhgorodcastle.com*

Folk Architecture and Life Museum
музей народної архітектурі та побут, *muzey˘narodnoï arkhitekturi ta pobut*

Yes, another one, but this one is arguably the best maintained in the country. Built over an old cemetery (yes, they covered up an old cemetery to preserve old houses), this open-air museum features twenty-four buildings, each an example of Romanian, Hutsul and Hungarian culture.

The hallmark of the museum is the wooden **St. Michael's Church.** Built in 1777 and originally located in the village of Shelestovo, it was moved three times before it found its place here. Renowned for its onion-domed steeple that is covered in wooden shingles, its condition is remarkable. *33a Kapitalna (33a Капитульная); Admission 12UAH Adults, 6UAH Students, 10:00-18:00, Closed Tuesday; +(38) 031 223 63 52*

Ukrainian Greek Catholic Cathedral

Located down the road from the Uzhhorod Castle, this church is worth a quick glimpse inside. Built in 1646 as part of a Jesuit Monastery complex, it was converted in 1773 into a Greek Catholic cathedral. Later, under the Soviets, it was changed again into a Russian Orthodox Church. Now it's experiencing another transformation as its interior is being painstakingly restored to its former glory. *33a Kapitalna (33a Капитульная)*

EAT

Mrs. Greenwich Pizza Café ("Місіс" Грінвіч Піца Кафе) Located in the city center, this pizza joint offers up homemade bread, compote, and the best pizza in town. Add to that copious choices of beer and free Wi-Fi (get the code from the waitress), and you have the makings of one popular hotspot. *59 Grushevs'kogo (59 Грушевського); Open 11:00-23:00; Pizzas start at 21UAH; Drinks at 6UAH*

Cactus (Кактус) Serving up traditional Ukrainian fare, Cactus offers free internet access, a decent beer selection, and an occasional live music show. Smoky and loud, it brings back visions of college, which is just what you want sometimes. *7 Korzo (7 Корзо); Entrées 14-35UAH, Drinks from 8UAH*

Uzhhorod Castle Restaurant (Ужгородський замок Ресторан, *Uzhhorods'kyy Zamok Restoran*) While the food and wine are nice, people don't come here for that. They come here to eat in a castle, because, honestly, how often can you do that? In the summertime you can dine on the terrace overlooking the moat, and in the winter a roaring fire is built in the interior dining hall. *33 Kapital'na (33 Капитульная); Salads from 20UAH; Entrées from 30UAH; Drinks from 8UAH; Reservations recommended; +38 (0312) 44-36-68; www.uzhgorodcastle.com;*

Carpathians

SLEEP

Unfortunately, Uzhhorod doesn't offer much as far as budget accommodations go. If you're in need of a room for cheap, your best bet is one of the *babushkas* out front of the train station (100UAH per night for a room is reasonable).

Old Continent Hotel ("Олд Континент" готель) Rid yourself of any preconceived notions about "Soviet" hotels. Located right next to the pedestrian bridge in downtown Uzhhorod, Old Continent boasts clean and airy rooms, a decent in-house restaurant, and an English speaking staff that is more than happy to assist you. *Shandora Petefi Square (4 Шандора Петефі); Single Standard: 590UAH, Double Standard: 770UAH, Royal Deluxe: 980UAH; +(38) 031 266 93 66; www.hotel-oldcontinent.com*

Hotel Atlant (Готель Атлант) This small, centrally-located hotel is a good value with spacious suites and cute single rooms. The twenty-four hour English speaking receptionists are friendly enough. Skip the overpriced breakfast for something picked up down the road. *27 Koryatovicha Square (27 Корятовича); Junior Suite: 450UAH, Luxury Suite: 515UAH; +(38) 013 261 40 95*

Mukachevo (Мукачево)

Mukachevo is a sleepy little town located about forty kilometers from Uzhhorod. Most people come here on a day trip to see the castle that lies on its outskirts. The city center is a little banged up and probably not the most comfortable place to stay. However, for those traveling further into the Carpathians, Mukachevo makes a convenient stop on the way to Yaremcha or Chernivtsi.

While it could be improved, the city center has its charms with iced pastel colored buildings and plentiful fountains; not to mention an additional communist star or two (which makes for an odd sight this far west). In early September, the town has a **Honey Festival,** and in January the town boldly challenges the popular Crimean wines with its own **Red Wine Festival**.

TRANSPORTATION

Train

Mukachevo is located on a main train line with Uzhhorod. Multiple trains stop in Mukachevo daily from Uzhhorod (2 hours). Trains to Kyiv (19 hours), Lviv (5 hours), and Bratislava (12 hours) also run daily. To get to the city center from the train station, take marshrutka #6, #16, or #18.

Bus

Faster than the train, buses run constantly between Mukachevo and nearby towns: Uzhhorod (1 hour), Chop (1.5 hours), and Chernivtsi (9 hours). The bus station is located about a kilometer and a half from the city center.

SIGHTS & ACTIVITIES

Mukachevo (Palanok) Castle
Замок Паланок, *Zamok Palanok*

Unlike most castles in Ukraine, Palanok shows its age and history it its slightly melancholic façade. Located on a 68-meter high volcanic hill, you'll see it long before you reach it. The first foundations were laid in the fourteenth century and past residents have included Serbian prince Durad Brankovic and the Regent of Hungary, János Hunyadi.

Tenants of the castle lived in the lavishly decorated "High Castle." Composed of over 130 rooms, the castle now houses a museum which displays artifacts from the region, as well as paintings and depictions of its former rulers in the upper chambers. The lower chambers hold recreations of typical Hutsul-style homes. On the second floor, there's an **Ecumenical Chapel** and the most beautiful **Statue of Jelena Zrinska** with her son, a young Ferenc II Rakoczi; the Hungarian aristocrat who would later lead an uprising here against the Habsburg Empire. *Open 09:00-17:00, Closed Mondays; Admission 8UAH; www.zamokpalanok.mk.uz.ua*

EAT

Most of Mukachevo's dining options exist along the pedestrian stretch of Myru Square (пл. Миру). Coffee and ice cream shops abound, but **Traktor** (Трактор, entrées 20-35UAH, beer 6-10UAH), another Western-themed place, offers good food on the cheap. Try their deep fried pineapple with chicken, and stick with the beer. Located in the center of the pedestrian street, look for the wooden Native American statue on the road.

SLEEP

Apollon Hotel (Аполлон готель) Located a short walk from the city center, Apollon is a quiet hotel that's pleasant enough. Offering Wi-Fi (if you can pick up the signal in your room), hot water, and comfortable beds, it provides all the basics but lacks charm. *11-b Partyzans'ka (Партизанська, 11-б); Standard room: 150UAH, Junior Suite: 350UAH, Suite: 350UAH; +(38) 031 314 35 72; www.alfa-apollon.com.ua*

Hotel Zirka (Готель "Зірка") Also located in the city center, Hotel Zirka (Star) may look like the place you'd be most comfortable staying at – housed inside a bright yellow, neoclassical building in the heart of the city center. The service, however, rapidly changes one's perspective. *10-12 Mira Square (10-12 Мири площі); Single Room (with bathroom) 325UAH; Double Economy: 384UAH; Double Standard: 480UAH; Apartment Suite: 2000UAH; +(38) 003 131 310 31; star-ar@mk.uz.ua; www.star-ar.mk.uz.ua*

Skole (Сколе)

Situated about 111 kilometers south of Lviv, Skole is a sleepy little town nestled into the gentle backside of the Carpathians. Perpetually covered in a bit of fog, this town has a dream-like quality about it (even if it is a little disheveled). Its position at the

Carpathians

base of the mountains makes it popular with campers, and its proximity to Tustan also draws the rock climbing and hiking community.

TRANSPORTATION

Located on the main line, trains run here daily via the following routes: Uzhhorod-Kyiv (4 hours from Uzhhorod), Lviv-Chop (2 hours from Lviv), and Kyiv-Chop (12 hours from Kyiv). Elektrichka from Lviv come here daily (2.5 hours). By car, Skole is located on the Kyiv-Lviv-Chop Highway (E471/M06).

SIGHTS & ACTIVITIES

Urych Rocks – Tustan
Урич Скелі, *Urych Skeli*

Most people come to Skole to climb the **Urych Rocks**, upon which the fortress of Tustan was built in the ninth century. Lax safety regulations (climbing over the barricades isn't frowned upon) make this a popular place with rock climbers and hiking enthusiasts. Furthermore, its odd placement (it is the only rock jutting out of the earth around it) makes it a special place. Mystical speculations abound regarding the twenty-five million year old rocks, with some believing that the rocks symbolize some sort of astronomical calendar.

The fortress itself was built here because of its location: a prime stop in the Galicia-Volyn Kingdom's trade routes through the Carpathians. In early September, the **Ukrainian Medieval Culture Festival "Tustan!"** is held here (www.tustan.com.ua). The event brings jousters, sword fighters, and fire breathers to this sleepy town. A small **craft market** before the entrance to the rocks happens Tuesday through Sunday. Located about twenty-five kilometers from Skole, getting here by taxi or car is quite easy.

SLEEP

Most of Skole's accommodations during high seasons are rooms in private homes.

Vicharyk Hotel This bed and breakfasts is a "house" that operates more like a hotel than your typical bed and breakfast. Guests can take advantage of the restaurant and small food store on the first floor. There is also a sauna to be completed in 2011. Running hot water, Wi-Fi, and satellite TV make this a great find. All rooms have their own bathroom except for the Double Standard. The owners don't speak much English but will go to great lengths to understand you. *43 Danyla Halyts'koho (43 Данила Галицького); Double Standard Low/High Season: 250/500UAH, Triple Room: 350/700UAH; +(38) 050 370 26 65; skole.vivcharyk@gmail.com; www.vivcharyk.com*

Nezabudka Homestay Located inside a cozy home, Nezabudka provides a low-key, homestay experience for those looking for a unique escape. The English speaking hostess is glad to arrange transportation for rock-climbing, ski-lifts, horseback riding, or even mushroom picking. Full kitchen downstairs is available for guest use. Bathroom facilities are shared. *11-b Haydamatskaya (11-b Гайдамацкая); Price/pp: Spring-Autumn: 50UAH pp; Winter: 150UAH; New Year's (12/26-01/20): 200UAH; (+38) 050 205 70 24 (ask for Maria)*

Perechyn (Перечин)

Nestled between the Transcarpathian Mountains, just a twenty-minute bus ride north from Uzhhorod, lies the small village of Perechyn. Meaning "crossroad," it lives up to its name on the weekends when nearby villagers flood this regional center for market days. Perechyn also swells with visitors in the summer months when tourists come through on their way from Lviv to Uzhhorod. A favorite with hiking and camping enthusiasts, Perechyn is a great place to channel your *Walden Pond* self.

SIGHTS & ACTIVITIES

The Statue of Fedor Feketa
Статуя Федір Фекета

Located in the central square, just past the castle-like Palace of Culture, you'll see the statue of Fedor Feketa. If you didn't already think this village was adorable, just wait till you hear the story behind this man: Feketa spent his life as a postman, walking thirty kilometers everyday delivering mail to the villages around Perechyn and Uzhhorod. He became a regional hero for his tireless devotion.

Central Square
Центральна площа, *Tsentral'na ploshcha*

A tourist information center is scheduled to open soon within the square, with plans as well to build a museum dedicated to the history of this region of Zakarpattia. The museum plans to have information on Transcarpathia written in four languages: Ukrainian, Slovakian, German, and English. For now, the area is a popular spot to park one's bike and recover after a leisurely ride through "the nature."

SIGHTS & ACTIVITIES

Cross Road
Хресна дорога, *Khresna Doroha*

Taking a walk on top of the "Cross Roads" is the best way to enjoy the charm of Perechyn and the breathtaking views of the mountains. To locate the road, walk south from the main square for about one minute and turn right on the street located just before the Greek Catholic Church (Греко-Католицької Церкви), which will be on your left. Cross the small stream and follow the road to the top of the hill to the entrance to the Bratislava Church and cemetery. Enter the main gates of the cemetery and follow the road as it loops around to the top. Near the top of *Cresna Doroha* is another road leading into the forest; a great place to hunt mushrooms and wild berries. Also very popular with the picnic crowd.

Camping

To get to the best camping spot, locate the Greek Catholic Church (Греко-Католицької Церкви) in the city center. Follow the road located next to the church (the church should be on your right) and go until it dead-ends. The train station will be on your left. Turn right and walk about a half of a kilometer until the road begins to curve to the right. Watch to your left for an archway going under the train tracks, located just before the curve. Go under the archway and follow the path to the Uzh River. In the summer, this is a lovely walk with fruit trees and flower gardens on either side.

EAT

Pidkova Korchma (Корчма "Підкова") Pidkova, or "horseshoe" tavern, is located just north of the center square. Look for the sign with the – you guessed it – horseshoe. Pidkova's cooks pride themselves on their Ukrainian, Hungarian, and Zakarpatska cuisine. The owner recently invited the Guinness Book of World Records to measure the giant horseshoe on the back patio. Perhaps by the time you get there, they'll have the plaque and you can check that one off your life's "to-do" list. *3 Mayakovsky (3 Маяковського); Entrées from 20UAH; Drinks from 8UAH; +38 (0501) 88-36-03*

Kantina (Кантіна) Located on the main road and across from the Palace of Culture, Kantina has a mishmash of dining spaces. An outdoor patio serves up *shashlik,* and inside there's a large, open dining room with vaulted ceilings. Further down the interior hallway lies the entrance to the "*raykom*" (speakeasy) dining room in which you may peruse old photos and flags of Soviet yesteryear and catch a game a football on television. Ask for the English menu. *25 Zhovtnya (25 жовтня); Entrées from 25UAH; Drinks from 8UAH; +38 (0314) 52-25-54*

SLEEP

Berizka Hotel and Restaurant (Берізка) Located near the central square, Berizka is set back just a little from the main road and behind a few buildings; watch for the sign. Offering basic rooms and a sauna popular with the locals, this is nice, subdued place. The bottom floor houses the local bakery, so waking up to the smell of fresh-baked bread is an added bonus. *2a Chervonoarmiÿš'ka (2a Червоноармійська); +(38) 031 452 10 58; labich-berizka.7@mail.ru; www.hotel-berizka.zaua.com*

Tyrianska-Dolyna Hotel, Restaurant, and Conference Center (Турянска долина) This hotel and restaurant is one of the first indications of entering Perechyn. Located on the outskirts of town, this small conference center complex offers public and private dining spaces, a large dance floor with live entertainment, outdoor dining terrace, a Russian sauna, Wi-Fi, and a pool room. In the restaurant, ask for "*pechena kartoplia,*" which are baked potatoes made in true Zakarpatska fashion: cooked in a fire and tossed with onions and slightly roasted *salo* (pig fat). The dining room can get noisy on the weekends so if you're sleeping here, try to get a room away from it. *122 Zhovtneva (122 Жовтнева); +(38) 031 452 22 63*

Verkhovyna (Верховина)

Disappearing as fast as it came, Verkhovyna remains – unlike its neighbors down the road – a quiet village. One could easily spend a day in reflection here, drinking hot tea and staring out over Mt. Smotrych.

But adventure travelers are also hearing about this magical land where locals are still excited to meet tourists. And hikers still make bets with each other over who found the best climbing route. Even if you're just passing through, make sure you stop and make time to see Roman Kumlyk, who resides here. He might just be the coolest thing about the Carpathians.

SIGHTS & ACTIVITIES

Roman Kumlyk

Granted the title of "Distinguished Artist" by the SSR, Roman Kumlyk is a musical legend in these parts. The man knows how to jam out on over sixty different types of instruments, and his house resembles a Hutsul museum with the walls covered in accordions, violins, dulcimers, and drums. On the weekends, he dons traditional garb and gives concerts on the second floor of his home. A veritable one man band, he's simply the most engaging, funny, and endearing performer I've met in Ukraine. And no doubt, he's the last artist to know how to play many of these ancient instruments. Look for the white house with a "watch for the dog" sign. *35 Franka (35 Франка); Concerts: 10UAH/pp, CD: 15UAH; +(38) 097 307 52 54*

Museum Hunting in Verkhovyna

The museum I was standing in was empty, the small display room showing off a couple of dusty painted *pysanky* and some "Hutsul" costumes with their tops gone; the local school was probably using them for something. I mumbled a curse word and headed back towards the door.

I returned to the woman who had directed me here (a *babushka* who made her money on the roadside selling cabbages on the weekend) to see if this was indeed the only museum in town. After a brief inquisition about my accent, I returned to the car with her hints and a cabbage. "She got you to buy one?" my friend Roma laughed as we carried along the dirt road.

Verkhovyna is a tiny village, a quick flash of chickens, goats, and homes to most visitors as they speed through here on their way to Kosiv or Yaremcha. Evidently, it's also home to this amazing museum, which we couldn't find anywhere. Eventually we passed by another woman selling sunflower seeds on the side of road. A little depressing since this was a dirt road in the middle of nowhere (how many cars could possibly pass by?). But she seemed happy enough with her Dixie cup sized portions, ready to be bought. I bought a cup as Roma rolled his eyes and asked her if she knew about any museum around here. She pointed up a muddy hill and told us to ask at the house up there.

By the time we reached the farmhouse, I was ready to call it a day. The mountains, while gorgeous, were incessantly raining down a light mist, and my shoes were covered in batter-like mud. Roma and I argued about who would knock on the door. "You're Ukrainian," I countered "it's weird if I do it. It's like "Hi, I'm this random American showing up on your doorstep in the middle of the Carpathians, wanting to know about a museum that may not exist." He huffed and then knocked as I hung back. The door swung open and then, Roma disappeared inside and I followed, wrestling off my muddy shoes on the porch before scurrying inside. What I saw next was completely unexpected.

A man in full Hutsul garb was seated at the foot of what looked like a xylophone, but with strings instead of bars. Behind him sat an engrossed audience of thirty teachers, all entranced, watching this elderly man do a combination of comedic standup and musical demos. He swirled around the room picking violins off the walls or suddenly whipping a flute out of a cabinet.

The "museum" everyone kept saying I had to visit was actually this man's weekly performance. Roman Kumlyk: the one man show.

SLEEP

Herdan With three privat ground transportation in the country e, wooden cottages and one large, main cottage with five private rooms, Herdan offers an eclectic mix of sleeping arrangements. Tucked away one kilometer from the center of town, this comfortable lodge makes for a romantic mountain escape. Call ahead and they'll even pick you up from the bus station. *8-10 Popovych St. (8-10 Попович); Double Standard Jan-March/March-Dec: 200/150UAH, Double Superior Jan-March/March-Dec: 250/200; Suite Jan-March/March-Dec:300/250UAH; +38 (067) 603-33-97*

Hotel Verkhovyna (Верховина) This comfortable mountain lodge offers roomy accommodations and breathtaking views. The staff is also more than happy to arrange hiking tours and camping trips for interested guests. The kitchen cooks up hearty mountain specialties and hot toddies nightly. Located just seven kilometers outside Verkhovyna at the base of the ski lifts, you'll need to catch a bus from Verkhovyna to Iltsi (Iльці), or you can take a taxi for 20UAH. *Singles from 200UAH, Doubles from 250UAH; +(38) 067 306 99 38; www.verhovyna.com*

Central Ukraine

Odessa (Одеса)

Odessa has a way of converting those who would otherwise like to dismiss Ukraine. Known as the "Pearl of the Black Sea," this seaport town has captivated its audience since it was founded by Catherine the Great in 1794. Archeological digs have found remnants of ancient Greek settlements and the Ottomans, Turks, Poles, and Lithuanians have all, at one time or another, made their claim here. Even with all that history, it wasn't until Odessa was founded as an essential trade port that the place really took off.

With the transport of goods came exposure to different cultures. By the nineteenth century, Odessa had become a cultural hodgepodge with Russians, Greeks, Ukrainians, Jews, Bulgarians, Armenians, Italians, and Germans all lending a unique flair to Odessa's scene. Even now, walking throughout the city can feel like you've hopped into a country that has a thing for the Mediterranean – with a slight dollop of Soviet-flare. Falafel and shawarma stands crowd the bottom floors of Italian designed buildings, while *babas* sell sunflower seeds alongside pouches of paprika and saffron. If there's such a thing as cultural schizophrenia, you'll find it here.

The fourth largest city in Imperial Russia by the nineteenth century (behind St. Petersburg, Warsaw, and Moscow), this city injects a bit of cool into Ukraine. With the largest "alternative" scene in the country, get ready for its renowned nightlife consisting of an elusive mélange of jazz quartets, nightclubs with hipsters – a breath of fresh air in the land of "face control" – and coffee houses with jam bands.

If you're planning on staying here for just a few days, prepare for a change of plans. C'mon man, this is Odessa! People name their children after this place, and when you get here, you'll know why.

TRANSPORTATION

Airport

The interior of Odessa's International Airport resembles more of a bus station than an international airport, but then again, you're not there to sightsee. A ride to the center (10km) will cost an unreasonable 100UAH. Buses stop across the street to the right of the main terminal and head towards the center (центр) and the train station (Ж.д. вокзал). Look for the signs in the windows.

Central Ukraine

Train

There are three daily fast trains to Kyiv (9 hours) as well as two regular trains (13 hours). Trains also run to Moscow (25 hours), Simferopol (12 hours), and Lviv (12 hours). There is also a train every other day to Kamyanets-Podilsky (15 hours).

Centrally located, you can walk to the city center comfortably depending on how much baggage you have. A taxi to the center will cost around 20UAH (that is, after a long haggle). Marshrutkas and trolleybuses stop in front of the McDonald's in front of the train station. Look for "центр" or take Marshrutka #221 and #175 to reach the center.

Bus

Arriving to Odessa by bus is…anticlimactic. The Central Bus Station is undergoing repairs and has been for as long as anyone can remember. Despite the chaos it still functions as a major hub with buses and marshrutkas running hourly to nearby towns. Buses from distant cities run daily and updated schedules can be found at www.bus.com.ua (available in Russian only). To reach the city center, walk out from the bus station, cross the street where the trolley lines are, and catch a trolleybus going right (if the bus station is in front of you).

Trams, Trolleybuses, & Buses

Odessa has one of the best, if most confusing, above ground transportation systems in the country. Buy your tickets from the bus driver for 1UAH along one of its nineteen routes (look for your destination or street name on the placard).

Border Crossing: Transnistria

Transnistria is breakaway territory located mostly on a strip of land between the Dniester River and the eastern Moldovan border to Ukraine. After it declared its independence in 1990, a brief civil war erupted lasting until 1992. It maintains its functional autonomy with military and slight economic support from Russia.

Unrecognized by Moldova (and most of the world), it creates a whole whirlwind of chaos for border-crossers. Entering Transnistria and exiting through Ukraine as a non-Moldovan or non-Ukrainian citizen is possible from the Moldovan capital of Chisinau via marshrutka. Guests can even stay within the region for up to three days without any official entrance fee.

It's coming from Ukraine (like say, Odessa) through Transnistria and into Moldova where the problems begin. You see, by entering Moldova via Transnistria you will not be given a Moldovan entrance stamp. Problems arise when one tries to leave; no entrance stamp means no exit stamp.

The Transnistria border guards are known for their appreciation of "little presents," generally two dollars will get your passport back with a stamp. Exercise caution and hide all your valuables. Ukrainian hyrvnia aren't that high in demand, but U.S. Dollars and Euros are.

For those who love a border-crossing story, the journey from Odessa to Chisinau is up there with some of the best!

Marshrutkas

These white, privately-owned buses careen down the streets of Odessa like badasses. Jumping curbs and scaring tourists seem to be the norm. A trip costs 1.50 to 2.50UAH. Pay when you exit.

By Sea

Ukrferry Shipping Company used to operate weekly ferries between Odessa and Istanbul, but stopped in 2010 due to economic difficulties. There have been rumors it will be up and running again before the next season, no word as of yet. Cruises still stop at Odessa's port on their way to Kyiv, or while heading towards Crimea and across to Turkey. For updated seaport schedules and destinations list it's best to head to the Odessa Sea Port Station's ticket office which is located on the ground floor of the building. Some ticket agents do speak English. Or check www.ukrferry.com.

No Subway?

Odessa is the third largest city in Ukraine (after Kyiv and Kharkiv) so it's a little odd that it has no metro. During the nineteenth century the area around the city was heavily mined for limestone. The resulting labyrinth is referred to as the "Odessa Catacombs" (see page 150). Later, they would be used by Partisans during the Second World War for housing, hideouts, and a means in which to traverse the city without being detected. So expansive are the catacombs that the breadth of these tunnels has still not been completely mapped out. Because of these tunnels, the ground beneath Odessa is so potholed and fragile that constructing a metro here is next to impossible.

SIGHTS

Locals are likely to give you a "must-see" list that simply involves statues, the Potemkin Stairs (of course), and some streets that make for nice strolling. Unfortunately that's what I am going to do, too. But don't fear! Part of Odessa's charm is that it forces visitors to succumb to its leisurely pace. A long morning coffee followed by an afternoon sunbathing on its beach and finished with window shopping and market browsing along its fabulous boulevards seems to be the ideal first day. After an uncomfortable train ride here, Odessa's international flair and European sense of leisure is an undeniably welcomed escape.

BUILDINGS AND MONUMENTS

Tolstoy's Palace
Толстой палац

This building has recently been filed for inclusion as a UNESCO World Heritage Site for its stunning examples of pre-revolutionary architecture. Built in1832 by Count M. Tolstoy and his wife, the couple is probably better known than the building. Responsible for building the first emergency medical service in town and the city's largest library, their cultural and humanitarian efforts made them the city's most prominent patrons of the arts. *4 Sabaneiv Mist (4 Сабанєєва Міст)*

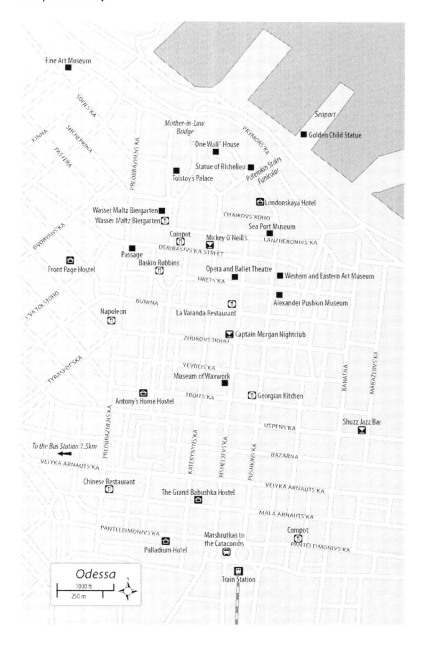

Fine Art Museum

SOFILS'KA

KINNA
SHCHEPKINA
PASTERA

PREOBRAZHENS'KA

Mother-in-Law Bridge

"One Wall" House

PRYMORS'KA

Seaport

Golden Child Statue

Statue of Richelieu

Tolstoy's Palace

Potemkin Stairs Funicular

Londonskaya Hotel

CHAIKOVS'KOHO

Wasser Maltz Biergarten
Wasser Maltz Biergarten

Sea Port Museum

LANZHERONIVS'KA

Compot
Mickey O'Neill's

DVORYANS'KA

Passage
Baskin Robbins

DERIBASIVS'KA STREET

Front Page Hostel

Opera and Ballet Theatre

Western and Eastern Art Museum

HRETS'KA

IVA TOLSTOHO

BUNINA

Napoleon

La Varanda Restaurant

Alexander Pushkin Museum

ZHUKOVS'HOHO

Captain Morgan Nightclub

TYRASPOTS'KA

YEVREIS'KA

Museum of Waxwork

KAMATNA

MARAZLIIVS'KA

Antony's Home Hostel

TROITS'KA

Georgian Kitchen

USPENS'KA

Shuzz Jazz Bar

PREOBRAZHENS'KA

To the Bus Station 1.5km

VELYKA ARNAUTS'KA

KATERYNYNS'KA

RISHELIEVS'KA

PUSHKINS'KA

BAZARNA

Chinese Restaurant

The Grand Babushka Hostel

VELYKA ARNAUTS'KA

MALA ARNAUTS'KA

Compot

PANTELEIMONIVS'KA

Palladium Hotel

Marshrutkas to the Catacombs

PANTELEIMONIVS'KA

Train Station

Odessa

1000 ft
250 m

Sea Terminal

Some take an odd comfort in this building's modernization which was completed in 2000. To me, it's a bit jarring: the contemporary glass and metal design seems so out of place in a city that's all popsicle colors and renaissance glory. Welcoming ferries and yachts, and also housing a free cultural center, it's sadly a little overtaken by the Odessa Hotel's omnipresent leering. *6 Prymorskaya (6 Приморская)*

Passage
Пасаж

This shortcut between Deribasivs'ka (Дерибасівська) Street and Preobarazhens'ka (Преображенская) Street has turned into the prettiest breezeway mall known to man. The interior, known for its architecture and design work on the ceiling, keeps visitors gazing up the whole time, much to the dismay of shopkeepers. An odd hidden gem, Passage is just another reminder that this city has architectural goldmines in seemingly every nook and cranny.

Deribasivs'ka
Дерибасівська

"You've never heard of this street?!" is often the phrase that will welcome you to the "world famous" Deribasivs'ka. Well, world famous in that everyone in Eastern Europe knows about it. Immortalized in countless Soviet films, it has also played as the background in an untold number of novels.

The street was named after Jose de Ribas, a Russian Imperial Navy admiral and a hero of the Russo-Turkish War. De Ribas was a unique mix of a man – half Irish and half Spanish – who fought for the Russians…what the hell right? Perhaps that's why this street has such an eclectic buzz about it. Cafés, bars, art galleries, and shops all crowd this lovely pedestrian street which is busy year-round.

Mother-in-Law Bridge
Тещин Міст, *Teschin Mist*

One of the longest bridges in the city, rumor has it this bridge was constructed by an aristocrat who wished to be closer to his mother-in-law's fabulous *varenyky*. Others swear it was constructed so she wouldn't have an excuse to stay the night. After all, the quick bridge back to her house was right there.

The answer? Well, I guess it depends on how much you like your mother-in-law. The bridge now is the spot in Odessa where newlyweds hang their locks and shackles. While the view isn't awe inspiring, the image of hundreds of locks can pull at even the most jaded of heartstrings. *21 Lanzheronivs'ka (21 Ланжеронівська)*

Opera and Ballet Theatre

Originally constructed in 1809, the Opera quickly established itself as the cultural backbone of the city. When it burnt to the ground in 1873 (yep, this too caught on fire), devastated locals quickly rallied to complete another one. The result is one of finest – if

Tchaikovsky is just one of many famous conductors who have graced this theater with their presence over its two hundred year history.

not *the* finest – theaters in Eastern Europe. Built in 1887 by architects Ferdinand Fellner and Hermann Helmer, who are also known for their works in Vienna, Budapest, Zagreab, and Dresden, this theatre's beauty is astounding and often sprouts arguments as to which is more impressive: the gorgeous exterior or its luxurious interior. *1 Tchaikovsky Pr. (1 Чайковського пр)*

"One Wall" House
"Одна стіна" Будинок, *"Odna stina" Budynok*

Coming upon this house it may look like any other slightly dilapidated, neoclassical building…but wait for it! If you stand in the right spot, to the left of the house looking back on it, a magical thing happens. The house appears to only have a front wall and no back or sides to it. One of the stories behind the "witch house," as it's also known, is that during construction the owners didn't have enough money to construct a fourth side wall, so the builders connected the front and back wall by forming a triangle. The resulting design makes for an interesting optical illusion. *4 Vorontsovsky (4 Воронцовський)*

STATUES

Gold Child Statue
Who doesn't love chubby babies? No one. Combine this love with Ukrainians fanaticism for all things eggs and you might just have the most appealing statue in all of Ukraine. Representing the "Golden Age," this incredibly chunky baby is popular with travelers who rub its toes for good luck. *Awe. 6 Prymorska (6 Приморская)*

Statue of Duc de Richelieu
Exiled to Russia in 1790 by Marie Antoinette from France, Richelieu seemed to have made the most of it. After joining the Russia Imperialist Army and fighting in the Russo-Turkish War, he was appointed the Governor of Odessa by Tsar Alexander I (take that Marie Antoinette!). You can't miss the statue of the toga-clad Richelieu, the base of which has coins that date back to the eras of Louis XIV, Louis XVII, and Catherine II embedded within it. *Prymorska (Приморская)*

MUSEUMS

Alexander Pushkin Museum
Пушкіна музей

Born in Moscow in 1799, Pushkin is recognized as one of Russia's greatest poets. Famous by the time he was twenty years old, he was renowned throughout the empire for his clever wit, incredible works, and insatiable appetite for women who, it seemed, couldn't resist him either. St. Petersburg's parlors soon filled with stories about the young writer – and not everyone liked what they were hearing.

It was when Pushkin developed a sense of political consciousness and began to present his ideas via his writing, that he won the Tsar's disfavor. He was exiled to southern Russia and three years later, in 1823, transferred to Odessa.

His exotic and handsome looks – his great grandfather was Ibrahim Hannibal, an Ethiopian man who was brought to Russia as a gift for Peter the Great and later became a nobleman – were raved about throughout the city. But it was his wicked, innuendo laced humor that had the women coming in droves and the men coming in for the kill. He drank to excess, slept with everyone (no wife was safe!), and always won in his gambling. Indubitably, every fortnight seemed to be perforated by someone challenging Pushkin to a duel.

The governor of Odessa was not a fan, and soon started to intercept his personal letters in an attempt to find something to accuse Pushkin of perpetrating – other than being awesome. When one of the letters contained a sentiment of atheism, he had it forwarded to the Tsar. Pushkin was then banished from the city.

Today, visitors to the Alexander Pushkin museum will get an insight into the thirteen months this esteemed Russian poet spent in Odessa. *13 Pushkins'ka (13 Пушкінська); Open 10:00-17:00, Closed Monday; Admission 10UAH; +(38) 048 222 74 53*

Fine Art Museum

Located in the former private residence of Count Pototsky, the building was turned into a museum by the city in 1899. Each of its twenty-six halls plays host to a bevy of impressive exhibits (the building itself is quite the splendid sight as well). But perhaps the most interesting here is it's subterranean grotto. *5a Sofiivs'ka (5a Софиевска), Open 10:30-16:30, Closed Tuesday; Admission 15UAH, 7.50UAH children; +(38) 048 223 82 72; www.museum.odessa.net/fineartsmuseum*

Museum of Waxwork

Is there anything creepier than wax statues? What about wax statues in old buildings? The Museum of Waxwork is Ukraine's answer to Madame Toussard's. *4 Rishelyevska (4 Рішельєвська); Open 09:00-21:00; Admission 25UAH, 20UAH students, 5UAH children; +(38) 048 222 34 36*

Regional History Museum

This museum is housed in a nineteenth century mansion and was founded in 1955. Over four thousand artifacts tell the story of Odessa from the fourteenth century onward. Not to miss is the second floor hall which holds maps, jewelry, paintings, weapons, and plans from "Old Odessa." *4 Havanna (4 Гавана); Open 10:00-16:00, closed Friday; Admission 10UAH; +(38) 048 222 84 90*

Sea Port Museum

Boasting a Cossack war ship, the original plans for the city, as well as recreations of dock workers' sleeping quarters, the Sea Port Museum is a pretty cool stop that recreates the history of this port town. *Myttna Polshcha (Митна площа); Open 10:00-17:00, Closed Sat and Sun; Free Admission; +(38) 048 729 38 57*

Museum of Western and Eastern Art

The best museum in the city – some would say the country – this art museum holds painting and sculptures by Peter Paul Rubens, Michelangelo, and Merisi da

Central Ukraine

Caravaggio. If you're wondering why the museums' name sounds familiar, it is probably because you've heard of the crime that was committed here. In 2008 the "Taking of the Christ," a painting worth over 100 million dollars, was stolen from here and has yet to be recovered.

"St. Matthew" and "St. Luke," two Frans Hal paintings, are on display here. The tale of their discovery is perhaps even more extraordinary than the famous heist. Their journey started when Catherine the Great purchased four Hal paintings during a trip to Holland in the eighteenth century. While being transported back to St. Petersburg, a terrible storm occurred destroying one ship in the fleet, and heavily damaging the other. All four paintings were believed to have been lost forever.

Over a century later, in the 1950s, a museum curator was at Odessa's Privoz Market where he saw a remarkable painting. Curious, he asked the lady selling the painting to come back to the museum with him so that his colleagues could examine the painting. The curators all realized immediately that this was a work of Frans Hal. When they asked her how much she wanted for it, she said six rubles. They gave her nine rubles instead. *9 Pushkins'ka (9 Пушкінська); Open 10:30-17:30, Closed Wednesday; Admission 5UAH; +(38) 048 722 48 15; www.oweamuseum.odessa.ua*

ACTIVITIES

Catacombs
Катакомби

The catacombs of Rome may be the most famous, but Odessa's catacombs are the world's largest (Rome's are 300 kilometers and Paris' a measly 500 kilometers when compared to Odessa's estimated 2,500-kilometer maze). Crazy, bored young folks have been known to pack a bag and attempt an expedition of their own here. Many of these excursions have resulted in emergency rescues and even death.

For those who like adventure, but not the whole death part, head to the village of Nerubayske (Нерубайське) and **The Museum of Partisan Glory**, which gives guided tours of the caves. To get there, take bus #84 from the Privoz Market. The tours (given in Russian) are 50UAH and lead visitors through a series of tricked out tunnels which illustrate how they were used during the Second World War (the tunnels were used extensively by the armed resistance against the Nazi-backed Romanian Occupation Army of Odessa). Inside the tunnels are bunkers, a hospital, and even a target range they used with mannequins dressed as Nazi's for targets.

On your way into the museum, keep an eye out for the propaganda posters by the stairs. One of them was signed by Fidel Castro when he visited the catacombs.

If you'd like a guided tour in English, **Diligence Travel** does a good private tour for small groups (970UAH for 2-3 ppl, 1090UAH 4-8 ppl) transportation is included. The entire tour takes about four hours. *Diligence: 4 Velyka Arnauts'ka (4 Велика Арнаутська); Open 10:19:00, Sat 11:00-15:00; (+38) 048 237 30 37; natain-com@eurocom.od.ua; www.diligence.com.ua*

Potemkin Stairs
Потьомкінські сходи, *Pot'omkins'ki skhody*

Prince Vorontsov commissioned these stairs for his wife in 1825 – because flowers are so blasé. The original construction consisted of two hundred stairs and ten ledges, but when Prymorskaya Boulevard was constructed seven steps had to be sacrificed. They now lie hidden beneath the pavement.

Designed to trick the eye, when viewed from the top, only the landings are visible. But when viewed from the bottom, only the stairs are visible.

The steps had their name changed in 1955 (formerly it was known as the Giant Staircase or the Richelieu Steps) in honor of the fiftieth anniversary of the Battleship Potemkin Uprising. Made famous in the 1925 film "Battleship Potemkin," the uprising took place when a mutinous battleship of the Russian Imperial Fleet landed in Odessa. Seizing the opportunity, socialist revolutionaries mobilized and sought to link up with the ship's fleet. However, their plans were thwarted when Imperial Forces led a counter attack in the streets.

The 1925 silent film culminates with a shot of Cossacks opening fire on the stair's pedestrians. According to first-person accounts, this never actually occurred, but the film did such a good job of portraying the bloodshed that it has become irrevocably associated with the battle. After all, an image of a baby carriage flying down a massive staircase is a little hard to shake off.

While historically interesting, it ranks a seven on the disappointment scale. The reason being that it is best viewed from the bottom, looking up where one finds a lovely view of the city peeking up from behind the top of the stairs. When viewing from the top down, one gets a lovely view of a hotel and a car dealership.

Funicular
Running up the length of the Potemkin stairs, the funicular was built in 1902. In later years, it would be replaced by an escalator (gasps of horror!). The new funicular was built in 2005 in honor of Odessa's 211th anniversary. Yep here anniversaries go paper, silver, gold, funicular.

BEACHES

Before the Soviet Revolution, the beaches of Odessa were crowded with the hotels and palaces of the wealthy. Once known as the "Riviera of Russia," the pleasure palaces have been seized and turned into clubs or sanatoriums, but the feeling of leisure and extravagance remains. Odessa has five beaches. They are listed below in order of proximity to the city center:

Langeron/Lanzheron Beach
Пляж Ланжерон

The oldest beach in the city, Langeron Beach takes its name after the count that had his summer home here. The closest beach to the city center, it begins right after the seaport border. Unfortunately nothing remains of the Count's palace except the

Central Ukraine

archway at the entrance of the beach. Much quieter in the summer than Arkadia Beach, this beach is popular with sunbathers.

Otrada Beach
Пляж Отрада

Otrada was the name given to his home by a Greek merchant who had a villa here. You can get to this beach by walking down Frantsuzsky (Французский) Boulevard from Asarov Avenue. In the summertime, the Otrada Beach Club is in full force for posh tourists who don't mind shelling out a cover fee for the use of a beach chair and a private pool. Also located here is the Chernomorsky Yacht Club. Established in 1875, it is the oldest sports organization in the city.

Dolphin Beach
Пляж Дельфин

South of the Yacht Club is Dolphin Beach, the "youth" beach of Odessa. Taking its nickname from the student housing that is located nearby, this beach is always filled with young kids attempting to get some sun before their exams.

Chkalovsky Nudist Beach
Пляж Чкаловский

If you like to do your sun tanning in the buff, head to Chkalovsky Beach, just north Arkadia Beach. Named after the sanatorium that's close by, you can find it by going to 85 Frantsuzsky Boulevard (85 Французский Бульвар) and heading to the beach that lies just below the sanatorium. This nude beach is devoid of restaurants and bars so if you want to stay a while, you might want to pack a cooler in lieu of your bathing suit.

Arkadia Beach
Пляж Аркадия

At the beginning of the twentieth century an enterprising executive constructed a restaurant at the end of this beach. Named "Arkadia," the restaurant became so popular with the wealthy that soon the beach surrounding the establishment took the same name. Nowadays Arkadia is busting with restaurants, cafés, bars, and nightclubs that stay open till dawn. A bustling maze in the summer, it's nearly impossible to find a spot to sit down. The cover fee (usually around 20UAH) for full-service – umbrellas, beach chairs, and bar service – is well worth it.

EAT

Food lovers rejoice! The farther south you go in Ukraine, the better the food seems to become. Suddenly spices make an appearance and, oh my God, is that ethic food made by foreigners? Get excited. Odessa was the first city to pop up along the food trail south, and it hits the spot every time (you just need to know where to go).

 Georgian Kitchen (Грузинская кухня, *Gruzinskaya kuhnya*) Georgian food is everywhere in Odessa. Unfortunately, it's usually overpriced and made by people who just think adding black pepper to things constitutes a title change. This restaurant is located in the basement floor of an apartment block and while it may not look impressive, it's the food you're here for. Reasonably priced Georgian favorites like *khinkali* and *khachapuri*, cooked authentically by, dare I say it, Georgians, make this place a can't miss. *34 Pushkins'ka (34 Пушкінська); Mains from 30-50UAH, Drinks 6-10UAH*

Chinese Restaurant (Китайський ресторан, *Kyttays'kyy restoran*) The closest thing Ukraine has to a Chinese a take-out place, this little dive café will satisfy all your fried meat and noodle cravings. The friendly (foreign) staff speaks some Russian but no English; the picture menus help. Try the lo mein (лапша, *lapsha*) which at 50UAH is enough to feed two people. Their sweet and sour chicken/pork (кисло-сладкий курица/свинина, *kislo-sladkii kuritsa/svinina*) doesn't disappoint either. Though not as fancy as other "Oriental" restaurants in town, the service isn't pretentious and you're just paying for the food and not the decor. Look for the Japanese lanterns on the outside of the building and the Christmas tree that's never been taken down. Though it looks a bit rundown on the outside, trust me, go inside! *94 Malaya Arnautskaya (94 Малая Арнаутская); Mains: 35-55UAH; Drinks 6-12UAH; Open: 11:00-21:00*

Wasser Maltz Biergarten ("Вассер Мальт") The most stylish brewery in all of Ukraine, the beer here is pricey (at around 25UAH a half liter) but it's all made in-house. The leather clad seats at the bar make for a great area to watch the piano player. But it is the lush booths that overlook the city garden that are the hot ticket. With an English speaking staff and a menu that's worth the prices, this place is popular with the local TEFL teachers and politicians alike. *6 Havanna (6 Гавана); Mains from 70-180UAH, Drinks from 25UAH; Open: Sun-Thursday 11:00-24:00: Friday, Sat: 11:00-01:00; www.pivnoysad.com.ua*

Compot (Компот) Named after the sweet Ukrainian drink (boiled down fruit and water – with sugar added of course), Compot is a cute Ukrainian take on French-style bakeries. With panini-style sandwiches, all sorts of pastries, daily soup specials, and coffee available to-go, Compote makes the perfect recovery spot. *Two locations: 20 Deribasivs'ka (20 Дерибасовская), 70 Panteleimonivs'ka (70 Пантелеймонівська); Pastries from 12UAH, Coffee from 12UAH; Open 08:00-23:00*

La Veranda (Ла Веранда) If you've got a craving for pasta, then this chain (they have another location in Prague) is the place to go. Authentic pasta and meat dishes, fresh salads, and carpaccio make for a welcome break from the usual Ukrainian fare. The atmosphere is informal, but super cute, resembling an Italian kitchen the color of lemon pastry cream. The one downside is that the wines are overpriced, but they do have a good international selection. *21 Bunina (21 Бунина); Pasta from 70UAH; Meat dishes from 100UAH; Wine from 250UAH a bottle, 70UAH Glass; Open 12:00-24:00; www.laveranda.com.ua*

Steak House (Стейк Хаус) A favorite restaurant along the "world-famous" pedestrian boulevard, Steak House (and you must pronounce "house" the way the locals do: "*haa-uss*") is easy to spot from all the tourists getting their picture taken with the painted cow out front. Inside, it's fancy-smancy right down to the bathrooms. My male friend enthusiastically informed me that the urinals are a trough with orange slices and petals strewn inside. There's also a ruler attached to the wall in the men's room for those who have – um – bets to settle. The steak is overpriced but in Ukraine just finding a place that offers anything resembling steak will suffice. This is prime people watching real estate, filled to the brim with the who's who of Odessa. *20 Deribasivs'ka (20 Дерибасовская); Steaks from 100UAH; Sides from 40UAH; Beer from 17UAH, Wine from 60UAH a glass; Open 11:00-24:00; www.steak.od.ua*

Baskin Robbins (Баскін Роббінс) What's that? Did your heart just stop? Normally I wouldn't recommend massive chains like this, but the arrival of Baskin Robbins was welcomed with unbridled excitement by ex-pats and locals alike. For weeks those little pink and blue deli cups symbolized that you've arrived…or are willing to shell out 40UAH for ice cream (big spender!). *44 Hrecheskaya (44 Греческая); Ice Cream from 30UAH; Open 10:00-21:00*

Puzata Khata (Пузата хата) If you're not sick of it yet, there's yet another one of these cheap, good cafeterias on the top floor of the Europa shopping center. The location has a great view, which makes up for the depressing interior. Being the cheapest place in the area to get a beer, it's also a popular pre-party spot. *44 Hrecheskaya (44 Греческая); Entrées from 16UAH, Drinks from 8UAH; Open 08:00-22:00*

Napoleon (Наполеон) If you're a coffee snob that is horrified by most of Odessa's coffee shops offering pastries *and* sushi, then come here for your fix. Located off of one of Odessa's loveliest streets, this coffee shop takes pride in, thankfully, just the coffee. English speaking staff seals the deal. *28 Preobrazhens'ka (28 Преображенская); Coffee from 20UAH; Open 10:00-23:00*

NIGHTLIFE & BARS

Mickey O'Neill's Irish Pub (паб "Міккі О'Ніллс") As with most cities, this "Irish Pub" claims to be the most popular spot for foreigners and ex-pats. While it's true that its doors and staff are always welcoming those who are seeking the familiar in a foreign place, it's also true that less than stellar locals know that tourists come here, and take advantage of it. It's a fun place but keep your wits about you. *13 Deribasivs'ka (13 Дерибасовская); Open 24hrs*

 Шyzz (Shuzz) Jazz Bar Walking in this place from the street you might get nervous and walk out convinced you have entered the wrong door. While at first it may look like a doctor's waiting room, continue through the white door on the back wall to the right and you've arrived (the kids smoking outside are a dead giveaway of this hidden bar). This jazz bar plays live music nightly and the folks that come here can only be described as Odessa's most eclectic and individualistic. Not a place to get dressed up and show off, just a place to chill, drink cold beer, listen to some music, and dance to something other than techno on the (small) dance-floor. Tap dance performances by Alex Gilko (look for him on Twitter) took place every night I was there. Full bar and friendly staff – you just have to get their attention. *22 Uspenskaya (22 Успенська); Open from 20:00*

Captain Morgan (Капітан Морган) A popular spot with wife-hunters, the scene at this club is the proverbial Eastern European mix of really attractive women and mediocre guys. With techno music blaring loud enough that you'll hear it the next day, this bar encourages its patrons to "drink and dance" (it says so on the banner). Bottom floor is the "lounge" area and the second floor is the dance floor. If you can get past the face control at the door, expect table shots and bad decisions to be made here. *30 Zhukovs'koho (30 Жуковского); 50-70UAH Cover; Bar opens at 21:00*

SLEEP

Luckily Odessa seems to be leading the way in Ukraine as far as hostel standards go. Exorbitantly expensive digs await you in the poshest of hotels, but there's a smattering of fun hostels to take the edge off. While this is a great city to splurge in, beware that Odessa's nightlife (like Arkadia Beach in the summer) has a way of making places to sleep obsolete.

Hostels

 Babushka Grand Hostel The Babushka is housed inside an apartment whose glory days are over. However, scattered about are remnants of its once grand past. Chandeliers hang from the ceiling, massive windows speak to its previous owner's wealth, and the ceilings in the bedrooms are speckled with the last breath of gold leaf. The staff is amazing and often host impromptu trips to their favorite jazz club. Rooms are basic with bunk beds, but the massive private room with its plush bed makes a fantastic small splurge. *60 Malaya Arnautskaya (60 Малая Арнаутская); Bunks from US$17, Privates from US$28/pp; babushka.grand@gmail.com*

Front Page Hostel Front Page takes its name from the previous owner's obsession with the news – as in the walls here are covered in shellacked newspaper articles. One room was covered in tasteful (really) Playboy spreads, that sadly now serves as the staff room. The largest hostel in all of Odessa, Front Page is a centrally located party hostel and its large kitchen plays host nightly to a bevy of international drinking games. The beds are a bit rough, but who cares when you're simply using them to crash at night. They also do a free weekly shuttle ride to their place in Kyiv for guests staying more than two nights. *42 Koblevskaya Street (42 Коблевская); Bunks from $15, Privates from $21/pp; info@tiuhostels.com*

Antony's Home Hostel More of a homestay than your typical hostel, Antony's is housed in a converted apartment building that retains much of its "home" feel. If you're in Odessa for its culture and history, rather than its clubs and bars, then this quiet hostel is for you. With a balcony overlooking the courtyard, a room for families and couples, as well as bunks, Antony's is a cozy break from hectic Odessa. *45 Troitskaya (45 Троїцька); Bunks from US$16, Privates from US$23 /pp; vld.maslov@gmail.com*

Hotels

Londonskaya (Лондонская) If you're going to splurge (I mean, really splurge) in Odessa, then this is the place to do it. Centrally located, every room has amazing views of the port and the pedestrian walkway the hotel is located on. The interior lobby screams "money!" without crossing the line into gaudiness. Rooms come with a mini-bar, Wi-Fi, satellite TV, and air conditioning. The hotel also houses a spa and sauna, pool, and fitness room. English speaking staff and a hotel bar that resembles something out of a Bond film round this place out. *11 Primorsky Boulevard (11 Приморський бульвар); Singles from US$166, Doubles from US$200, Junior Suite from US$250, Senior Suite from US$360; www.londred.com*

Palladium (Паладиум) Located a five minute walk from the train station, this hotel is bright and modern, but you'll have to take public transport or a taxi to get to the center from here. At night, though, you might not have to leave it at all. With their own substantially sized and popular nightclub "*Itaka*" attached to the hotel (free entrance for hotel guests), this place is its own nightspot destination. *4 Italyanski Boulevard (4 італійських бульвар); Standards from US$100, Junior Suite from US$130, Suite from US$180; www.hotel-palladium.com.ua*

Apartment Rentals

Odessa Apartments With airport pickup (free for five night stays and longer, US$20 if not) and a staff that works to find something within your price range, Odessa Apartment is a safe bet. Make sure to specify the area of town you'd like the apartment to be located in and check out their English website for availability. *1 bedroom flats from US$44, 2 bedrooms flats from US$65, 3 bedrooms flats from US$120; +(38) 67 708 55 01; info@odessaapts.com; www.odessaapts.com*

Off the Beaten Path: Central Ukraine

Central Ukraine is a region seldom visited by tourists, although many of them pass through here on their way to Crimea. One of the poorest regions in the country, it is filled with villages that were named during better times when this area was the breadbasket of Europe. Villages named Peace, Grape Land, and Straw Hat amass a blur through bus windows, disappearing by the time they were acknowledged. For those who aim for more than just a drive-thru, there are some rather unique highlights. Kherson has pleasant, uncrowded beaches year-round and is incredibly cheap when compared to other cities. At Askaniya Nova, you can ride in the back of a horse-drawn carriage and see camels, zebras, and bison lounge about in their massive nature preserve.

Kherson (Херсон)

If locals seem downtrodden here, it is likely because they're still a little exasperated that they're not Odessa. Odessa's fate as the culturally laden port city (and the money that comes along with it) was seemingly promised to Kherson when it was founded by Grigory Aleksandrovich Potemkin (whom "Potemkin Villages" is named for, see box) in 1778 by order of Catherine the Great. The city was created to fortify the southern borders of the Russian Empire. To strengthen it, a commercial shipping yard was added as well as plans to create a Black Sea fleet that would have its base here. The city was christened Kherson after Chersones, the ancient Greek settlement in Crimea. But with the foundation of Nikoleav and Odessa, Kherson lost its footing as the main trading port of Russia. Today, Kherson is known mainly as a shipbuilding area.

TRANSPORTATION

Daily trains run to Kyiv (12 hours) and Simferopol (8 hours). Odessa is a short (3 hours) bus ride away from Kherson's main bus station.

Potemkin Villages

Considered to be a historical myth, the popularity of this tale and its refusal to die probably has to do with the imagery it evokes. According to legend, Grigory Potemkin constructed fake village façades to fool Empress Catherine II during her visit to Crimea in 1787. The myth's basis most likely has its origins on Potemkin encouraging villagers to spruce up the place for the Empress's arrival. But after hundreds of years of exaggeration, locals will now tell of entire villages being constructed for the Empress's enjoyment, or of oil paintings being dragged down to the Dnipro River at night and fires placed before them so she had something to marvel at as her boat cruised by. After all, the better this area looked to her, the better Grigory Potemkin looked as well.

Nowadays, Potemkin is associated with the USSR's attempts at dissuading critical opinions by leading foreign visitors on "tours" to exceptional places and presenting them as if they were the norm.

SIGHTS & ACTIVITIES

Unfortunately for an Oblast capital, there's not much to see or do in Kherson. A pretty enough town, the twenty-minute walk down **Ushakova** Street (Ушакова) from the train station to the city's main drag, **Suvorova** (Суворова) is well taken care of and enjoyable. In the summertime, this pedestrian boulevard is filled with café tables and locals indulging in ice cream or a cold beer.

Calypso Beach Club

If you're in town during the summer, it's definitely worth checking out the beaches as they are uncrowded and clean (when compared to Crimea). **Club Calypso** serves as a nightclub in the summertime and during the day it becomes a pay beach complex. Paying the entrance fee here is worth it as its patrons are generally a little more relaxed and the full bar doesn't hurt either. *1 Prydneprovsk (1 Придніпровський); Open from 11:00 in the summer; Admission 5-15UAH*

EAT

John Howard's John Howard's is a cool pub right on the main road of Kherson. The staff is friendly enough and they have Wi-Fi, beer on tap, and french fries – need I say more? While the outside terrace is bustling in the summer, this English style pub is the city's best refuge in the winter. *30/1 Ushakova (30/1 Ушакова); Beer 10-35UAH; Entrées around 21UAH; www.pub.johnhoward-pub.com.ua*

Who was John Howard?

Locals will tell you that the philanthropist, born in London in 1726, contracted typhus while caring for patients and died in Kherson. In truth, Howard was very interested in prison reform and spent his years traveling nearly seventy thousand kilometers visiting hundreds of jails while reporting his findings in his papers *The State of Prisons*. When he came to Kherson in 1790, he visited the local prisons and contracted typhus; dying shortly thereafter. He was buried on the shores of the Black Sea and though he requested a small funeral, once word of his death spread, hundreds came; including the Prince of Moldova. After his death, he was honored by being the first civilian to have a statue in St. Paul's Cathedral in London.

Lenina Pizzeria On the weekends there is often a wait to enter this Italian place, famed in the area for its sold-by-the-slice pizza. Good selection of toppings, cheap beer, and a cozy atmosphere set this place off. *51 Lenina (51 Ленина); Open from 11:00; +(38) 055 226 17 05*

Celentano's Newly opened, this place is all the rage with the locals. One of the few oblast capitals without a McDonald's, anything "chain" is worshipped here and Celentano's is no exception. Plentiful seating and right on the main pedestrian walkway, you could do far worse. *15 Suvorova (15 Суворова); Pizza from 21UAH; +(38) 055 226 32 65*

SLEEP

Diligence Hotel ("Диліжанс" готель) The best hotel in the city (even when compared to the "starred" hotels), this cozy place is just one block off the main road and is easy to get to from the train station. The hotel's restaurant is good and with free Wi-Fi, an accommodating staff, and in-house laundry service, it's the place to

Central Ukraine

stay in Kherson. *39 Gogolya/17 Girskogo (39 Гоголя / 17 Гирского); Double Standard: 43 Euros, Double Suite: 53 Euros, Double Luxe: 86 Euros (breakfast included); +(38) 055 249 92 36; www.hotel.diligence.mail.ru*

Fregat Hotel (Фрегат готель) Another one of those mass buildings from the Soviet Era, the Fregat Hotel is overtly proud of itself. While it is clean and shiny, it's perhaps well past its glory days. If you don't stay here it might be worth checking out their in-house tourism company for guided tours to Askaniya Nova if you only want to go there as a day trip. The rooms are simple, with most providing a fantastic view of the river. *2 Ushakov (2 Ушаков); Singles from 350UAH, Doubles from 400UAH; +(38) 055 249 05 22; office@HotelFregat.com; www.hotelfregat.com*

Askaniya Nova

Covering more than eleven thousand hectares, Askaniya Nova (Аскания-Нова) Biosphere Reserve boasts the only steppe in Europe that has never been touched by a plow (bam!). The reserve is home to over four hundred kinds of flowers and thirty species of birds. Not to mention an unexpectedly odd collection of animals: zebras, llamas, American bison, buffalos, South American camels, Indian and African antelopes, and deer. You have to constantly remind yourself that you're in Ukraine. The reserve is especially famous (in certain circles) for having the largest group of Przewalski's horses in captivity.

Established in 1828, the reserve was bought by the Falz-Fein family in 1856. The family had a ten-year-old son, Friedrich, who would later be referred to as the "Askaniyan Darwin." Friedrich's fascination with exotic animals began when he started breeding the animals his father had given him as presents. As he grew, so did his passion and soon the wealthy Friedrich was consulting experts about which animals to import to add to his collection. By the mid-nineteenth century, Askaniya Nova was the third largest private zoo in Europe.

Tragedy befell this untamed area when the reserve was confiscated by the Red Army in March of 1919. The last owner, the wife of Friedrich Falz-Fein, was shot and killed when she refused to leave.

The reserve was then turned into a national park.

TRANSPORTATION

To get to the reserve, take a marshrutka to Nova Kahovka from Kherson. Private marshrutkas leave regularly from in front of Kherson's train station (just look for a sign reading "Н. Каховка") and take about one and a half hours. Unfortunately, from there you have to get a taxi to the reserve which is seventy-five kilometers from Nova Kahovka. A taxi should run around 225UAH.

TOURS

The most exciting (and worth the money) are the "safaris" through the reserve. All other tours mostly consist of looking at plants, which is nice, but not what you came here for. Kanna Hotel organizes tours from April 15th to November 10th from 08:00

to 17:00. The park shuts down completely during droughts due to fire hazards, so it's wise to check on the status of the parks openings. Ask for the "Gazel" trip (a trip through the wild animal reserve in a minivan) or the rustic guided tour in a horse-drawn carriage. You can book one in front of the zoo at the reserve. All tours must be reserved three days in advance. For more, visit www.askania-nova-kanna.com.ua.

SLEEP

Kanna Hotel (Канна Готель) Clean and basic, this hotel is pricey due to its location near the park. *22, Krasnoarmeyskaya Str., Ascania village (22, Красноармейская ул. Аскания); Basic room: 300UAH; Deluxe 340UAH; + (38) 055 386 13 37; kanna-hotel@mail.ru; www.askania-nova-kanna.com.ua*

Crimea

An Autonomous Republic, Crimea (Крым, Krym) is its own special entity in Ukraine. Here, Russian is the language of choice, minarets rise above the tree lines, and crowded summer beaches nestle up to palace-crowned cliffs. For history buffs, there's the valley that Tennyson would immortalize and the port city which brought The Plague to Europe. For romantics, there's seaside palaces that played host to foreign dignitaries and doomed Tsars. A beautiful, slightly overlooked area by Western tourists, Crimea demands your full attention...and knows how to keep it.

A note on Language

The Russian-Ukrainian divide is perhaps most felt in Crimea. In the 2001 census, 58 percent of Crimea's population identified themselves as Russians, while those identifying as Ukrainian made up only 25 percent. On the streets, Russian is the language you'll hear and signage and billboards are likely to be in Russian as well. Because of this, transliterations in this section will be in Russian, not Ukrainian. However, city names will use their Ukrainian (and not Russian) spelling in English. For instance: Yevpatoriya rather than Evpatoria.

HISTORY

The history of Crimea is best explained as a never-ending series of people who came here shouting "mine, mine, mine, mine!" The better question is "who hasn't laid claim to Crimea?" From the Crimean Khan's palace in Bakhchisarai, the Genoese fortress in Sudak, to the Greek ruins of Chersonesos, it's possible to attempt a retelling of its history through snapshots of buildings alone.

Or you can try to write it:

The ancient Greeks knew this region as Taurica, named after the Tauri (an off-shoot of the Cimmerians) who inhabited the mountains in the area. The Scythians arrived in the seventh century BC and quickly occupied the inland. The Greeks settled around the coast, building colonies like Chersonesos (near modern Sevastopol), Yevpatoriya, and Feodosiya. By the first century BC, most of these colonies were incorporated into the omnipresent Roman Empire.

In AD 250, the Goths arrived and then, a century later, the Huns showed up and did a good job of pretty much destroying everything. Around AD 450, the Alan tribes invaded but liked the place so much they stayed, becoming allies with the then reigning Byzantine Empire, which ruled the southern shore from the sixth to the twelfth century.

The Crimean Khanate

It was the 1240 Mongol invasion that blew away all previous invasions; the Mongols quickly conquered Crimea along with Kievan Rus'. Two centuries later, control over the territory had passed on to their descendants: the Crimean Tatars.

Around this time, Crimea was renamed by the Crimean Tatars, taking its name from the city of Qırım (known today as *Stary Krym*, Old Crimea) which served as the capital of the Golden Horde. It also began a period of seemingly infinite invasions, though they mainly revolved around the struggles between the Turkish and the Slavic peoples for control of the region.

After the Golden Horde was dissolved, the Crimean *khans* (rulers) began competing for control. In 1441, Haci Giray Khan established the Crimean Khanate and proclaimed Bakhchisarai as its capital. When the Turks invaded in 1475, the Crimean Khanate was named protectorate and Crimea became a vassal state of the Ottoman Empire.

This autonomy gave the area freedom and the Crimean Tatars began an era rich in culture, traditions...and slave trading. The trafficking of humans was one of their main economic activities and forays into Russia, Poland and Ukraine for supplies royally pissed off the neighbors. Some speculate that residual grudges relating to this long-ago practice are the result for the continued prejudice towards the few remaining Tatars in the area.

Why are there so few remaining? Well, Crimea's precarious position between Russia and the Turks wasn't always such a good thing. When Russia began to move further south after the Pereyaslav Agreement (see "The Khmelnytsky Uprising" on page 13) the Crimean Tatars were forced to choose Russian "protection." Although Catherine the Great originally promised Crimea would simply be a "protectorate" of Russia, she just went ahead and annexed it fully to the Russian Empire in 1783.

The Crimean Tatars were threatened by the sudden presence of the Christian Russians, who enacted harsh vendettas against the Tatars. Many were forced out of their homes or towns so that Russian nobility and the elite from nearby countries (like Ukraine and Belarus) could move in. Over the next one hundred years, the regions original Tatar population (estimated to have been four to five million people) would decrease to just one-tenth of its original size, with most fleeing to Turkey. Crimea was suddenly filled with palatial vacation houses for the wealthy and had an imperial navy on the way. With the downfall of the Ottoman Empire, Russia's expansionism into Crimea was being closely watched by Britain and France, and they didn't like what they saw at all.

The Crimean War

Crimea is perhaps best known to Westerners because of the Crimean War (1854-56). The ball was already rolling towards a face-off with France and Britain, but the thing that turned the ball into a bomb was when Russian troops began to occupy the

Ottoman vassal states of Moldavia and Walachia. When the Russians destroyed a Turkish fleet in 1854, France and Britain feared that Russia would take Istanbul. So, already having ships in the Black Sea, they went quickly into battle and declared war. While Austria remained neutral, they did threaten to enter on the Ottoman side unless Russia got the hell out of Moldavia and Walachia. And they begrudgingly did.

While Russia withdrew, the allied troops landed in Crimea with the goal of capturing Sevastopol. The battles that ensued were renowned on both sides for being marred by stubbornness, disregard for the dead or injured, and somewhat foolish gallantry (See "Valley of Death" on page 174). When the port was taken in 1856, negotiations began and concluded with the signing of the Treaty of Paris; ending the war.

Twentieth Century

The heyday of Crimea as a retreat for the wealthy and its credibility as a Mecca for artists (a favorite of Tolstoy) was somewhat blemished by the ever-changing hands of governmental rule. After the Bolshevik Revolution in 1917, the Crimean Tatars rushed to establish an independent Crimean State. Their state was short-lived as the Crimean Autonomous Soviet Socialist Republic was formed in 1921. Under Lenin's rule, the Tatars were allowed to use their language and practice their traditions. This mild-cultural renaissance ceased when Stalin came into power at the end of the 1920s, when it became clear that all non-Russians were seen as threats and needed to exercise caution (although, as an odd side note, Stalin himself was born in Georgia, not Russia).

During World War II, German invaders took Crimea. After the war the Tatars (which then constituted about 25 percent of the population) were accused by the Soviet government of collaborating and aiding the Germans. They were then forcibly removed from their homeland and resettled into Uzbekistan. It's estimated that half perished en-route to their new "home."

The Republic of Crimea was dissolved and recognized only as an Oblast in 1945. In 1954, in remembrance of the Treaty of Pereyaslav between Russia and Ukraine, it was transferred to Ukraine. The following decades would see the expansion of Crimea's popularity and a dramatic rise in the quality of life in the area. Perhaps that's why 88 percent of the population supported preserving the Soviet Union in 1991 (the highest percentage in Ukraine).

Later that year, President Gorbachev was put under house arrest in Crimea during the August Coup. The Coup hastened the disintegration of the Soviet Union, introduced Boris Yeltsin as the new leader, and catapulted Crimea into the world spotlight yet again.

Although Crimea is an autonomous entity, it is still Ukraine's entity. Home to an ethnic Russian majority and Russia's Black Sea Fleet, if a war was to happen between Russia and Ukraine, it would likely start here. Although business development has lessened political tensions in the area, they are still there, buried beneath tourism hype and cotton candy stands.

When Ukrainian President Viktor Yanukovych extended the lease on Russia's navy base in Crimea for a "discount on gas prices" in April 2010, Ukrainian nationalists took it as a sign that Ukraine was now back under Russian influence. The lease was scheduled to expire in 2017, but has been extended until 2042.

For now, Crimea is proudly claimed by Ukraine, and Crimea – if somewhat unenthusiastically – accepts this.

Simferopol (Сімферополь)

Simferopol is a hotbed of activity in the summer. Acting as the main hub for Crimea to the rest of Ukraine, it can get a little hectic. Inevitably you will pass through here on your journey and while there aren't many "must-see" things within the city, it is pleasant enough. Cheaper than its neighbors, it offers a few budget accommodations and a plethora of restaurants.

TRANSPORTATION

Air

Crimea's Simferopol Airport (SIP) is among the most popular ways to enter the country. With daily flights from Kyiv, Istanbul, and Moscow, it makes for the easiest way of getting to Crimea (especially if that's the only place you're going to go in Ukraine). Periodic domestic flights occur in the summertime, so check the online timetable (www.airport.crimea.ua) for updated schedules.

Airline tickets can be bought at the Kiyavia office. *22 Sevastopolskaya (22 Севастопольская); Open Monday-Friday 09:00-18:00; Saturday 09:00-17:00; golubets@ticket.crimea.ua; www.airport.crimea.ua*

To get to the city center from the airport (located just over eleven kilometers away), take trolleybus #9, or marshrutka #49, #50, #98, #113, or #115. For a cab, you'll need to cough up 70UAH. Direct marshrutkas to the most popular cities (Yalta, Sevastopol) on the coast leave directly from the front of the airport. Look for the signs on the buses and pay the driver.

Train

The train station in Simferopol makes a grand entrance: all coke machines, neon signs, and Turkish architectural embellishments. No wonder it's plastered all over their postcards.

Word of warning: buy your train tickets in advance in the summer months. *Platzcart* and *kupe* sell out quickly and if tickets are available at the last minute from Kyiv or Odessa, they're usually *SV* which cost three times as much as any other ticket.

Regular trains run daily to Kyiv (17 hours), Dnipropetrovsk (5 hours), Lviv (21 hours), Kharkiv (16 hours), and Odessa (12 hours). The number of trains available doubles in the summertime.

Crimea

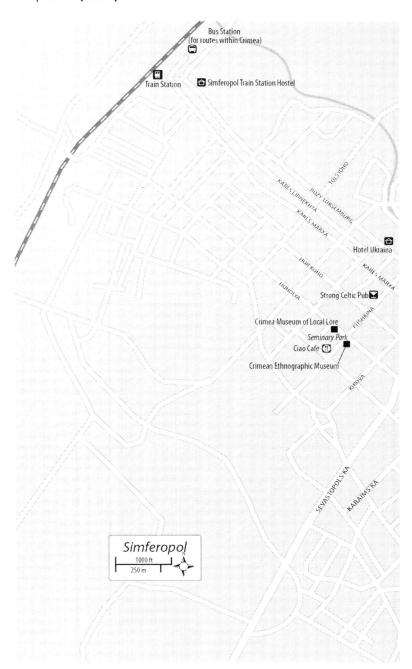

Bus Station
(for routes within Crimea)

Train Station

Simferopol Train Station Hostel

TOLSTOHO

ROZY LUKSEMBURG

KARL'S LIPKNEKHTA

KARL'S MARXA

Hotel Ukraina

HOR'KOHO

KARL'S MARXA

IJDHOLVA

Strong Celtic Pub

PUSHKINA

Crimea Museum of Local Lore

Seminary Park

Ciao Cafe

Crimean Ethnographic Museum

KIROVA

SEVASTOPOL'S'KA

KARAIMS'KA

Simferopol
1000 ft
250 m

Central Avtovokzal

KYIVSKAYA

KUIBYSHEVA

PEREMOHY

Hotel Victoria

SHPOLYANS'KOI

Dekabristov

FRANKA BLVD

KIROVA

NABEREZHNAYA

Celentano

Cafe Marakand

HASPRYNS'KOHO

Silpo

Hotel Valencia

Kebir-Dzhami Mosque

VOROV'SKOGO

CHEKHOVA

CHERVONOPRAPORNA

KRYLOVA

Scythian Neopolis

FUTBOLISTIV

Crimea

Rioni Cafe

Elektrichka (slower commuter train) leave from the train station to Sevastopol (2 hours) with stops at Bakhchisarai. They also have connections to Yevpatoriya (2 hours).

Bus

Getting here by train is recommended. However, once here, the bus is your friend. If you're traveling throughout Crimea, you will have to take a bus at one point.

The bus station in front of the train station (next to the McDonald's) is where you'll want to go if traveling within Crimea. Buy your tickets from the yellow kiosk (just look for the massive queue) and then find your bus in the parking lot in front of it. Buses here leave to destinations like Yalta (2 hours), Yevpatoriya (1.5 hours) and Sudak (2.5 hours) every thirty minutes in the summer.

For long distance buses, head to the Central Avtovokzal (Центральный Автовокзал, *Tsentral'nyi Avtovokzal*). Buses to Kerch (4 hours), Feodosiya (3 hours) and Sevastopol (2 hours) leave regularly. Buses leave daily to Odessa (12 hours) but they're best avoided as the long trip is dreadfully uncomfortable in the sweltering summer months. Central Avtovokzal is located at 4 Kyivskaya (4 Киевская).

SIGHTS & ACTIVITIES

Scythian Neopolis
Неаполь скифский, *Nyeapol' skifskii*

On top of a twenty-hectare hill, about two kilometers outside of the city, lies the ruins of an ancient Scythian tribe. Nowadays excavations seemed to have ceased, so all that remains is one deteriorating building, a few picnickers, and a view looking back on the city, which doesn't look all that majestic. Still if ruins are your thing, this might do something for you. The ruins are located between Vorovskogo (Воровского) Street and Krasnoarmeyskaya (Красноармейская) Street, off of Bataeva (Батаева). A taxi to the site from the train station will cost around 15UAH.

If you feel like a leisurely walk back to the city center from the ruins, take a stroll along the **Salgir River** (Река Салгир, *Reka Salgir*). The longest river in Crimea, it cuts the city in two, flowing aside Naberezhnaya (Набережная) Street. In the summer, it is lined with beer tents and cafés.

Kebir-Dzhami Mosque
Кебир-Джами мечеть, *Kebir-Dzhami Mechet*

Restored in the early 1990s, this mosque dates back to 1502 and is one of the oldest buildings in the city. The mosque is located in the Old Quarter (Старый квартал, *Staryi kvartal*) of town and is a remnant of when this area was heavily populated by Tatars. Back then, this section of town was known as the Ak-Mechet (White Mosque) quarter. Nowadays this white chalk mosque is fully functioning. *4 Kurchatova (4 Курчатова).*

Museums

Simferopol has a few museums for a rainy day. The **Crimea Museum of Local Lore** (14 Gogol, 14 Гоголь; Admission: 8UAH; Open 09:00-17:00, Closed Tuesday) and the **Crimea Ethnic Museum** (18/12 Pushkina, 18/12 Пушкина; Admission: 5UAH; Open 09:00-17:00, Closed Tuesday). have several interesting exhibitions that detail the different inhabitants the peninsula has seen over the centuries.

AROUND SIMFEROPOL

Below the plateau of **Chatyr-Dag** (Turkic for "tent-mountain") on the Simferopol-Alushta highway, is a bevy of caves worth exploring. Like french macaroons, its lower side is riddled with pockets and crevasses that expand beneath its surface to reveal hundreds of wells and caves. The grandest is the "**Marble Cave**" which was discovered in 1987 and is now regarded as one of the best, and most visited, caves in all of Europe. Relatively shallow (the cave is only sixty-eight meters deep), it's the result of two subterranean riverbeds collapsing one on top of another. Now the two-kilometer long cave is divided into "floors" and "rooms" with names like the "The Pink Room," and the "Hall of Hope." Its trickling geological shapes cling to the walls looking like the melted columns from a Dali painting, and its floors resemble strange, alien flowerbeds.

Definitely check out the cave of **Emine-Bair-Khosar** (Well of Maiden Emine). Known for its dramatic fairy green colored lake, its giant calcite columns, and its "Hall of Idols. This one should not be missed.

Onix Tours The caves are operated by Onix Tours who give the tours and rent out the necessary equipment for viewing. Cave viewings start at 30UAH. To see all the rooms of the Marble Cave will run 210UAH (equipment included). The caves of Emine-Bair-Khosar cost 70UAH to go on all routes. Beds (starting at 50UAH per night per bed) in a simple wooden house on the premises can also be rented for those interested in staying the night (or two) to enjoy the surrounding area. To get here from Simferopol, take a bus to the village of Zarechnoye (Заречное) or arrange transportation through Onix Tours. *+(38) 065 225 63 48; info@onixtours.com.ua; www.onixtour.com*

EAT & DRINK

Rioni Café (Риони кафе) This quaint restaurant has all of your Georgian favorites (khinkali, khachapuri, kebabs) in a cute, but not overdone atmosphere. Most of the staff is Georgian and helpful with providing descriptions of the dishes, but their picture menu is the best aid. Be sure to get a side of *lobio*: red beans prepared with spices and topped with feta cheese. The only drawback is their wine prices, which are way too pricey! *50a Polygon (50a полигон); Entrées from 50UAH; Open from 11:00-till; +(38) 065 227 37 27*

Strong Celtic Pub (Сильное кельтское Паб, *Sil'noe kelt·skoe*) Located in a basement, this dark, oaky tavern is the Irish pub every large city must have. The waiters might slightly ignore you, but their kilt uniforms are quite cool. The food menu is decent, but this place is more for drinking. With a fireplace in the middle and a stereo that plays the Beatles and Pink Floyd, it's a cool place to come and chill for an evening. *11 Pushkina (11 Пушкина); Entrées from 30UAH, Beer from 15UAH; Open 11:00-24:00*

Crimea

Ciao Café (Чао Кафе) With an outdoor terrace and a pastry case filled with over sixty types of sweets, this is the perfect spot in the city for that midday pick-me-up. Inside, leather booths make for a great place to snuggle up with a cappuccino in the winter. *Inside Seminary Park, 7a Samokisha (7a Самокиша); Coffee from 20UAH, Pastries from 15UAH; Open 09:00-21:00; www.dessert.café-one.com*

Café Marakand (Кафе Мараканд) Welcome to your first introduction to Tatar cuisine in Crimea. Go heavy on the *plov* (a baked rice dish with meat, spices, and herbs) and *lagman* (a delicious beef soup with vegetables and thick, spaghetti-like noodles) to prepare for the upcoming winter. *17 Vorovskogo (17 Воровского); Entrées from 20UAH, Drinks from 11UAH; Open from 11:00, Closed Sunday*

On the Cheap

Chains abound in Simferopol for those looking to save their pennies until they hit the exotic (and more expensive) points of Crimea.

Silpo (Сильпо) Check out the cafeteria on the first floor of this massive grocery store. Upstairs, the place overflows with peanut butter, cream cheese, sliced bread, and other coveted, hard-to-find ex-pat favorites. Downstairs they serve up pizza, hot entrées, soup, coffee, and desserts for a steal. *19 Kirova(19 Кирова); Entrées from 12UAH, Drinks from 8UAH; Ground Floors: 10:30-19:00, Grocery: 24hrs*

Celentano (Челентано) With one located across from the train station, Celentano is a friend to every backpacker. Many a night has been spent here drinking cheap beer and eating relatively okay pizza, waiting for the last train out of town. *5/7 Karla Marksa (5/7 Карла Маркса); Pizza from 35UAH (individual size), Drinks from 8UAH; Open from 10:30*

SLEEP

While Crimea is becoming a hostel hotspot, the seasonality of the area means that many hostels are only open in the summer. Check www.hostelworld.com or www.hostelbookers.com for new hostels in Crimea. It's very likely that hostels will continue to sprout around this area.

Simferopol Train Station Hostel Located literally next to the train station, this is a good choice for those looking for cheap accommodations before leaving town. Popular with wife-hunters, though, so single females traveling by themselves might be more comfortable staying elsewhere. The American owner and his family (which sometimes stay there) are friendly and I've heard good things from many hardcore backpackers. Free Wi-Fi, free drinking water, and twenty-four-hour check-in are all a plus. *15/1 Lenina (15/1 Ленина), Apt 6; Bunks from US$17, Apartment US$43; +(38) 063 225 28 96; crimeahostel@gmail.com*

Hotel Victoria (Отель Виктория) With a bright lobby, free Wi-Fi, sauna, pool, fitness center, and sparkling clean bathrooms (I mean, so clean you could sleep in them!), this unassuming hotel was a pleasant surprise. English speaking staff – they try anyways – and breakfast is included. *17a Dekabristov (17a Декабристов); Single/Double Junior Suite: US$46/60; +(38) 065 260 00 64; www.viktoria-hotel.com*

Hotel Ukraina (Отель Украина) Some people mock this place for being over-the-top (they are really proud of the recent remodels), but I kind of loved it. A bit opulent, this hotel wants to make you feel like you're in Versailles – or at least that's what the receptionist told me. Get ready for a lot of gold and marble, and some green pillars thrown in for good measure. Wi-Fi, a bar and restaurant in the lobby (skip the coffee), free breakfast buffet, and friendly staff. A nice – albeit pricey –

retreat in this commuter town. *7 Rozy Luksemburg; Standard Single/Double 470/640UAH, Business Standard/Double 570/700UAH; +(38) 065 253 22 53; www.ukraina-hotel.biz/en*

Hotel Valencia (Отель Валенсия) Centrally located and independently owned, this hotel takes pride in its eclectic appearance, having attentive staff, and hosting some past VIP guests (some of whom were famous Soviet actors I was unfamiliar with, much to their dismay). Cool bar downstairs, good location and free Wi-Fi. They can also arrange apartment rentals in the city center. *8 Odesskaya (8 Одесская); Single from 250UAH, Doubles from 350UAH; + (38) 065 266 19 51; www.simferopol-hotel.com*

Sevastopol (Севастополь)

Perhaps better known for not being known, Sevastopol was one those magical sounding Soviet "secret-cities" closed off to the public until 1997. Home to the Black Sea Fleet and their families (and that's all!), it was pampered like an only child. The results of which are easy to spot upon arrival. The wide boulevards are kept as tidy as a serviceman's barracks.

The townspeople currently seem to be more relaxed than in previous years. The results of which, I'm sure, have to do with the recent lease extension on the port, which is the town's economic security. With the Black Sea Fleet remaining until 2042, the city's Russophilic tendencies show no sign of slowing down. Its adoration for Russia probably stems from the fact that it was once the showpiece of the Russian Empire. Needless to say, political discourses vary tremendously from the ones heard in the coffee-shops of Lviv.

A perfect jumping off spot to Crimea's must-see spots like Bakhchisarai and Chersonesos, and littered with remnants of Crimea's historical battles, Sevastopol is well worth the trip.

HISTORY

Sevastopol's beginnings can still be seen in the ruins of Chersonesos, which was the largest Greek port on the Black Sea. A vital center for trade in Kyiv-Rus' times, it's no wonder that, centuries later, Catherine the Great would see this area's location as a prime reason to take it from the Turks in 1783. The city's history intoxicated Catherine, convincing her that by building here she would intertwine Russia's destiny with Greek history. She demanded that a new town be built around the old ruins. She hoped this new city would one day become the main port for the Russian Empire's navy, which she believed would be the most powerful in the world. Hopes of a growing fleet here were dashed with the Crimean War when, in 1854 to 1855, the city was attacked by the French, British, and Turks.

After holding out for 349 days, the city was finally defeated. The Crimean War was over and the place lay in ruins. The terrain around Sevastopol where the battles were fought is still littered with placards, cemeteries, and monuments. Those interested in the Crimean War should check out the battlefields of Inkerman and Balaclava (see page 174).

Crimea

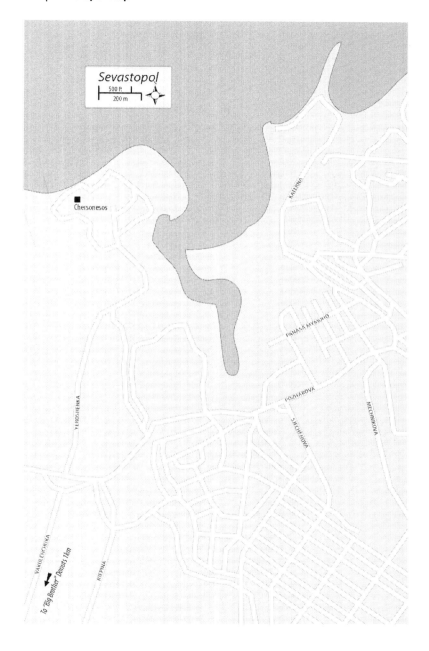

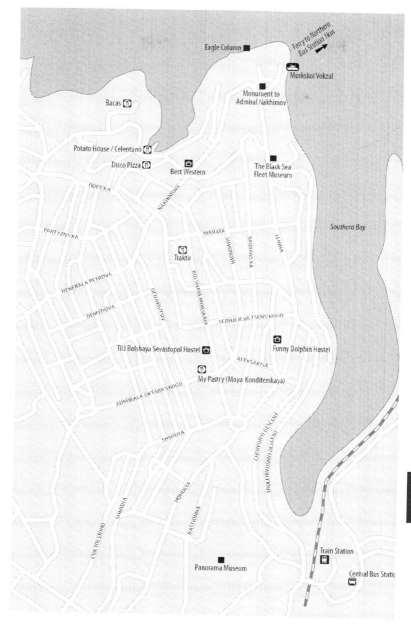

Eagle Column

Ferry to Northern Bus Station 1km

Morskoi Vokzal

Monument to Admiral Nakhimov

Bacas

Potato House / Celentano

Disco Pizza

Best Western

The Black Sea Fleet Museum

ODES'KA

NAKHIMOVA

Southern Bay

PARTYZNS'KA

MARATA

SUVOROVA

RADYANSKA

LENINA

Traktir

HENERALA PETROVA

OCHAKIVTSIV

BOLSHAYA MORISKAYA

DEMYDOVA

SERHIEJEVA TSENS'KOHO

TIU Bolshaya Sevastopol Hostel

Funny Dolphin Hostel

ALEKSAKISA

My Pastry (Moya Konditerskaya)

ADMIRALA OKTABR'SKOGO

CHERVONYI DESCENT

SHMIDTA

TROLEIBUSNYI DESCENT

LVA TOLSTOHO

SHMIDTA

HOHOLYA

BASTIONNA

Train Station

Panorama Museum

Central Bus Station

Crimea

In 1945 the city was again devastated by the Germans after a 250-day siege. Lenin bestowed upon Sevastopol the honor of being a "Hero City" for holding out so long. If you're thinking everything in Sevastopol looks so shiny and new, it's because it is – only ten buildings date back to before that attack.

TRANSPORTATION

Train

Two trains leave and arrive daily from Kyiv (17 hours). Trains for Moscow (24 hours) and St. Petersburg (32 hours) are available daily during the high season. There is no direct train from Odessa to Sevastopol. All trains stop en route in Simferopol. From there you can take seven daily *elektrichka* to Sevastopol (2.5 hours).

To get to the city center from the **Sevastopol Train Station** (1 Vokzalnaya Ulitsa, 1 Вокзальная улица; +(38) 069 248 79 26), walk over the tracks on the metal pedestrian bridge and queue up with the rest of the folks at the bus stop. Take any marshrutka or trolleybus with the sign "5km" or "Центр" on it.

Bus

Arriving and leaving by bus is the best option if you are traveling within Crimea. During the high season, buses zigzag across the peninsula, inundating the roads with fast and last minute transit options. From the **Central Bus Station** (11 Vokzalnaya Ulitsa, 11 Вокзальная улица, +(38) 069 248 81 99) buses leave regularly to Bakhchisarai (1 hour), Yalta (2 hours), and Simferopol (2 hours).

If you're coming from a city in the north like Yevpatoriya (2 hours), your bus might arrive at the **Northern (Северный, Severnaya) Bus Station** (Zakharov Ploshad, +(38) 069 271 50 04). In such a case you will have take a ferry across to the city – the ride is actually quite nice. The ferries depart from right in front of the bus station and run constantly. Tickets cost 3UAH each way.

Ferry

Ferries used to run regularly to Odessa and Istanbul but the recent economic downturn has shut down many of the routes. Transportation by boat remains unreliable. If they do start up again, their schedule will be available at the Morkskoi Vokzal (Sea Station) located at 5 Nakhimova (5 Нахимова). Current information can be found online at www.morport.sebastopol.ua.

SIGHTS & ACTIVITIES

Most travelers will find that they commute out of Sevastopol for day trips, rather than sightsee within the city itself. However, for avid war history fellows there are some sights worth seeing.

The **Monument to Admiral Nakhimov** is hard to miss in the square named after it. Dedicated to the man who led the city's defenses, this spot is where the masses gather during holidays, performances, and celebrations. In the center of the roundabout is the six-meter bronze statue of Nakhimov who lost his life by an enemy sniper during battle.

Down by the waterfront on Primorskii (Приморский) Boulevard you'll see the melancholic **Eagle Column** rising dramatically atop a pile of boulders ten meters out in the water. It was built in memorial to the ships which purposefully sunk themselves here in the bay in 1854 to prevent enemy ships from entering the harbor.

The most popular of Sevastopol's wartime attractions is the **Panorama Museum** (Панорама музей) located on the hill at the end of History Boulevard. It opened in 1905 to commemorate the fiftieth anniversary of Sevastopol's defense during the Crimean War. Inside the museum is a massive 360 degree painting of the battle fought here on June 6th, 1855. It was designed to give viewers the feeling that they are standing on a hill overlooking the action.

The downstairs museum displays remnants of the Crimean War such as cannonballs, artillery, and various uniforms. You can also rent audio guides in English from here. *Istorychni Boulevard (Історичний бульвар); Open Tuesday-Sunday 09:30-17:00; Admission Adult/Child 20/10UAH*

The **Black Sea Fleet** can be seen in the Southern (Южный, *Yuzhnyi*) Bay. But for those who speak Russian and want more info, then **The Black Sea Fleet Museum** is for you! Littered with historical artifacts, photos, and replica ships, it's especially interesting to a certain few. *11 Lenina (Ленина); Open Wednesday-Sunday, 10:00-17:00*

EAT & DRINK

The food scene in Sevastopol was a dreary sight for a while. Years of being closed off bred a one-dimensional, oddly repetitive food culture. If you've been to one place, you've been to them all. Luckily new places have been opening every season, each with their own special gimmick (for better or for worse).

Bacas (Бакас) Situated on the water, this "Fish and Wine" place is outfitted in the ever-popular nautical theme. But the food is good, the service attentive, and the view spectacular; especially in the evening when the boats are docking. In the summer, they open the terrace and bands plays. If you're not a fish person, they also do great *shashlik. 2a Kapitanskaya (2a Капитанская); Entrées from 75UAH, house wine from 52UAH (per liter); Open from 12:00; +(38) 069 253-50-59*

My Pastry (Моя Кондитерская, *Moya-Konditerskaya*) For your coffee and sugar buzz, head to this cute little coffee shop and try to snag one of their cozy side booths. With forty kinds of pastries (ogle them in the pastry case before you decide), you can easily work your way into a diabetic coma here. *4 Admirala Oktabr'skogo (4 Адмирала Октябрьского); Coffee from 21UAH, Pastries from 17UAH; Open 08:00-18:00*

Potato House / Celentano Bringing together the country's two favorite fast (and cheap) places under one roof, this mega-building is one of the city's most popular spots. At night it's a good pre-gaming spot as its close to some of the city's best clubs. And during the day it's awash with tourists and locals clamoring to get a good table to watch the ships come in (it is located on the pier). *Artbuhta (Артбухта); Entrées from 30UAH, Drinks from 8UAH; Open from 10:30*

Traktir (Трактир) A cheeky little place with thick wooden tables, Russian military uniforms on the walls, and remembrances of the Crimean War, Traktir sticks to the familiar. The borsch is good and their garlic rolls (*pampushki s chesnokom*) should not be missed. *8 Bolshaya Morskaya (8 Большая Морская); Mains from 25UAH, Drinks from 8UAH; Open from 11:00; +(38) 069 254 47 60*

"Big Brother" (Большой брат, *Bol'shoĭ brat*) Donuts! You didn't really know you missed them until they were no longer available. Luckily, fried dough has made its way to Ukraine and is now being served at this oddly named, brightly colored joint. The traditional sweet stuff is available in flavors like chocolate glaze, caramel crème, and jam-filled, as well as some more exotic ones (mushroom donut anyone?). *29 Vakulenchuka (29 Вакуленчука), on the second floor of the "TC" building; Donuts from 3.80UAH; Open from 10:00*

Disco Pizza (Диско Пицца) I never figured out if this was actually the name of this pizza place, but that doesn't matter. What does matter is that two restaurants located in the back corner of the pier – behind Potato House – combine to form a courtyard of sorts. At night, a DJ plays here and locals dance at this impromptu club venue. Patrons look on from their tables, eating pizza and drinking liters of beer. It's a weird, do-not-miss spot. *Artbuhta (Артбухта); Pizza from 30UAH, Drinks from 10UAH; Open from 12:00*

SLEEP

TIU Bolshaya Sevastopol Hostel Open seasonally, this place is always changing locations. The Western owners are friendly, the coffee free, and the massive group outings to bars in the evening are a nice bonus. Though the beds are uncomfortable, most people are too knackered by the end of the night to notice. *Location in 2010: 38 Bolshaya Morskaya (38 Большая Морская), apt. 16; Bunks from US$22; info@tiuhostels.com; +(38) 098 669 47 83*

Funny Dolphin Hostel The first hostel in Sevastopol, this hostel is trying to stay open year-round. Ukrainian-owned, the hostel is clean, tidy, located in a quiet neighborhood, and the hosts are as friendly as can be. Better for those who like a more "chill" experience, the beds are comfortable and the atmosphere calm. Call in advance if you're arriving at an odd time so they are there to let you in. *5 V.Kuchera (5 В. Кучера), apt. 2; Bunks from US$17, Private from US$40*

Best Western Sevastopol Built in 1952, the building Best Western resides in is considered to be an architectural gem. With panoramic views of the Sevastopol Bay, English-speaking staff, free Wi-Fi, and buffet breakfast, this hotel beats all Western expectations. *8 Nakhimova (8 Нахимова); Standard Single Low/High Season: 560/680UAH, Standard Double Low/ High Season: 630/765UAH; +(38) 069 253 90 60; www.sevastopol-hotel.com.ua*

Around Sevastopol

VALLEY OF DEATH

Thanks to the Tennyson poem – "Cannon to the right of them / Cannon to the left of them…Into the jaws of Death / Into the mouth of Hell / Rode the six hundred" – the Charge of the Light Brigade has long been immortalized. It's a symbol of bravery, foolish gallantry, and perhaps the last true "glorious" battle.

The "Valley of Death" is now a vineyard, regarded highly for the wines it produces from this once blood soaked ground. The Charge of the Light Brigade took place on it during the **Battle of Balaclava** on October 25, 1854. The battle began when the Russians marched from Sevastopol into Balaclava; an effort which could have forced the British out of Crimea. Before long the Russians blew through six Turkish redoubts and had gained control of the Turkish cannons. At first they were met by the 550 men of the 93rd Highlander division who formed a "thin, red line" in the valley, but soon it appeared like the Russians were regrouping on the eastern end of the valley.

Soon after that, the British Cavalry received a command from British officer Lord Raglan telling them to stop the Russians from carrying away the guns. The message was vague (which group of Russians exactly?). But messages were often misconstrued during battles and so the leader of the brigade went along, leading his men into the valley, surrounded on three sides by Russian soldiers. It was an ill-fated mission to take the guns that were still in the Russian's hands. Certain doom awaited them as they charged down the valley and into the arms of the awaiting Russian army. Yet, none halted.

Communications had improved to the point where British citizens were getting reports of the battle a mere three weeks after the events occurred. Tennyson was inspired to write his poem after reading London Times' reporter William Howard Russell's eyewitness account in which he said: "At 11:00 our Light Cavalry Brigade rushed to the front…Surely that handful of men were not going to charge an army in position? Alas! It was but too true – their desperate valor knew no bounds, and far indeed was it removed from its so-called better part – discretion…At 11:35 not a British soldier, except the dead and dying, was left in front of those bloody Muscovite guns."

To see the Valley of Death, where some memorials are still scattered about the hills, take marshrutka #107 from Sevastopol to the battlefield located on the M18 from Sevastopol to Yalta. There's also a World War II diorama on top of Sapun Gor Hill which overlooks the valley.

CHERSONESOS

XEPCOHEC

A breathtaking sight, it's easy to see why Catherine the Great was so enamored with this place. When you first enter the grounds, the scattered ruins (that, sadly, aren't sectioned off and are crumbling beneath tourist traffic) aren't that impressive. But a walk around the back side will reveal small bluffs that sweep into the sea and rocky inlets where believers bathe their feet as Greek ruins lay overhead. Founded in 422 BC, remains of the city's ancient amphitheater and temples can also be seen.

The old and new here collide in the Ukrainian fashion as antiquity is covered up with new concrete and churches. The restored **St. Volodymyr's Cathedral** is an omnipresent force in the area, quickly upstaging the Greek ruins in its quest for attention. A favorite pilgrimage sight, it was here that Volodymyr the Great was baptized into Christianity, bringing the Russian Orthodox Church into existence.

To get to Chersonesos, simply take marshrutka #22a (running from 7:20 to 20:50, 30min ride, 2UAH) from Sevastopol. The route stops at the front entrance of the ruins. Currently there are two prices listed for visitors: one for Ukrainians and one for foreigners (this will not be the first time you see this in Crimea). As of now, foreigners pay 40UAH. *Open May-October 09:00-19:00, November-March 09:00-16:00; +(38) 069 223 15 61;info@chersonesos.org; www.chersonesos.org*

Balaclava (Балаклава)

Balaclava (Turkish for "fish nest") has a naturally occurring inlet hidden behind its harbors. If you know where to look, the rolling hills dip and open into an underwater cave that is the perfect hiding spot for pirates, or submarines.

Homer talks about this place in the Odyssey: A place where pirates live in the coves, tricking passing boats into entering the secluded harbor before nabbing them. The Soviets also used the underground grottos to their advantage by tucking away nuclear submarines, obscuring them from the roaming eyes of satellites.

Better Known As...
Most people know the name "Balaclava" as the term for the full-faced masks British mothers knitted for their sons fighting here during the Crimean War. They marked the boxes full of them "Balaclava" at the post-office and the name stuck.

Entering this harbor town in the spring or summer, cafés line the harbor and vendors crowd the sidewalks selling sailor hats and postcards. Fishing vessels, yachts, and charter boats cozy up in the harbor; each offering rides to nearby beaches with names like "Silver" and "Gold." And all the while, a wondrous backdrop of gently sloping hills ensconce the bay and within them a secret. Well, a secret that's now open to the public.

TRANSPORTATION

Balaclava is about fifteen kilometers from Sevastopol. From the bus or train station in Sevastopol, take marshrutka #9 or #20 to the "5km" bus stop. A chaotic place, "5km" provides bus interchanges throughout the region. The bus (marshrutka #9) you're looking for is located in the back, left corner.

If you want to avoid the hassle altogether, you can always haggle with a taxi. But expect prices to be atrociously high.

SIGHTS & ACTIVITIES

Fortress of Cembalo
Крепость Чембало, *Krepost Chembalo*
Walking by the Bay of Balaclava, you'll see the ruins of this fifteenth century Genoese fortress perched on the hillside. Parts of the grounds surrounding the ruins are precariously sectioned off as it looks like they could tumble at any time. However, much of the area is open for those in search of an amazing view of the surrounding area.

Naval Museum

Военно-морской музей, *Voenno-morskoi muzyei*

Opposite the bay from the cafés and vendors is "Facility 825," a secret Soviet hideaway where submarines would dock for repair without anyone knowing. Today, the six-hundred-meter long meandering tunnels are open to the public and house the Navel Museum, which is one of the country's must-do things.

Shortly before his death, Stalin approved the building of a secret nuclear submarine base. Losing the arms battle with the U.S., the Soviets went quickly into action constructing a facility that could withstand the force of "five Hiroshimas" deep into the mountains of Balaclava. In the summer of 1957, they began the transformation of the city. Working twenty-four hours a day, miners and constructionists quickly niched out roads, inlets, lock-chambers, workshops, and arsenals in the mountain. In the event of a nuclear attack, the facility could hold ten thousand people as well as an entire division of nuclear submarines for three years. And the whole thing took just four years to build.

Founded in 2002, the museum now gives guided tours of the complex. *1 Mramornaya (1Мраморная); Admission Adult/Child 25/10UAH; Open 10:00-17:00, Excursions on the hour*

Beaches

In the summertime, ferries docked in the bay of Balaclava offer rides to the nearby beaches of Silver Beach (Серебряный, *Serebryanyi*, 15 minutes) and Gold Beach (Золотой, *Zolotoi*, 30 minutes). These generally run every hour from 08:00 to 18:00 and start around 10UAH. Look for the boats docked along the pedestrian walkway with signs advertising boat rides to the beaches.

Silver Beach is the most popular area, although it provides no shade from the

Balaclava and Florence Nightingale

In November 1854, Florence Nightingale arrived, along with other volunteer nurses, in Balaclava where the main British camp was setup during the Crimean War. What greeted her was a seriously overworked staff, crowded conditions, and horribly wounded soldiers who were being poorly cared for. Medicines were scarce, hygiene was disregarded, and mass infections (typhus, typhoid, cholera, and dysentery) were rampant. The death rate at the camp was staggering.

Nightingale tirelessly cared for the wounded soldiers and made constant rounds late into the evening. A reporter from *The Times* observed her at work and wrote about Nightingale: "She is a 'ministering angel' without any exaggeration in these hospitals, and as her slender form glides quietly along each corridor, every poor fellow's face softens with gratitude at the sight of her. When all the medical officers have retired for the night and silence and darkness have settled down upon those miles of prostrate sick, she may be observed alone, with a little lamp in her hand, making her solitary rounds." After this write-up, she became synonymously known as "The Lady with the Lamp."

Credited with laying the foundation of professional nursing, International Nurses Day is now celebrated on Florence Nightingale's birthday.

Crimea

sun. Gold Beach stretches along the coast for eight hundred meters and while it is less crowded, the sand isn't as fine.

Some people choose to walk along the path that runs from the ruins of Cembalo, through Cape Aya to Silver, Gold and even farther to Figs Beach (Инжир, *Inzhir*). To get to Silver Beach along this path is a sweaty forty-five-minute walk in the sun. Gold Beach is a good hour and a half walk.

The last beach along the cape is the magical sounding "Lost World" (Затерянный Мир, *Zateryannyi Mir*) but it's impossible to walk there. You'll have to take a forty-minute boat ride – just be sure you arrange for them to come back to pick you up!

At the end of the main promenade in Balaclava there is also a free, public beach (although sun bathing on a slab of concrete doesn't really seem that appealing when compared to the "Lost World").

SLEEP

Balaclava is easy to do as a day trip from Sevastopol. But for those interested in overnight stays, here are a few options.

Hotel Listrigon (Отель Листригон) Perched on top of a hill overlooking the bay, Hotel Listrigon offers fantastic views, decent service, and cheaper prices than its neighboring competitors. The rooms are divided into "A", "B", and "C" class, with "C" class being a communal apartment with shared bathroom. Breakfast is included for "A" and "B" class, which also have private terraces. *7 Noyabrya 5-D (7 Ноября 5-Д); A/B/C/ Class starting at 300/280/100UAH per 2 ppl in low season, 460/440/150UAH per 2 ppl in high season; +(38) 067 692 11 79; www.listrigon.com*

Hotel (Resort) Dakkar (Отель Даккар) A favorite with posh tourists, this hotel has the best service in town as well as a number of good, if seasonal, cafés and restaurants on premises. With Wi-Fi and clean rooms with all the essentials, you'll relax easy here. Is it worth the price? The fully booked rooms in the summertime seem to say yes; just don't dwell on that question too long. Breakfast included. *13 Kalicha (13 Калича); Doubles from 500/600UAH Low/High Season, Junior Suites from 700/800UAH Low/High Season; +(38) 069 263 77 63; www.dakkar-resort.net*

Golden Symbol (Золотой Символ *Zolotoĭ Simvol*) Golden Symbol is a tiny hotel nestled next to the harbor where yachts dock daily. The eight rooms are breezy, modern, and well kept. The bar downstairs has great food and lively conversations at night. Feels like an Eastern European take on a New England style inn. *1A Nazukina (1А Назукина); Double Standard from US$50, Suites from US$70; +(38) 069 263 72 24; www.goldensymbol.com*

Yevpatoriya/Evpatoria (Євпаторія/Евпатория)

Don't let the sanatoria (Soviet "health" resorts) that ensconce this town detract you from visiting. Bust through this tacky film into the city's interior and soon you'll discover a city rife with history, displaying a veritable grab-bag of cultural and religious influence; with some nice beaches to boot.

Still a little bit of a secret to outsiders, Yevpatoriya's mishmash of influences collide here to form a city consisting of random architectural styles and religious buildings, ancient squares, a unique food culture, and a party atmosphere that goes till dawn. After visiting, you'll find that you almost want to keep this magical place to yourself.

HISTORY

Known as Kerkinitida when the Greeks had control of it (around 500 BC), this city was a vibrant center of trade. Little remains of this phase, probably because the Scythians had such a great time attacking it all the time. Eventually they gained control of the city and, like what often happens with new loves, quickly lost interest. The city then fell into a peaceful state of disuse for the next thousand years. It wasn't until the Ottoman Turks crowned it Gozlev and established it as a center of Black Sea trade that the city became vibrant again.

The Tatars heavily invested in development of this area and built twelve mosques in the city. They also heavily fortified its defenses, but that did little to stop the

---

A Hitchhiker's Guide to Ukraine

I have ridden in a car, balancing on top of boxes of beets. In speeding taxis where the driver laughed at me for looking for a seatbelt – he had cut them out. I've ridden in a horse-drawn carriage to a bus stop. I've taken trains that have broken down. And I've wedged myself into the back of a van filled with plywood and mattresses to get from Sevastopol to Odessa when the train was sold out.

When traveling in Ukraine, there is a point in every trip when you think: "Well, this is odd." And one day, this happened.

Crimea in the summertime. The people! I was trying to get to Yevpatoriya and the bus was sold out. Luckily, I had managed to get my ticket the day before and so I was just sitting in my assigned seat, ticket in-hand, as the ticketless passengers argued with the driver outside. Eventually everyone took their seat before the masses piled in; each begrudgingly accepting their standing room only status. They filled in every void until the walkway was jammed with bodies. I heard a woman say something loudly before the standing passengers started shuffling about. Suddenly I saw an infant – around nine months old – being passed back like a bucket from passenger to passenger, before being handed to the guy sitting next to me. Maybe he was the father? Nope. He looked at the baby and then handed her off to me. The baby didn't cry, or act like this wasn't anything other than completely normal. I looked around and made eye contact with a woman up front – the mother – who was standing. When she saw I had her baby, she relaxed and told the driver he could go.

And so there we were – me and this baby – on a road trip to Yevpatoriya. I named her Sophia and we had a grand time (although my accent really confused her). After our two-hour journey, her mother collected her, said thank you, and that was that.

In smaller towns in Ukraine, people leave strollers outside of grocery stores and ask others to watch their babies while they run to the bathroom in restaurants. In the West, we're often quick to condemn these acts as "foolish," but I think it speaks to Ukraine's sense of community; of their pride in watching out for one another. And for one bus ride I was the trusted stranger, who *of course* would help hold the baby. In reality, it made me rather sad knowing that I could never do that back home; trust a stranger that much with the most precious thing in my life. But in Ukraine...

ongoing Cossack raids. When all of Crimea fell to the Russian Empire in 1783, Gozlev went with it. In 1784, Catherine the Great had the city's name changed to Yevpator after an ancient Slavic monarch. It was during this time that the city began to flourish as the country's preeminent spa town. Fashioned after the resorts in Switzerland and Italy, suddenly Russian aristocracy no longer had to leave their country to get "the very best."

TRANSPORTATION

From May to September direct trains from Kyiv (12 hours) run regularly to Yevpatoriya's train station. Buses run regularly during the high season to/from Simferopol (2.5 hours), Feodosiya (4.5 hours), Yalta (4 hours), and Sevastopol (2 hours). Buses sell out quickly here in the high season so it's best to buy your departure tickets in advance.

SIGHTS & ACTIVITIES

Dzuhma-Dzhami Mosque
Джума-Джами мечеть, *Dzhuma-Dzhami Mechet*

Located on the city's main street of Revolyutsii (Революции), you can't miss the Dzhuma-Dzhami Mosque. Originally built in the sixteenth century, it was here that the Crimean Khans were crowned. Returned to the Crimean Tatars in the nineties, today it is a recently restored working mosque; and the only multi-domed mosque in the country. The mosque is generally open to visitors and in the summer free tours are given. Visitors should remove their shoes at the door. Women will need to put on a full body robe and cover their hair before entering. Robes and shawls are provided free of charge before the main door.

Dervish Monastery
Дервиш монастырь, *Dervish monastyr*

Recently closed for renovations, the Dervish Monastery should be open again soon. Dating from the fifteenth century, it is here that Sufism (a mystical dimension of Islam) was practiced. Intense states of meditation were held here by the monks for days and even weeks, and certain spots within the structure are supposed to have different "channels of energy." Visitors are allowed to walk around the complex, but women must cover themselves. *18 Kareavaya (18 Караева); Open May-September*

Turkish Bath
Турецкая баня, *Turetskaya banya*

The Turkish bath in Yevpatoriya worked for almost five hundred years. Up until 1987, residents of Yevpatoriya were able to enjoy it. Closed for repair in the early nineties, it has yet to be reopened. However, visitors may roam the area, taking in what little breath of antiquity the place has left. Recently the female bath entrance has been restored, giving a glimpse into what a remarkable retreat this place must have been. *50 Krasnoarmeyskaya (50 Красноармейская)*

Karaim Kenassa
Караимские Кенасы, *Karaimskie Kenasy*

Built in the nineteenth century, this complex is the last remaining building of the Karaites. Modern Crimean Karaites, of whom there are less than fifteen hundred remaining, consider themselves to be decedents of a group of Khazars who around the tenth century converted to a form of non-Talmudic Judaism. Today the Karaim Kenassa is a complex building, which weaves together areas of worship with nature. Quite unlike any other center of worship, it's overtly familiar and sublimely foreign. Shrines open into magnificent gardens and then close off again into secluded cloisters for prayer. Open to visitors, this area of worship should not be missed. *68 Karamskaya (68 Карамская); Open May-September 10:00-17:00; Admission 5UAH*

DO

The **pedestrian walkway** that follows the coastline along Frunze (Фрунзе) Street is the place to go to in the summer as open-air nightclubs, discos, bars, and street vendors take their places. Get some ice cream and take a stroll along the coast, or buy a bottle of Crimean wine and get a spot in the cool sand.

In the summertime, marshrutkas abound taking bikini-clad tourists to the local beaches all around Kalamita Bay. The most popular is **Solnyshko (Солнышко) Beach,** but for those wanting more seclusion try to find one going to the "Wild Beaches" in the area of Chaika (Чайка). Located at the very end of the main strip (about twenty minutes from the city center), the beaches here are unattended, but relatively less noisy and crowded than the city beaches. Just look for the marshrutkas marked with the beach's name.

EAT

Karaman (Караман) Located next to the Karaim Kenassa, this place has the city's best *chebureki* (a thin, wonton like dough filled with meat or cheese) and *plov* in the area. Look for the little stall window next to the temple. *68 Karamskaya (68 Карамская); Quick bites from 8UAH; Open: 10:00-20:00, Closed Mondays*

Dzheval Café (Джеваль Кафе) Located next to the mosque, this restaurant has the best Tatar food in the country. Try the *tuzla masal* (35UAH), a mix of tomatoes, carrots, eggplant, herbs and garlic tossed with walnuts. Their *tavuk kobetesi* (a layered Crimean Tatar pie stuffed with chicken and potatoes) is also amazing. Being a traditional Tatar restaurant, they don't serve alcohol. However, they do have an enormous amount of outside seating replete with pillows and lounge chairs which make this a great place to come to enjoy a hookah in the evening. *13a Karaeva (13а Караева); Entrées from 40UAH, Drinks from 10UAH; Open from 11:00; +(38) 095 850 37 32; www.odun-bazar.com*

Literature Café (Литература кафе) Decked out in 1920s swag and paying homage to Russian poet Anna Akhmatova, this café serves up hot lattes, an ever-changing array of sweets, and some heartier specials nightly. *21/16 Anna Akhmatova (21/16 Анна Ахматова); Coffee from 20UAH, Pastries from 15UAH; Open 10:00-21:00 +(38) 065 694 43 07*

Crimea

SLEEP

Yevpatoriya's former life as the playground for Russia's aristocracy is evident it its hotel choices that still cling to their "health resort" roots. In the summertime, you'll also find numerous *babas* crowding the bus station offering up rooms in their homes for rent. If you're looking to save some money and are up for an adventure, this is your best option. When haggling with them, prices should start around 100UAH. In high season, however, prices rise drastically.

Dolce Vita Guest House A quick walk from the city center and just two minutes from the beach, this guest house has individual apartments (two-story lofts and one-level studios) for rent. Popular with families, this posh place has all modern conveniences. Breakfast included. *6 Tokarev (6Токарев); Closed November 1st-April 30; 2 people, 2-story apt, Low/High Season: 350-500/550-1050UAH; 2 ppl, one-story apt, Low/High Season: 400-700/650-1200UAH; +(38) 065 696 07 29; www.dolcevitacrimea.com*

Hotel Planeta (отель Планета) A modern hotel with a swimming pool, Hotel Planeta stays true to its past. Popular as a Russian "health" resort, it offers a full-range of health treatment options unseen in the Western world. One could pass on those and simply enjoy the swimming pool and sauna, nearby beach, and even on-site petting zoo. The beach is open June 1st to August 31st. Rate also includes three meals daily. *29/73 Kosickogo (29/73 Косицкого); Double Jr. Suite, Low/High Season: 450pp/600-700ppUAH; Double Standard, Low/High Season: 300pp/400-500ppUAH; +(38) 065 253 12 22; www.planeta.crimea.com*

Hotel Liana (Отель Лиана) Two hundred yards from the beach, Hotel Liana offers cute accommodations in a comfortable setting. With a swimming pool and sauna, clean rooms, and decent prices, this hotel is one of the better deals in the city. *5 Kosickogo (5 Косицкого); Double: 600-800UAH; Apartment (up to four people): 1000-1350UAH; +(38) 065 692 81 74; www.evpatoriya.com/liana*

Hotel Ukraina (Отель Украина) The most centrally located hotel in town, Ukraina's location on the main strip makes it a fun place to stay in the summer. It also has a few rooms with the cheapest rates in town (however, the cheapest fares will have

---

Kazantip Music Festival

The longest, craziest, and most unusual electronic dance and music festival in Europe, Kazantip is quickly becoming the most popular thing about Ukraine. Over 150,000 people fly in from all over the world to enjoy this non-stop, twenty-four hour party on the beach. Taking place on the outskirts of the tiny town of Popovka, in the "Republic of Kazantip," the festival is basically a land onto itself.

The festival happens yearly around July or August, taking up over sixty thousand square meters of beach and attracting over thirty restaurants and bars, six dance floors and over three hundred DJs.

While most guests coming to the festival crash right on the beach, many opt to stay in festival-provided housing (they also have rooms "for girls only"). Those wanting to save some money can stay in the nearby town of Yevpatoria and bus into the festival daily (a fifteen-minute ride). It's recommended if you're coming to the festival to book your rooms early as this festival basically rents out all available rooms.

Log on to www.kazantip.com for more information on lineups, room reservations and tickets.

you using communal showers). Great for those looking for a beach escape in high season, yet still want to have money left to go out at night. *9 Krupskoy (9 Крупской); Single from 280UAH, Doubles from 400UAH; +(38) 065 699 40 25; www.hotel-ukraine.net.ua*

Bakhchisarai (Бахчисарай)

It's hard not to feel like you are entering some secret territory when creeping into the secluded town of Bakhchisarai. Meaning "Garden Palace," this windswept land was once the capital of the Crimean Khanate.

Over the past few years, many Crimean Tatars have moved back here, opening shops and restaurants that are decidedly not Russian in an attempt to repatriate this area. Minarets sweep the skyline, tile roofs slant beautifully off buildings, honey-drenched desserts are sold on the sidewalks, and the smell of spices make the whole place reminiscent of the Middle East.

Walking through the old town, the city condenses down to a skimpy strip of road that makes its way along the base of a canyon. Looking up, you can see that the tops of them have been etched out into the honeycombed "Jewish Fortress" of Chufut-Kale, and topped with the country's most mesmerizing church: the Uspensky Monastery.

During the day, buses carrying pilgrims kick up the dust and breeze through here, hitting all the must-see "stops" before rushing out again. The magic time in this town is at dusk, when the streets grow quiet, hookahs are set up, and the windows are open to let in the fresh night air.

SIGHTS & ACTIVITIES

Khan's Palace
Ханский дворец, *Hanskiĭ dvorets*

After the Crimean Khanate was brought under Ottoman Rule, the capital of the Khanate was moved here. For the next three and half centuries, trade flourished and prosperity grew (and with that the palace). The palace's elaborate structural elements were designed by Ottoman, Persian and Italian architects in the sixteenth century, with most of the construction completed by use of slave labor. During this time, Bakhchisarai exploded as a cosmopolitan and religious center. At its height, the city contained thirty-two mosques, which Catherine the Great did a great job of destroying when Russia took over in 1783.

Catherine the Great, however, did see something special, technically "romantic," about Khan's Palace and thus spared it from destruction. One of only three Muslim palaces found in Europe (the others being Topkapi Palace in Turkey and the Alhambra in Spain), a visit to Khan's Palace is a must.

When visiting, make your way through the wall of vendors and soon the palace's minarets and tiled ceilings reveal themselves. A little too extravagant in some places – a remodel was performed after a fire in 1736 destroyed much of the original construction – it seems some parts were rebuilt by a Russian aristocrat who went to

Crimea

Turkey and thought "hey, I think I'll make me something like this back home." If you can ignore the modern embellishments that sometimes detract from the authenticity (like the massive fake flower arrangements and gaudy statues), you'll enjoy it.

The ticket center to the Khan's Palace is located within the main entrance on the right. Base tickets are 50UAH for adults and 25UAH for students and children. Individual tickets are also sold to the Palace's other attractions, mainly the mosque.

You enter the palace through the "**Divan**" (Persian for "council") **Chamber** that was built in the sixteenth century. It was here, amongst the stained glass windows and plush couches, that matters of State in the Crimean Khanate were addressed and settled. The inscription over the door reads: "The door of Divan. Khan Selamet Guirei, a son of Khan Khadji Selim Guirei, 1742."

The Crimean Tatar National Movement

Mustafa Jemilev, Chairman of the Crimean Tatar Mejilis (parliament) and recognized leader of the Crimean Tatar National Movement, said when he received his Nobel Peace Prize nomination that he hopes his award "will draw attention to the situation in the Crimea, namely the allocation of land to returnees, and…the need for nonviolent solutions to all problems in the Black Sea region."

The problems Jemilev refers to have been around for quite some time. The ongoing tragedy began when over two hundred thousand Tatars were forcibly deported en masse to Central Asia by Stalin in 1944 (Stalin had falsely accused them of collaborating with Nazi Germany). After the collapse of the Soviet Union, many Tatars began their slow return.

Upon their return, they found the land which once was theirs taken, having been turned into resorts or pegged for later development projects. The then recently formed Ukrainian government did not have camps for the Tatars and many were forced to live in makeshift homes, often without running water or electricity.

On the outskirts of Simferopol, one can see little stone huts cloistered together, haphazardly built and clinging to one another on the hillsides. Many of these are the results of Tatars seizing plots of land after their application to build houses had been refused. These acts of defiance are growing as they struggle to build communities and reestablish themselves here in a land in which, many say, authorities are of no help.

With a regeneration of pro-Russian candidates serving in Ukrainian offices, Crimean Tatars are increasingly worried. Many even feel that certain anti-Tartar propaganda is being pushed into the public realm. Perhaps because of this, over ninety thousand Tatars remain in exile to this day; they are afraid to come back to their Crimea.

Many NPOs and movements have been organized, striving to educate Crimeans about Tatar culture to fight the intolerance that sometimes accompanies ignorance. Still, while progress has been made, one can't help but notice how Tatar history seems to be completely overlooked in certain Crimean museums and historical texts (just like Jewish history elsewhere in the country seems to be ignored). An inconvenient and melancholic story, it seems most Crimeans are content in never mentioning the Tatar plight.

For more information on Tatar culture, current events and news and information visit www.iccrimea.org or cidct.org.ua/en.

From there, the palace opens into a courtyard that holds its most famous attractions: the **Fountain of Tears** and the **Golden Fountain**. Built in 1733, the gold-leaf marble of the Golden Fountain is a lovely and slightly overlooked site; like the sibling of a celebrity. The inscription on the fountain says: "Khan Kaplan Guirei, let God forgive him and his parents," and "Let God give them, youths of paradise, some pure drinks." Interpret that as you will.

On the far wall in the corner, amongst the flicker of camera flashes, is the Fountain of Tears. Built in 1733 and made famous by Alexander Pushkin's poem, it's always presented with two roses: one red (for love) and one yellow (for chagrin). It's a little hard to appreciate its design as the fountain isn't hooked up to proper plumbing. But what can you do? The sentiment is still lovely.

From there you pass through the Summer House (eighteenth century) with its ornately carved wooden ceiling and central marble fountain, and the Small Mosque (sixteenth century). Then it's out through the vegetable garden (which still produces luscious looking vegetables) and into the only surviving Harem (there were originally four). Built in the eighteenth century for the Khan's mother, this building was once attached to the main building via an ornate gallery. You'll also pass through a series of "Dwelling Rooms" that are splashed with rugs and various apparatuses from past lives.

The main museum ends with a hall containing traditional dresses of the Crimean Tatars, recreations of typical homes, and snippets of life. "The Bride Room" recreates a Tatar wedding day when the bridegroom's family would come to view the Bride's dowry. The museum, however, mentions nothing of the deportations the Tatar's went through, but it does offer an insightful and well-done glimpse into their culture.

Exiting out into the main courtyard, you'll see the Main Palace Mosque (to the

---

The Fountain of Bakhchisarai

Catherine the Great probably thought the palace was "romantic" because of the Fountain of Tears. The story behind its creation is one marked by true love, or utter contempt.

The love part started when the last of the Crimean Khans, Giri, became consumed with an enslaved "war prize" in his Harem. The girl – a young Polish woman whose beauty was supposedly unrivaled – did not return the sentiment. So devastated was she in her situation that she refused to do anything, let alone be with the Khan. And so, after just one year there, she died.

The Khan was inconsolable and soon he began to weep uncontrollably day and night. People started to worry. After all, this Khan was renowned for his unapologetic strong will. The courtesans finally had had enough of his blubbering and had a fountain constructed for him. They presented it to him by placing it by the girl's tomb, explaining that the fountain would do the crying for him from then on.

Years later, in 1820, Alexander Pushkin would visit the palace and pen "The Fountain of Bakhchisarai" upon hearing the story. The poem's popularity solidified the palace in the hearts of Russians everywhere and possibly spared it from destruction.

left) and, next to it, the Khan's Cemetery. In the back corner is the Mausoleum to Dilara Bikez, who may have been the Polish girl so lovely, she broke the Khan's heart.

Kahn's Palace is located at 129 Lenina (129 Ленина) and is open 09:00-17:30. Admission is currently 50UAH for adults and 25UAH for students and children. The palace also has a website (in English): www.hansaray.org.ua.

Uspensky Monastery
Успенский монастырь

Located two kilometers from the Khan's Palace, it's possible to take a leisurely hike up the hill here, or simply catch the marshrutkas that go along the main drag. When you come to a cluster of Tatar restaurants that sit in front of a rather dramatic wooded hill, climb up the paved road along with the other tourists. After a ten-minute climb, you're there!

Built into the limestone, Uspensky Monastery is perhaps the country's most intriguing church. Ornate mosaics are fixed into the side of the mountain, a dramatic staircase explodes out of the mountain side, and the gold domes of the church seem to seep forth from the rocks. A working monastery now (it was once closed by the Soviets), it was built in the ninth century by Byzantine monks. Climb the stairs to the small chapel located in the top of the cave and watch as monks hold services here as they have done for centuries. Women should cover themselves in the scarves provided. Donations are accepted and photography is not permitted in the upper parts of the monastery.

As you exit, watch for the pipe that pumps out water. Pilgrims crowd it, filling two-liter bottles with the water that's "blessed."

Chufut-Kale
Чуфут-Кале

Continue walking down the path that you took up to the Uspensky Monastery and after one kilometer you'll be at the "Fortress of the Jews." This two-hundred-meter high bevy of cliffs and plateaus is honeycombed with the remnants of cave cities that have sheltered people for centuries.

The first to inhabit this area were the Christianized Alan tribes between the sixth and twelfth centuries. The area was christened Kyrk-Or (Forty Fortresses) because of the number of monasteries they built in the area. From then on, it seemed every nationality that passed through here stayed a while. The Armenians and the Karaites also left their mark on the city. It was here that the Crimean Khanate had its first capital in the fifteenth century. When the capital was moved down the road to Bakhchisarai, the Khan declared that the Turkish-Jewish Karaites could sell and trade freely in the capital during the day, as long as they returned here at nightfall. Thus, this is how the area earned its nickname: "Fortress of Jews." The Jewish Karaites would occupy the mountain until the mid-nineteenth century.

Today, the cave city makes for great exploring. Entering from the southern gate, you'll come to the fourteenth century Karaim Kenassa (prayer houses), a mausoleum, burial chambers, and the ruins of countless homes etched out of the rock.

Tepe-Kermen
Тепе-Кермен

Founded in the sixth century, this collection of over 250 cave structures is located about two miles up from Chafut-Kale. Known as the "Castle on the Summit," it's the oldest of Crimea's cave cities. To get here, follow the ridge up from the eastern gate of Chafut-Kale and stay on the ascending path.

Mangup-Kale
Мангуп-Кале

For those who have a serious hiking bug, Crimea's most fantastic cave city is located twenty-two kilometers south of Bakhchisarai. This city served as the ancient capital of the Feodor and was the largest city in Crimea for over five hundred years. The plateau it is built upon is in the shape of a hand, with four "fingers" rising up, and sheer drop-offs on three sides. An impressive site, the fortress here was built in the sixth century by Crimean Greeks and wasn't abandoned until the fifteenth century. Popular with hikers, campers, rock climbers, and mountain bikers, this area is an adventure lover's dream world.

To get here, take a marshrutka from Bakhchisarai to Zalisne (Залісне) and walk about one kilometer from the southernmost tip of the town. On your left you'll see four rocks peeking out from the wooded area (the four "fingers). At the base of the hill is a seasonal lodge but most visitors camp "unofficially" in and around the mountain.

For those looking for organized adventure tours of the area, Ukraine4U (www.ukraine4u.com) offers biking tours, hiking, and camping excursions throughout Crimea and the rest of Ukraine.

SLEEP & EAT

Bakhchisarai's appeal is in its relative secluded feel, so you won't find any big resorts here. Shack up a night or two at one of the cozy inns below and be sure to check the family-owned restaurants next to the hotel.

Ashlam-Saray Hotel (Ашлам Сарай-отель) The Hotel Ashlam is a cozy inn tucked next to the restaurant Esfane, which the owners also operate. The rooms are simple with Middle Eastern decorations. Bathrooms are shared, but have hot/cold running water twenty-four hours a day. The owners can also organize camping and cave excursions. Great for those wanting greater insight into Tatar culture. Please note that this place is observant to Muslim traditions and no alcohol is allowed on the premises. *1 Basenko (1 Басенько); Double Room: 80UAH, Triple Room: 110UAH, Quadruple: 140UAH; +(38) 050 883 51 99; www.ashlama-saray.com*

Hotel Dilara Hanum (Отель Диляра ханум) Located seven hundred meters from the Khan's Palace, this small hotel offers up ten rooms. The hotel is run by a fantastic Tatar family that makes guests feel at home. Though the hotel itself is basic, the service is incredible, with the owners going out of their way to make guests feel comfortable. They also have two rooms located in the heart of the old town next to their restaurant, "Musafiri." *43 Ostrovskogo (43 Островского); Economy room: US$10/pp, Standard room: US$40 per room; Luxe Room (up to 6 ppl): US$100; +(38) 065 544 71 11; www.bahchisaray.net/node*

Hotel Merab (Отель Мераб) Hotel Merab has nine cozy "standard" rooms in their guesthouse. Communal kitchen and patio are open to guests for use as well. In the evening, their restaurant (located next door) cooks up great food while guests lounge around smoking hookah and watching the sunset. Located in the old town this hotel has Wi-Fi and hot/cold running water. The hosts can also arrange transportation to nearby sites or camping trips. *125b Reki (125b Реки); 2 bedroom: 300UAH, 3 bedroom: 360UAH; +(38) 067 731 52 35; www.meraba.crimea.ua*

Yalta (Ялта)

At dusk, the streets in Yalta explode with neon colored wigs, street performers, *babas* selling individual cigarettes, and men with monkeys looking to entertain. The restaurants here are over-glitz and expensive, the rooms outrageously priced, and the crowds – oh the crowds!

However, underneath its shallow surface, this city has a heart of gold. To try and deny its appeal is impossible. *The* destination in Crimea, all roads lead to Yalta.

> Anyone that has ever seen *Pinocchio* is likely to suddenly, and oddly, remember that scene when he runs away to the carnival as they take a night stroll through Yalta.

HISTORY

The story of Yalta supposedly began when a group of Greek sailors became caught in a storm on the Black Sea. So terrible was their situation that they thought they would surely perish. But as fate would have it, the men slowly drifted to shore and when one man saw the faint outline of Aiyu-Dag ("Bear Mountain") through the twilight he began to yell *Yalos! Yalos!* (meaning "shore" in Greek). A short-lived Greek colony called "Yalta" was formed where the men landed.

The city remained pretty much dormant until the Russians and tuberculosis came along. This sunny, warm retreat became *de rigueur* for all those suffering from "the consumption." Seaside sanatorii sprang up to take the chill off of those who could afford it. In the 1900s, wealthy aristocrats spent their summers in Yalta as a sign of patriotism. The Tsar's summer palaces were also built here.

Enthusiasm for this place has yet to dwindle, and even with its exorbitantly high-costs, Ukrainians and Russians alike still come back year after year.

TRANSPORTATION

If you come to Crimea, you will end up here whether you want to or not (as all roads seem to wind through Yalta eventually). Currently the longest (and most boring) trolleybus in the world takes visitors the nearly ninety kilometers from Simferopol to Yalta (an epic three-hour adventure) while marshrutkas whizz down here constantly from Simferopol's train station (1.5 hours). Buses also come frequently from Sevastopol (2 hours), and Feodosiya (5 hours). All buses arrive at Yalta's Avtovoksal (8 Moskovskaya, 8 Московская). To get to the city center, take trolleybus #1, #2, or #3. Get a window seat so you don't miss out on the views!

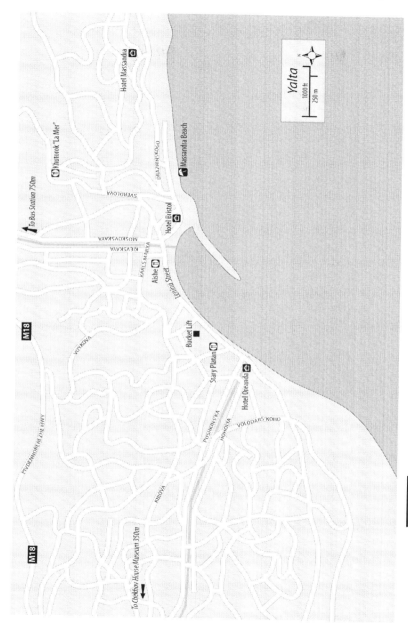

Yalta

N

1000 ft
250 m

Hotel Massandra

Khutorok "La Mer"

Massandra Beach

DRAZHINS'OGO

SVERDLOVA

To Bus Station 750m

Hotel Bristol

MOSKOVSKAYA

KIEVSKAYA

KARLS MARKA

Aishe

Lenina Street

M18

VODOVA

Bucket Lift

Stary Platan

Hotel Oreanda

PUSHKINS'KA

MOHOVYA

VOLODARS'KOHO

PIDGENBORICH ZHE HWY

KIROVA

M18

To Chekhov House Museum 350m

SIGHTS & ACTIVITIES

Lenina Street

Lenina (Ленина) Street is the city's main artery, gushing out the typical tourist attractions that have made this town famous. Peruse the myriad of stalls, grab a beer or some ice cream, and take in the fabulous Crimean sunshine. The city's most terrifying attraction is the **Bucket Lift** (17 Lenina, 17 Ленина) that haphazardly propels guests up into the stratosphere, providing great views of the coast – if you can enjoy it through all the "I'm going to die" thoughts running through your head.

For a more subdued experience, continue to the end of the promenade to **Primorsky Park** (Приморский парк) which offers a calm green oasis in the midst of all the neon. Walking through the cypress forest, you'll stumble upon some old monuments and sanatoria as well as a few park benches that offer solitude for quiet reflection.

Chekhov House Museum

Дом-музей Чехова, *Dom-muzyei Chekhova*

The entrance to this museum doesn't look too promising. Soon after entering, however, you'll understand why this museum is worth missing a day at the beach.

Chekhov came to Yalta to work from 1898 to 1904. A long-term sufferer of tuberculosis who reveled in Yalta's recuperative atmosphere, Chekhov is often credited for the rise of Crimea's popularity among Russia's highbrows. When he wasn't landscaping the home's majestic gardens, he was penning short stories here like *The Cherry Orchard* and *Three Sisters* and entertaining guests like composer Rachmaninoff and the writer Leo Tolstoy. Simply put, an invitation to Chekhov's "White Dacha" was *the* hot ticket, and now it's open to the public.

To get to the museum, take trolleybus #1 to the "Пионерская" (*Pionerskaya*) stop, or take marshrutka #4, #6, #8a, or #17 to the Museum of Anton Chekhov ("Дом-музей А.П.Чехова") stop. *112 Kirova (112 Кирова); Open 10:00-17:00, Tuesday-Sunday: June-September, Wednesday-Sunday: September-May; 20/10UAH, Adults/Children; +(38) 065 439 49 47; www.yalta.chekhov.com.ua*

Beaches

Most hotels and sanatoria include entrance to private beaches in their room rate. Public beaches are located all along the boardwalk. The city's most popular (and crowded) beach is located in front of the Hotel Oreanda (35 Lenina, 35 Ленина). With barely any room to stand here during the afternoon, it is best to arrive early. **Massandra Beach** (Массандровский пляж) is the second most popular in the city and about a fifteen-minute walk from the city center. It offers free public sections and VIP pay sections.

Livadia Palace

Ливадийский дворец, *Livadiiskii Dvorets*

In the suburbs of Yalta is the impressively subdued Livadia Palace. The Renaissance Revival-styled building is perched atop a hill romantically overlooking the Black Sea. Pathways wrap around the complex, trailing the way through its expansive manicured lawns, making the palace's name seem like a somewhat obvious choice – "livadia" means "meadows" in Greek.

Built for Tsar Nicholai II in 1911 as a summer home, this pleasure palace was used by the Tsar's family for a mere four summers. During that time, paths along the "Tsar's Path" were built. Now it's an overgrown seven-kilometer stretch that leads from the palace to Swallow's Nest. The path, referred to as "The Sunny Path," was constructed in the belief that exercise would help cure the family's tuberculosis. But alas, TB wouldn't be the cause of their demise. Bolshevik troops arrested the entire Romanov family in 1917 and executed them the following year in Ekaterinburg. A demure chapel located off of the "Sunny Path" now commemorates them as martyrs. A few family photos and mementoes of the ill-fated family are all that remain in the palace's private apartments.

The palace is perhaps better known for hosting the Yalta Conference in 1945. Soviet leader Josef Stalin, British Prime Minister Winston Churchill, and U.S. President Franklin Roosevelt all met here over nine days – the main discussions happened in the palace's White Hall – to outline the fate of post-war Europe. In the end, Germany was divided and ceded parts of Poland to the USSR. Photographs from the conference hang on the walls, along with a few candid shots, bringing to life the fact that this unexpected spot in Ukraine once hosted the world's most powerful men.

After the conference the palace fell into disuse. When President Nixon visited in the 1970s, the Soviets scrambled to gather up furniture and antiques to fill the halls and presented it as if it had been a museum the whole time. In actuality, it didn't function as one until 1994.

Bus #26, #27, #32, and #47 run to the palace from the central bus station. Ask for the "Livadia Palace" (Ливадия дворец, *Livadiya dvorets*) stop on the main road. From there, cross the main road and head down the path towards all the tour buses. Taxis from the city center cost a staggering amount because of all the tourism, and parking a private vehicle at the palace costs an outrageous 50UAH.

While admission to the Palace Grounds is free, entrance to the Interior Palace (Open 10:00-18:00, Thursday-Tuesday) is 40UAH for adults and 20UAH for children.

Swallow's Nest
Ласточкино Гнездо, *Lastochkino Gnezdo*

Perched on the Aurora Cliff, overlooking the Ay-Todor Cape, Swallow's Nest is a decorative castle that has captivated its audience for years. From afar, the castle looks majestic, even spell-like. Tottering literally over the Black Sea, it's like a child's play palace. The original structure on the cliff was a wooden cottage, but when German oil tycoon Baron Steingel acquired it, he had it torn down and built the whimsical neo-Gothic miniature as a present for his mistress.

Crimea

Since then, it has been used as a private library, a museum, a background for movies, and has even survived a major earthquake. Today, there is also a disappointing and overpriced Italian restaurant inside.

While it may not be the most impressive thing in Crimea, it's certainly the most recognizable as photos of this place seem to be synonymous with Ukrainian guidebooks. Like it or not, this is Crimea's most iconic symbol.

The castle is located about ten kilometers from Yalta. The best way to see the castle in all its glory is to approach it via the sea. In the summer, ferries run constantly during the day from Yalta's seaside promenade located on Набережная (Naberezhnaya). Buses # 26 and #27 also stop in front of the castle on their way to Vorontsov's Palace.

Vorontsov's Palace
Воронцовский Дворец

Located sixteen kilometers from Yalta, in the town of Alupka, Vorontsov's Palace is one of Crimea's most stunning complexes in a region full of dazzling escape homes for the wealthy.

The sprawling manner is an intoxicating mix, melding the design of a classic British castle with Moorish accents. It was built as the summer home for the immensely wealthy regional governor, Prince Mikhail Voronstov. The son of a count, he spent his childhood in London before returning to serve in the Napoleonic and Russo-Turkish wars. He built this home from 1828 to 1846 by use of serfs who were brought here from his other prominent manner in Odessa.

Inside the palace, visitors will find the museum in which documents, antique drawings, and lithographs of the construction are displayed. The living quarters, billiard room, dining hall, library, and the guest wing are all open for exploration.

It is the sprawling gardens behind the palace, with picturesque views of the Black Sea, which are the main attraction. Leading down to the garden is the **Grand Staircase** flanked by six marble lions. One of the lions is affectionately referred to as the "Churchill Lion," as Churchill reportedly said it looked like him when the British delegation stayed here during the Yalta Conference.

Turning around, you'll notice the palace's most stunning Middle Eastern design features: two minaret-style towers that jut out. On the far side, on the palace's interior wall, an inscription says "There is no Conqueror, except Allah," in Arabic.

To get here, buses #26 and #27 connect Alupka (Алупка) to Yalta. While admission times change seasonally, the palace is generally open Tuesday through Sunday, from 09:00 to 17:00. Admission is 30UAH for adults and 15UAH is children. For more information, see: www.worontsovpalace.com.ua or call +(38) 065 472 22 81.

AROUND YALTA

Uchan-Su Waterfall (Водопад Учан-Су) means "flying water" in Tatar and the water really does leap off a cliff here; spraying tourists who look up at it from the viewing platform. This is Europe's highest waterfall (98 meters) and is located on the halfway mark up Mount Ay-Petri, about eleven kilometers outside of the city. To get here, take bus #30 from the main bus station and get off at the "waterfall" (водопад, *vodopad)* stop.

If you stay on the bus it will continue up to the summit of **Mount Ay-Petri** (1233 meters), which offers sublime hiking paths (that are also popular with mountain bikers) as well as breathtaking views of the sea, the "drunken forest," and Crimea's "Grand Canyon."

For those looking for a more impressive ascent, then Crimea's **Cable Car** (www.kanatka.crimea.ua) is the way to go. You'll get amazing views and a bit of a scare (luckily, these seem a bit sturdier than the bucket ride in Yalta and even safer than most marshrutkas). Definitely an experience, it's the most spectacular way to ascend the mountain. From the bus station in Yalta, take bus #27 or bus #32 from downtown Yalta to the "канатки" (*kanatki*) stop. Open seven days a week from 11:00 to 16:00. A one-way ticket costs 50UAH for adults and 25UAH for children.

Massandrovskii Dvorets
Массандровский дворец

Looking like a French chateau, this resplendent lodge is the thing fairy tales are made of. Approaching it, it's hard to imagine you're anywhere but the French countryside – although the Russian speaking tourists give the location away. Finished by Tsar Alexander III in 1889, it was known throughout the Russian Empire as being the world's most kick-ass kitchen garden – Stalin would later appoint the place for use as his *dacha*.

The restored interior is open to guests, but it is the sprawling gardens that are hard to resist. The fertile grounds here are also used for agricultural production as one of Ukraine's most popular wineries, Massandra Vineyard, resides on property. They're known for their sweet, white Madeira wine.

To get here, take trolleybus #2 across from Yalta's main bus station. The palace is open from 09:00 to 16:00, Wednesday to Sunday. Admission is 40UAH for adults and 20UAH for children.

EAT

You won't go hungry in Yalta. Food stands and stalls cater to the most popular of cravings along Naberezhnaya (Набережная) Street. If you can subsist on pizza, ice-cream, cotton candy, and corn-on-the-cob for a few days, then you'll never have to leave the boardwalk. For those who enjoy a bit more variety, check out the places below.

All of Ukraine's chains (Pizza Celentano, Potato House) have numerous stores in the city and outlets on the waterfront. There's even a McDonald's on the main thoroughfare that serves McLavash...yes!

Stary Platan (Старый Платан, Old Sycamore Managed by Massandra Vineyards)
This wine cellar doubles as a restaurant known for its wine pairings. If you're a wino and gunning to try all of Crimea's staples, this is your dinner spot. *Located in the basement at 1 Ekaterininskaya (1 Екатерининская); Open 11:00-23:00; Small plates from 50UAH; Wine from 40UAH a glass*

Khutorok "La Mer" (Хуторок) Built on the sea, this is the most well-known of the Khutorok chains. The interior of the place is designed to look like a ship, but thankfully restrained. An odd mix of Tatar cuisine meets Russian classics is on the menu but the food is done well. The jovial atmosphere and smiling locals make this a popular spot. Try the potato pancakes (*deruny*) with mushrooms and bacon, or the veal stroganoff in creamy tomato sauce. *9 Sverdlova (9 Свердлова); English menus are available. Entrées from 70UAH; Beer from 20UAH; +(38) 050 398 40 40; www.hutorok.yalta.ua*

Aishe Айше If you're not going to make it to Bakhchisarai, then go here to get your fill of Tatar cuisine. Their *lagman* (spicy beef soup with vegetables and thick noodles) is fantastic and the entrées are affordable and authentic. *9 Lenina (9 Ленина); Entrées from 35UAH; Open 10:00-23:00; +(38) 050 696 38 25*

SLEEP

Hostels

The first 'backpackers" hostel in Yalta opened up last year, and many more are on the way. Hostels here are most likely to be seasonal (May to September) and change locations every summer. Check www.hostelworld.com or www.hostelbookers.com for the most up-to-date listings and addresses.

Hotels

Hotel Bristol (Отель Бристоль) Remolded in 2003, this is the town's oldest hotel and at three stars, one of its best deals. Rooms are comfortable and have en-suite bathrooms and air conditioning. The hotel has a pool and gym, and is located just one hundred meters from Massandra Beach. The restaurant downstairs serves up great Tatar food and you can even snag free Wi-Fi from their in-house pizzeria. *10 Roosevelt (10 Рузвельт); Standard Single 545/875UAH Low/High Season; Double Standard 650/980UAH Low/High Season (although prices seem to be lower if you book through hostelworld.com); +(38) 065 427 16 09; www.hotel-bristol.com.ua*

Hotel Massandra (Отель Массандра) Located right by Massandra Beach, this hotel is a short twenty-five-minute walk from the city center – but with that seclusion comes tranquil evenings. Most rooms have balconies that overlook the rolling hillside and some come equipped with air conditioning (for an additional price). Rooms are basic, clean and have comfortable beds. This place has a friendly staff, too. For those looking for a relaxing, rather than rowdy, beach holiday, this is the place. *48 Drazhinskogo (48 Дражинского); Standard Single: 390/590UAH, Low/High Season; Double Standard: 490/690UAH, Low/High Season; +(38) 050 324 22 57; www.hotel-massandra.com*

Hotel Oreanda (Отель Ореанда) With all the *mafiya muzhchin*, mistresses, and high prices, it can be easy to think you're in Monaco when entering this glitzy resort. But if you have money to burn, then go for it here my friends. Everything is luxurious, from the extravagant restaurant, to the views of the sea, and the private beach. It seems "more is more" is the catchphrase here. *35/2 Lenina (35/2 Ленина); Classic Single/Double 860/1330UAH Low Season, Classic Single/Double 1280/1960UAH High Season; +(38) 027 427 42 50; www.hotel-oreanda.com*

Hotel White Eagle (Отель Белого Орла, *Otel Belogo Orla*) Much more a boutique hotel than anything else, White Eagle is a bit off the beaten track, tucked into the woods up a hidden path. With breakfast included, comfortable rooms, and an English speaking staff, this six-room boutique hotel built into a Russian mansion is hard to resist. *13 Prov Krutoy (13 Пров Крутого); Open during the summer; Single/Double US$120/US$160; +(38) 050 324 21 61*

APARTMENTS

Serious negotiating skills are needed for dealing with the throngs of individuals who wait daily at the bus station to rent out their flats. In the low season, US$50 is the average, but the price soars in the summer with average flats going for US$100 (the price may rise even more for foreigners). Alternatively, the apartment companies below can help you arrange something in advance.

Hotel Vista (Отель Виста) Hotel Vista has spacious apartments that are great for large groups. Located in the city center. *Apartment for two ppl 680/760UAH Low/High Season; Apartment for four ppl: 740/820UAH low/high season; +(38) 065 427 35 18; www.vista.crimea.ua*

Sergey Sorokin (Сергей Сорокин) Sergey has studio apartments, as well as two and three bedroom apartments for rent in Yalta's center. For pictures and info, check his website. *Studios from US$50/US$130 Low/High Season; Two bedrooms from US$55-US$170 Low/High Season; For apartment info, call Sergey Sorokin +(38) 067 793 91 00; www.mt.crimea.com*

Travel 2 Sevastopol This English speaking company has a good reputation and a large number of apartments to rent in the city center. Rooms cannot be rented more than two days in advance – something you will encounter a lot of in Crimea. Just go with it. *Average price from US$45-US$100 per night (one bedroom); US$60-US$140 per night (two bedroom); +(38) 050 649 83 60; www.travel2sevastopol.com*

Sudak (Судак)

By the time the roads hit Sudak, the tourist crowd has thinned out. Not to say there's nothing here worth seeing. An important stop along the Silk Road in the thirteenth century, Sudak is a lovely little town with a grand fortress. But the most memorable opportunity is a day trip to its nearby isolated beaches, romantically called the "New World" (Novy Svit) and the sparkling wines that they produce in the area.

Transportation

Buses run frequently to Sudak from Simferopol and Feodosiya (2 hours). In the summertime, tickets to/from Sudak should be bought early as they sell out quickly. Buses from Sudak to Novy Svit (Новый Свит) depart from Sudak's bus station as well.

SIGHTS & ACTIVITIES

Sudak Fortress
Судакская крепость, *Sudakskaya krepost*

When the Turks landed at Feodosiya Bay in 1475 and began raiding all the Genoese fortresses, it was Sudak's that fell last. Built by Genoese inhabitants between 1371 and 1469, the fortress was considered impenetrable. Using the surrounding natural defenses, the fortress was built on a sheer cliff, with only one natural entrance on the northern side.

One of three surviving Genoese fortresses in Crimea (the others being in Balaclava and Feodosiya), it's the most impressive. Of the original fourteen towers, ten are still surviving; the most popular being the **Devich'ya (Maiden) Tower**. The story

Crimea

behind its name, like most things in Ukraine, is a love story. At one time there was girl who lived here whose beauty was known throughout the region. When she was betrothed to the King, she refused, for she had fallen in love with a poor shepherd boy. Her father, naturally, had the boy arrested and locked away in the castle. The girl bribed the guards and lay next to the wall for days; starving herself. Her father finally realized that his daughter was amazingly stubborn and so he freed the boy, sent him to Turkey, and told his daughter that if he returned in a year, it was true love. If not, she would marry the King. When the boy didn't return in a year, the girl refused to believe that he had abandoned her. When she confronted her father about it in a mad rage, he admitted that he had the boy murdered. The devastated girl then climbed to the top of the Devich'ya Tower and threw herself off.

The fortress is also home to the **Festival of the Genoese Helmet**; one of the most intense medieval fairs out there. Taking place annually at the end of July and beginning of August, the fair's 2010 festival attracted over one hundred thousand people. What better place to have a Renaissance fair than at a medieval fortress?

The fortress is located at Sudaksaka Krepost (Судакская крепость) and is open 09:00-20:00, June through September; and 09:00-17:00, October through May. Admission is 20UAH for adults and 10UAH for children.

Rock Climbing

Crimea offers some great routes for experienced climbers around the Sudak area (climbers should be comfortable doing at least a 5c route). Those under thirty years of age might be interested in checking out the Ukraine Rock Climbing Festival. Organized yearly around September, it takes young, experienced climbers on group rock climbing trips as part of an annual Global Youth Summit. Check out www.theuiaa.org for more information.

Those headed to the area on their own, or in small group, can organize their own rock climbing tours with Sergey Sorokin (his contact info is on page 195). Climbers can bring their own gear, or he can supply it. He can also help find routes that cater to your personal abilities. Check out www.mt.crimea.com for excursion info.

EAT

All the major restaurants in Sudak are located along Naberezhnaya (Набережная) Street. Most of them open for the season and are rife with gimmicks – enter the ubiquitous Karaoke machine – to attract tourists. Most restaurants charge around 40UAH for entrées. At 21:00, many of them close the kitchen and the building turns into discos.

SLEEP

Hostels

Like most hostels in Crimea, the ones in Sudak are fairly new and seasonal. Check www.hostelworld.com or www.hostelbookers.com for up-to-date information and availability.

Moving Bubble Hostel Owned by the same guys who run Kyiv Central Station Hostel, this hostel provides a cool getaway in the cozy town of Sudak. Situated close to the beach, the beds here are fairly comfortable, the kitchen and the bathroom large, and the staff friendly. The outside patio is a popular place to converge at night to pop open bottles of Novy Svit bubbly. *3 Yablonevaya (3 Ул. Яблоневая); Private Room US$25/pp, Mixed Dorm US$20/pp*

Hotels

Hotel Bastion (Отель Бастион) Located at the base of the fortress, this hotel has five buildings spread across its private lot. With a variety of excellent price points, an in-house tourism office that can help set up excursions throughout Crimea, and a friendly staff, you may find yourself staying longer here than expected. Breakfast, air conditioning, en-suite bathroom are included in all rooms. *3 Ushakov (3 Ушаков); Double Standard (with balcony) 260/450UAH High/Low season; Double Deluxe Room 385/685UAH Low/High Season; +(38) 065 669 45 24; www.hotel-bastion.info*

"Hotel Royal" Though it looks like a tacky shopping plaza on the outside, inside it's a refreshing twenty-seven-room hotel with comfortable rooms and massage showers. Five minutes from the beach, it's quickly becoming a popular place to stay. *11 Molodezhnaya (11 Молодежная); Junior Suite 200/500UAH Low/High Season; +(38) 095 429 68 88; www.bogema.crimea.com*

Novy Svit (Новый Свит)

Seven kilometers outside of Sudak, Novy Svit is best seen as a day trip. Situated between the Falcon Mountain (*Kush-Kaja* in Tatar) and Eagle Mountain (*Koba-Kaja*), the sandy coastline here is framed with juniper trees and pine forests, hiking trails, and amazing beaches.

Marshrutkas here can feel like school buses rented out for a class trip with tourists clad merely in bikinis, or men carrying all sorts of flotation devices. The winding path leading through the mountains to the village of Novy Svit can be a hair-raising experience, but with all those tight turns come great views.

SIGHTS & ACTIVITIES

Golitsyn Trail

Голицын Трейл, *Golitsyn Tryeil*

For those looking for something to do other than the beach, take a walk down the coast to Mt. Orel. The base of this mountain has lost its isolated appeal as of late, becoming very commercialized, but it does lead the way to the town's famous grotto where Prince Golitsyn would hold his parties in the nineteenth century. If tourist hotspots aren't your thing, then walk down Naberezhna (Набережная) and look for the Golitsyn Trail

Crimea

(Голицын Трейл) sign. Once on the trail, the cheesiness stops. The path takes hikers up along the mountain, providing panoramic views of the Crimean coast and the three bays that graze it: Green Bay, Dark Blue Bay, and Blue Bay. In front of Blue Bay is the so called "Tsar's Beach" where it's said Nikolai II liked to bathe.

Golitsyn's Grotto
Грот Голицына, *Grot Golitsyna*

Walking along the trail, you'll come to the Golitsyn's Grotto, which, in actuality, is simply the result of Golitsyn's failed attempt to make a tunnel that would connect this cave to his wine cellars. After he gave up, he christened the cave a "grotto," and turned it into a reception hall replete with chandeliers and candles. Other caves along the path have been carved out and used as wine cellars.

For those interested in more intense hiking trips around Novy Svit, Hotel Bastion in Sudak can organize excursions. Since some of the trails in Novy Svit are located within the **Novy Svit Botanic Reserve**, having a guide is sometimes required.

Be sure not to leave the area without trying the local sparkling wine. While sometimes incredibly sweet, there is nothing more refreshing on a hot Crimean day.

SLEEP

Hotel Golitsyn Situated in Golitsyn's gorgeous mansion with rooms that overlook the Green Bay, this hotel is perfect for those wanting to stay in Novy Svit a bit longer. The building's interior is minimally decorated with natural wood and the balconies open fully to let in all that gorgeous mountain air. Friendly staff, massive breakfasts, and lush bathrooms complete the feeling of a beach escape. *5 L. Golitsyn (5 Л. Голицына); Rooms from 500UAH; +(38) 065 663 33 59; www.hotel-golitsyn.com*

Feodosiya (Феодосия)

A sleepy little town that explodes with visitors in the summer, Feodosiya is a fun summer resort town. A smaller version of Yalta, expect all the usual cheesiness but with a dash of history to make one feel less guilty about loving it so.

Prince Golitsyn and Novy Svit Wines

Prince Golitsyn had royal blood in his lineage and was a lawyer by education, but his passion was wine making. Following his passion paid off for him as he is credited with introducing wines to the Russian public who, at that time, had little enthusiasm for the drink. Knowing this, he arranged distribution halls in Moscow and St. Petersburg where any student, worker, or peasant could try, free of charge, the unfamiliar drink.

In 1878 he acquired the land in Novy Svit and constructed three kilometers of underground wine cellars while planting chardonnay, riesling, pinot meunier and pinot noir vines. Today, the simple vineyard has grown into the town of Novy Svit and his old mansion has been transformed into a hotel. His champagne is still produced in the artisan way: hand riddled and bottle fermented for three years.

In 1896 his sparkling wines rocketed to fame throughout the empire when they were served at the coronation of Tsar Nikolai II. They remain popular to this day.

Founded by the Greeks in the sixth century, the town was originally known as Theodosia. Later, the name was changed to Kaffa when it was bought by Genoese merchants in the thirteenth century. During that time, trade flourished and Kaffa emerged as home to one of Europe's largest slave markets. But with all those people milling about came exposure to various diseases. When Mongol tribes from the Asian steppes invaded the area in 1347, they brought the Black Death with them.

The Mongol army was already feeling the effects of The Plague and when they attacked the city, they reportedly initiated one of the first cases of biological warfare: throwing their dead counterpart's corpses over the walls and into the town. The disease that spread devastated the city. The wealthy fled, heading to Italy, and with that migration, they introduced The Plague to Europe.

In the latter part of the fourteenth century, the Crimean Khanate was able to take control of the city, annoyed after the Italians kept "intervening" in their internal affairs. They rebranded the city "Kefe" and soon it was one of the most important Turkish ports on the Black Sea. When the Russian Empire gained control of Crimea, they renamed the city "Feodosiya" (a Russified version of the original name: Theodosiya).

TRANSPORTATION

In the summertime, buses frequently run from Simferopol (2.5 hours), Sudak (2 hours), and Kerch (2 hours) to Feodosiya's main bus station located four kilometers from the center. The bus station in the town's center is where local marshrutkas leave for nearby places like Koktebel and the Kara-Dag Bio-Reserve (pg 204).

SIGHTS & ACTIVITIES

Genoese Fortress
Генуэзская крепость, *Genuezskaya krepost*

The remains of the Genoese fortress here are not as impressive as the one in Sudak. However, that doesn't deter the tourists. Located at Vul Gorkogo (Горького), the remains of the massive defense walls and towers, as well as an ancient bridge that used to lay over the fortress' moat, can be seen.

Mufti-Jami Mosque
Муфтий-Джами Мечеть, *Muftiĭ-Dzhami Mechet*

The original mosque on this site was built in 1623 and served as the main temple for the Crimean Tatars in the area and, at one time, housed the town's Turkish baths. The mosque has since been restored, with some of the Mosque's original minarets still intact. It's located on the corner of Lenina and Furmanova (Ленина и Фурманова).

Ivan Aivazovsky Fountain and Museum
Иван Айвазовский фонтан и музей, *Ivan Aĭvazovskii fontan i muzyei*

Ivan Aivazovsky is a famous Russian painter of Armenian descent who was born in Feodosiya. He is renowned for his seascape paintings, which amount to over half of

Crimea

his oeuvre. Many of his canvases depict the moody currents of the Black Sea from nearby shorelines.

His impact on the city where he was born is still remembered by the **fountain** located in the town's Jubilee Park (Юбилейном парке). Generally fountains in Ukraine aren't really symbolic, but this one is different. You see, in 1886 the city was in the midst of an amazing dry spell; the city's water source had all but dried up. By 1887 the situation had gotten so severe that the city was resorting to importing barrels full of water from Sevastopol. That autumn, Aivazovsky donated the water supply from his other estate and helped fund the laying of a pipeline. By the end of the project, Feodosiya was receiving over fifty thousand buckets of water from Aivazovsky's estate a day. The fountain was designed by the painter and funded by him that year as a memorial to the drought.

For those interested in seeing his more famous works, stop by the **Aivazovsky Museum** which displays hundreds of the artists' works. *2 Galeryeya (2 Галерея); Open 10:00-16:30 Thursday-Sunday, 10:00-13:30 Tuesdays, Admission 20/10UAH Adults/Children*

Beaches

Entering Feodosiya from the west of Crimea, you'll see the Crimean Mountains slowly descend into a more flat terrain: but that doesn't make the beaches here any less popular. Surrounding Feodosiya are fifteen kilometers of sandy beaches. The official adult "bathing" season begins May 23 and ends October 15. Koktebel Bay beaches and beaches along the Sea of Azov can also be done as day trips from Feodosiya.

EAT

Charochka and Kumi Café (Чарочка у куми) With a colorful atmosphere and live music, this café serves up traditional Ukrainian fare. The staff is extremely friendly and the prices are reasonable. Try the pelmini sautéed in butter and onions and topped with dollops of fresh sour cream. Not by any means "beach body" friendly food, but oh man, it is good. *38 Karla Marksa (38 Карла Маркса); Entrées from 20-30UAH, Drinks from 9UAH; Open from 11:00; +(38) 065 623 05 35*

"Father Billy Saloon" This Wild West themed saloon is a weird slice of Americana in Eastern Europe. Cowboy themed everything, country music and Russian disco jams collide in this massive joint. During the day it's a full-service café that serves up cheap salads, sandwiches and pizza. But at night, it turns into one of the city's most popular disco clubs. *4 Fedko (4 Федько); Entrées from 30UAH, Drinks from 10UAH (daytime); Open from 11:00; +(38) 065 623 50 26*

SLEEP

Hotel Alye Parusa (Алые Паруса) This lovely fifty-two-room hotel overlooks the water and has immaculate rooms. The breakfast buffet is unbeatable and the service is exceptional. Guests are spoiled with plush bathrobes and slippers, Wi-Fi access, pool and gym, and in-house tourism excursions. *47-B Aivazovsky (47-B Айвазовского); Single 450/750UAH Low/High Season, Double 650/1280UAH Low/High Season; +(38) 065 622 95 29; www.a-parusa.com*

Hotel Villa Angel (Отель Вилла Ангел) With nine private rooms located on Golden Beach, this hotel is more like a series of private apartments. Each room comes with a full kitchen and balcony and is decorated in a weird traditional Ukrainian/beach hybrid. The final result is more welcoming than you might imagine. Good for larger parties and for those who speak Russian. *Rooms from US$35-US$85, Low/High Season; +(38) 067 976 04 44; angelcrimea@mail.ru; www.angelcrimea.com.ua*

Hotel Lidiya (Отель Лидия) This thirty-four-room, three-star hotel is the popular choice for Russian jet-setters and the odd international guest. Built in 2001, it is centrally located with great views of the bay and the surrounding mountains. The in-house restaurant is a popular night spot and use of the pool on the third floor (odd, but true) is included in price. The one downfall here is the somewhat tiny rooms. *13 Zemskii (13 Земский); Single: 317/463UAH Low/High Season, Double: 463/728UAH Low/High Season; +(38) 065 622 11 12; www.lidiya-hotel.com*

Alushta (Алушта)

Located twenty-eight miles from Simferopol, Alushta is the most popular holiday spot for locals. In the wintertime, the town has a mere forty thousand inhabitants, but from June to October it easily triples. Stalls open along the small promenade and outdoor discos shake off their winter tarps as tourists begin to gather on the shoreline.

Far from having the nicest beaches in Crimea, Alushta is popular with Ukrainians because it's one of the cheapest places to vacation in the summer. In a region full of resort towns, Alushta still remains very much a village that happens to have a beach and some seasonal restaurants. For those that speak Russian and are just looking for a relaxing retreat, you might be interested in coming here rather than Yalta. Think of Yalta as Disney World and Alushta as Coney Island.

TRANSPORTATION

Marshrutkas from Simferopol's main train station run here constantly during the summer as well as trolleybus #52 from Yalta (1 hour).

SLEEP

Alushta Home Stay Igor and Valentina rent rooms in their large, breezy home in Alushta. While they don't have Wi-Fi, the rooms are comfortable and private. The house is located in a quiet neighborhood not far from the main strip of town and it has a fantastic outdoor kitchen that is home to many a barbeque in the summertime. You will need to know Russian to book a room with them, but they are extremely helpful having hosted many international guests. *D6 Kooperatyvni (D6 Кооперативные); Starting at 50UAH pp; +(38)098 387 10 23 (Igor); domalushta@mail.ru*

Radisson Hotel Alushta This Western hotel chain opened their four-star resort in one of Alushta's most historic buildings, which was built in 1913. Plus, this hotel is the only one in town that is actually located on the beach. With breakfast included, in-house restaurant and coffee shop, complimentary Wi-Fi, and a great pool, the Radisson is the ritziest place in town. *2 Lenina (2 Ленина); Rooms start at 129 Euros; +(38) 065 602 62 26; www.radissonblu.com/resort-alushta*

Crimea

Koktebel (Коктебель)

Koktebel's name derives from a Tatar saying that means "Land of the Blue Alps," and that romantic implication is hardly sullied when you see the place.

No wonder Russia's intelligentsia flocked here. Writers, poets, and painters made this place the Haight-Ashbury of the Soviet Empire. Writers Maxim Gorky and Osip Mandelstam came here in the summers to visit Poet Maximimilian Voloshin at his home.

Now Koktebel is a hipster's paradise. In the summer, stalls open on the streets, tourists flood the beaches, and the newly built resorts are booked solid. Like most "artist colonies," this one has sold out – but that doesn't mean it has lost its charm. Coming here is a breath of fresh hippie air, in sometimes rigid Ukraine.

TRANSPORTATION

The easiest way to reach Koktebel is via marshrutka from Feodosiya's (20km) main bus station that leave every half hour in the summertime. It's also possible to get a marshrutka from Simferopol's train station (2 hours) although these leave less frequently. It's wise to buy your tickets in advance as they are often sold out.

SIGHTS & ACTIVITIES

M. Voloshin Museum
М. Волошин музей

This home of painter, poet, and philosopher M. Voloshin has been turned into a museum, which displays his works and tells the story of the artist's life. Voloshin (1877-1932) is partly why Koktebel gained such a bohemian reputation. He studied in Paris with revered artists, but returned to Crimea where he was a strong philanthropist. *Naberezhnaya (Набережная); Open Tuesday-Sunday 09:00-17:00; +(38) 065 623 65 06*

Paragliding and Hot Air Ballooning
Koktebel is the home of Soviet aviation and aerospace engineering as its hills were the trial zones for many of their first flights. Today, daredevils and adventure seekers come here to paraglide from the close Uzun Syrt Mountain. You'll see placards all over the street selling the paragliding tours, but **Turavtoservis** (Туравтосервис) is one of the most popular places in the city to book a trip through. They are located at 28 Desantnikov (28 Десантников) and can be reached at +(38) 065 623 62 22.

For those looking for a tamer air experience, consider a hot air balloon ride. The **Aeronautics Federation of Crimea** can help with that. Book online at www.crimea-balloon.net or call three days in advance: +(38) 050 530 65 06 (ask for Viktor).

Koktebel Beaches
Koktebel's beaches were most famous for their "bare-all" mentality and tent cities. Legally you can camp on the beach, making this a communal-living paradise.

However, recent expansions of resorts have cramped the **Eastern Beach** (nude beach) so getting there early is a must. The Eastern Beach (Восточный пляж, *Vostochnyi plyazh*) is about a thirty-five-minute walk down the shore from the center.

For those that like clothing, Koktebel's **Central Beach** (Центральный пляж, *Tsentral'nyi plyazh*) is the most popular. Crowded by mid-morning in the summer, this beach has changing stalls, cafés and "VIP" zones that offer chairs with an admission fee.

For more isolated beaches, it's better to head to the shores of Kara-Dag Nature Reserve.

Koktebel Jazz Festival

Koktebel is becoming famous for hosting Ukraine's largest and best jazz festival. Started in 2003, it attracts over one hundred thousand people yearly for this three-day beachside festival. Usually held in September, it's a must-see if you're in the area. Check www.koktebel.info for upcoming festival information.

SLEEP

Koktebel is another one of those resort towns where you can show up without a reservation and get a room from the *babas* at the bus station. Look for the signs that say "housing" (жилье, *zhilye)* then get your bargaining on.

Himik Химик For those that don't mind roughing it, Himik offers wooden platform "summer homes" on the beach as well as over six hundred places to pitch a tent on the shores of Koktebel. During the Jazz Festival, this is one of the most popular places to stay as it's a short ten-minute walk down the beach from the festival. After all, is there anything more bohemian than sleeping in a tent on the beach and waking up for a jazz festival? *140 Lenina (140 Ленина); Open seasonally; camping sites from 30UAH; +38) 050 300 08 14; www.koktebel-himik.com.ua*

As El Hotel (Ас-Эль Отель) Resembling a Turkish bathhouse, the blue As El Hotel is a pleasant place in a city that abounds with places to stay. Smallish rooms (the cheapest are not air-conditioned), they have a variety of price-points for those watching their pennies. *127 Lenina (127 Ленина); Single: 400-800UAH Low/High season, Double 600/900UAH Low/High season; +(38) 067 184 76 18; www.as-el.com.ua*

From Those in the Know - Chuck McConnell

At Koktebel, I stayed in a delightfully quiet place named Usadba (www.usadba.su). My Ukrainian friends had shown me this place and the proprietor knew them and was agreeable when they negotiated an amazingly good rate for me to have my own unit. The African decor seemed oddly out of place in Crimea, but the setting was perfect – a fenced courtyard around a central garden. Breakfast and lunch were provided by Usadba, and we were able to cook amazing dinners in their kitchen. I felt lucky to have been shown this place.

Crimea

Kara-Dag Nature Reserve (Кара-Даг)

Kara-Dag barely registers on the maps of Ukraine. Just a tiny dot is all that signifies its existence, and yet coming here can feel like you're entering another world entirely. Formed by an extinct volcano, the earth here seems to have responded in its own unique way. Coves and grottoes dip and rise, surrounded by lush foliage and an exquisite array of fauna. Bottomless gorges give way to stone structures that explode from the earth, creating what seems more like modern art installation pieces than nature's work. Walking around the 575-meter-high Mt. Kara-Dag feels like you're walking on the dark side of the moon.

Meaning "black mountain" in Tatar, this eclectic wonderland of stone chaos was almost destroyed in the early twentieth century. Overgrazing animals and rapid deforestation were killing this once pristine land. In 1924, geologist AF Sludsky wrote about the rapid decline of the area: "People did everything to ruin the jewel located in their hands, to deprive it of light and leave it without dressy clothes." Luckily, this habitat was recognized for what it truly was: a messy, chaotic wonderland. It is now a protected nature reserve.

Kara-Dag Monster

Ireland has the Loch Ness Monster and Ukraine has the Kara-Dag Monster. According to local legend, a mythical creature – with the head of a snake and the body of a log – has been hanging around the eastern part of Crimea. It has been spotted over the centuries by a number of people, and some say it is even referred to in ancient Crimean texts. Of course, its existence has never been proven. The Kara-Dag monster apparently bites dolphins in half, so keep your eyes open!

KARA-DAG TOURS

Anyone can visit the Aquarium, Dolpharium, and Gardens that border the entrance to the Kara-Dag Reserve (Open Wednesday-Monday, May-September, 09:00-20:00). But to enter the reserve, you will have to have a guide.

Tours from the Kara-Dag Bio Reserve depart every day (except Tuesday) from May through September between 08:00 and 09:00, and 15:00 and 16:00. The tours last around four hours and cover a total distance of around seven kilometers. Tours are conducted in Russian (but you're there for the landscape more than the talking anyways) and are limited to twenty people per group. Tours cost 40UAH for adults, 20UAH for children. Reservations can be made by calling +(38) 065 622 62 87.

Excursions from Feodosiya, Sudak, and Koktebel are often sold on the main thoroughfares of those cities. While likely twice as expensive, these can be easier as transportation on a private shuttle is often provided. However, you will need to speak Russian to book an excursion on the street. For non-Russian speakers, it's worth checking out the larger hotels in Feodosiya and Sudak for excursion information in the high season.

Be sure to bring sunscreen, a hat, and walking shoes with you on the tours. Some tours from Feodosiya arrive via ferry, so a bathing suit might be handy.

During the tour you'll see the lava formations that have been given whimsical names: like "Devil's Finger" the "King and the Earth" and the most iconic "Golden Gate," which is a black stone arch that emerges dramatically from the sea.

Kara-Dag Nature Reserve is located near the village of Shepetovka (Шепетовка) and can be reached via marshrutka from Koktebel, Feodosiya, and Sudak's bus station. Just look for marshrutkas marked "Кара-Даг" in the summer.

Kerch (Керч)

At 2,600 years old, Kerch is the oldest city in Ukraine. Nestled between the Black Sea and the Sea of Azov, and isolated by its terrain and the former Soviet Union (during which time it was a closed-city), Kerch has maintained its distinct character.

The last major Crimean city on the map before Russia begins, most people come here to stand on the top of the city's Mithridates Hill and see the old empire in the distance. The city can be visited as a day trip from Feodosiya or Koktebel.

With that slightly eastern divergence comes uncrowded beaches and solidarity, seldom found in Crimea in the summer.

HISTORY

In the seventh century BC, Greek colonists founded Crimea's most ancient town, Panticapaeum (present-day Kerch). The town flourished and became one of the most prosperous in the region. It was also the first to produce actual money, minting silver coins around the sixth century. In 480 BC, the town became the capital of the powerful Bosporan Kingdom. During that time, the Greeks prospered and built many settlements here. The remains of these settlements still make Kerch an archeological goldmine.

The Bosporan Kingdom thrived and was recognized as a major world power through the first century BC until a forty-year war with Rome devastated the local

---

Legends of Kerch

Locals like to talk about Kerch's thick history. Some of their favorite stories cite that the hero of the Trojan wars was born on the Kerch straits. Another legend seeks to explain how this isolated land was found:

In ancient times, the Greeks controlled the size of their settlements by asking all but the eldest sons to leave and find new homes. And so, 2,600 years ago, a group of Greek men set sail from Greece in search of undiscovered territories. During their voyage a massive storm ravaged their boat. So terrible was the storm that the brave men retreated to the underbelly of the boat to wait it out. After two days the storm finally subsided and when the men came up they found their boat had made it to land, sitting on top the Kerchian Peninsula. The men found the area to be lush with greenery and situated between two seas from which they could fish, so they stayed and established their new home.

economy. Still the Bosporans would not be defeated until 43 BC when Roman Emperor Julius Caesar conquered them in Asia Minor. That battle is reportedly where the Emperor penned his famous, cryptic saying "Veni, vidi, vici," (I came, I saw, I conquered).

By the fourth century, the Huns had conquered what was left of the Bosporan Kingdom and the area began its tumultuous existence, forever being conquered and influenced by new cultures. The Byzantines, the Venetians, Genoese, Turks, Mongols, and Armenians all came through here and all left their own individual marks.

During the Crimean War, the area was heavily devastated. And during the Second World War, the Soviet Union recognized the city as one of thirteen "Hero Cities" having lost over thirty thousand inhabitants.

SIGHTS & ACTIVITIES

Mount Mithridates
Гора Митридат, *Gora Mitridat*
Located in the city center, this hill dominates the skyline. The entrance to the stairs is guarded by a pair of griffin statues (a symbol of the city). After that, it is a breathless 432 stairs to the top (94 meters). At the hill's summit, you can see the ruins of the ancient acropolis: the site of an ongoing archaeological dig. You can also see the **Glory Obelisk** at the peak. Erected in 1944, it's a memorial to the soldiers who served in the "Great Patriotic War."

Church of St. John the Baptist
Храм Святого Иоанна Предтечи, *Hram Svyatogo Ioanna Predtechi*
Located opposite the post office in Lenin Square (Площадь Ленина) is the oldest surviving church in Ukraine. During the first century BC, fleeing Christians, who were being persecuted in Rome, first appeared in the Bosporan State. This Byzantine church was erected in 717 as a tribute to that era and it's still used for church services. Also located near the main post office in Lenin Square is the city's **Hero City Monument**. On top of the monument is another golden griffin.

SLEEP & EAT

Downtown Kerch has no shortage of cafés and restaurants. Most are located along Dubinina (Дубинина), Lenina (Ленина), and Teatralnaya (Театральная) Street.

Hotel Zaliv (Отель Залив) Located a block away from the beach, this hotel has everything you need and a friendly staff that can help you book excursions. Comfortable rooms, free breakfast, and a great location really boost its appeal. *6a Kurortnay (6а Курортная); Singles from 350UAH, Doubles from 450UAH; +(38) 065 616 34 94; www.hotel-zaliv.com*

Meridian Hotel (Отель Меридиан) An eight-floor hotel in downtown Kerch, this hotel is a ten-minute walk from historic downtown and a fifteen-minute walk from the beaches of the Black Sea. The hotel's café keeps odd hours, but nearby is a great supermarket. Comfortable rooms. *9 Marata (9 Мараta); Singles from US$50, Doubles from US$65; +(38) 065 616 1507*

Eastern Ukraine

The Eastern part of the country appeals to those who find solace in Ukraine's Soviet roots. A little rowdier and less accommodating than the rest of the country, traveling in the East can be a brutal lesson in self-reliance. For those who travel smart, it has some highlights worth venturing out for. Check out a concert in an old salt mine (pg 222) or a football match at the country's best stadium, Donbass Arena (pg 221).

A Note on Language

Since Russian is the primary language spoken in some of the following cities the transliteration for Kharkiv, Donetsk, Luhansk, and Dnipropetrovsk will be in Russian, not Ukrainian. While Ukrainian is understood, and sometimes spoken, foreigners will have an easier time using Russian.

Kharkiv / Kharkov (Харків/Харьков)

Entering Kharkiv from the outlining countryside can feel like you've transversed some hidden cosmopolitan vortex; all villages and fields, and then suddenly the city is upon you. Home to over 100,000 students and some of the country's brightest young professionals, the fountain of youth might just be within Kharkiv's bustling metros and expansive parks. At night, all that youthful energy is expelled in the interior of its luxury bars and labyrinth-like clubs.

The city was founded in 1656 as a Russian military stronghold. Rapid expansionism and industrialization made it the obvious choice to serve as the Ukrainian S.S.R.'s capital after the Russian Revolution in 1917 (the capital was later moved to Kyiv in 1934). During World War II, over 70 percent of the city was destroyed after it was captured twice by the Germans. It survives today as Ukraine's second-largest city.

If you thought eastern Ukraine was nothing but slate-colored industrial wastelands with dreary residents, you thought wrong. With lush parks and expansive squares, Kharkiv is the preeminent college town of Eastern Europe and its youth brigade is out to win you over.

Eastern Ukraine

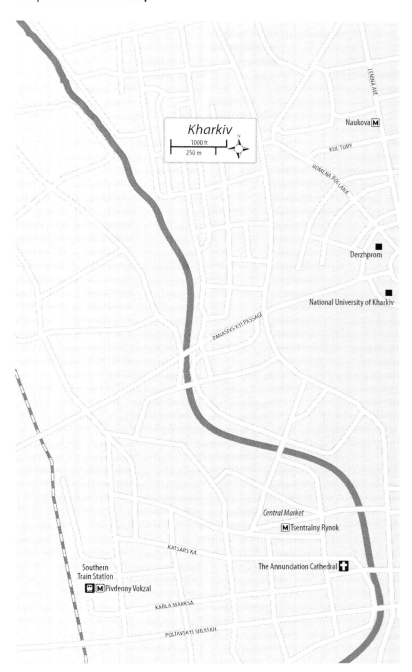

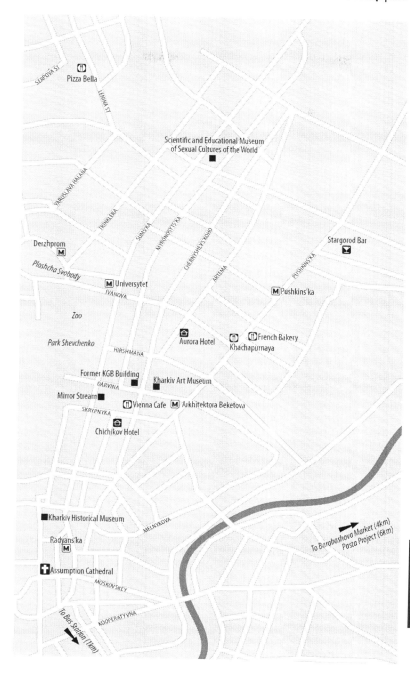

SERPOVA ST

Pizza Bella

LENINA ST

Scientific and Educational Museum
of Sexual Cultures of the World

YAROSLAVA HALANA

TRINKLERA

SUMSKA

MYRONOSYTS'KA

CHERNYSHEVS'KOHO

Derzhprom
Ⓜ

Stargorod Bar

Ploshcha Svobody

Ⓜ Universytet

IVANOVA

ARTEMA

PUSHKINS'KA

Ⓜ Pushkins'ka

Zoo

Park Shevchenko

HIRSHMANA

Aurora Hotel

Ⓘ Ⓘ French Bakery
Khachapurnaya

Former KGB Building

DARVINA

Kharkiv Art Museum

Mirror Stream

SKRYPNYKA

Ⓘ Vienna Cafe Ⓜ Arkhitektora Beketova

Chichikov Hotel

Kharkiv Historical Museum

MELNYKOVA

Radyans'ka
Ⓜ

To Baraboshova Market (4km)
Pasta Project (6km)

Assumption Cathedral

MOSKOVSKEY

To Bus Station (1km)

KOOPERATYVNA

TRANSPORTATION

Airport

Kharkiv recently inaugurated a new international terminal in anticipation for the 2012 UEFA European Football Championship. What was a chaotic, Stalinist building is now a chaotic, Stalinist building with better flights to Kyiv and Ivano-Frankivsk and sporadically to international cities like Moscow, Vienna, Sophia, and Istanbul. If you're headed into eastern Ukraine, flying here may be worth looking into. For up-to-date flight info, check out www.hrk.aero.

Marshrutkas for the quick trip to the town center wait in front of the main airport exit. For a longer, more interesting ride, take bus #115 which runs to metro stop Prospekt Gagarina (Проспект Гагарина). Bus #152 and #255 run to metro stop Akademika Barabashova (Академіка Барабашов). Bus #119 heads towards Prospekt Pobedy (Проспект Победы). Buses usually operate from 6:30 to 22:30.

Train

Still one of the best ways to travel out East, all trains arrive at the Pivdenny Vokzal (Південний вокзал) Southern Railway Station. Express trains to Kyiv leaves twice a day (07:00 and 16:30) and take six hours. Slow trains also run to Kyiv throughout the day and take about eight hours. Many trains run daily to Donetsk (7 hours) and Dnipropetrovsk (6 hours) along with one or two daily to Odessa (14 hours) and Simferopol (17 hours).

To get to the center from the train station (you're practically there), simply get on the metro at the Pivdenny Vokzal (Південний вокзал) stop.

Bus

Getting to Kharkiv by bus from Kyiv is easy. If you're coming from Kyiv's airport, it's possible to take an Autolux bus directly from the airport to Kharkiv (6.5 hours,

---

From those in the Know – Barbara Trecker

They say Kharkiv is a city of a thousand universities – or is it one hundred thousand university students? Either, or both, may be true.

Unless you're in the old *rinok* areas (which are decidedly ancient and haggard), the city emanates a collegiate, youthful feel. There are frequent outcroppings of buildings belonging to various academies, universities, colleges, and learning centers. Quite a different air from the frosty villages and feudal farmlands immediately outside the city limits, where life seems to deal rather harshly with the inhabitants and, in turn, visitors.

A lovely green park graces the center of the city, which is a fifteen-minute walk from the main train station. Along the way, you may hear chants emanating from an unusual red and white striped church, plunked like a UFO near the mangy Central Rinok.

Other than that, Kharkiv is not much of a walker's city. Luckily the metro is golden: clean and pleasant stations, and easy to navigate with simple lines.

Be sure to check out the giant central plaza which features sand sculptures in the steaming summers, and ice sculptures – massive sculptures that are worthy of a detour – in the frozen northland winters.

120UAH). Gunsel also has private coaches that go daily to Kyiv. Buses from nearby towns – like Poltava (2.5 hours, eight daily), Dnipropetrovsk (4.5 hours, twenty daily), and Zaporizhzhya (6.5 hours, twice daily) – also travel to Kharkiv's central bus station daily.

Autolux *22 Prospekt Gagarina (22 Проспект Гагаріна); +(38) 057 732 54 71; autolux.ua*

Gunsel *7 Prospekt Gagarina (7 Проспект Гагаріна); +(38) 057 719 97 19; gunsel.com.ua*

Kharkiv Central Bus Station *22 Prospekt Gagarina (22 Проспект Гагаріна); +(38) 057 732 65 02*

Metro

The Kharkiv Metro is an attraction itself. Consisting of twenty-eight stations on three lines, it's quite easy to navigate. If you're going to snap pictures of the tile work, chandeliers, or stained-glass windows that are present in some areas, do so discreetly as pickpockets love that stuff. Present cost for one token is 1.50UAH.

SIGHTS & ACTIVITIES

PLACES & MONUMENTS

Ploshcha Svobody
Плошша Свободы, *Freedom Square*

The ninth largest square in the world, and the second largest in Europe (take that Moscow's Red Square!), Ploshcha Svobody is where everything seems to happen in Kharkiv. From mass demonstrations and protests, to concerts and holiday shows, the action is here. The **Derzhprom** (*Gosprom* in Russian, meaning State Industry Building) is its central figure. The first skyscraper in the Soviet Union, it was constructed in the 1920s. The building's magnitude – a series of concrete slabs connected by a mish-mash of gray pedestrian crosswalks – gives the city center a slightly eerie chill. In the past, surely its burdensome presence served as a reminder to citizens that someone was watching.

When facing the building, on the right, you'll see the **Karazin National University of Kharkiv.** This university lends the city its fantastic student vibe and boats a cluster of one thousand international students from over fifty countries. Of course there's a **Lenin Statue** here which is where people meet when they say "see you at Lenin." *Metro Stop: Derzhprom (Держпром / Госпром)*

The Mirror Stream
Зеркальная струя, *Zerkal'naya Struya*

In front of Kharkiv's Opera House is a fountain that locals take great pride in. Constructed in 1927 in honor of the Great Patriotic War, the fountain has a pavilion and a garden in front of it and is included in UNESCO's encyclopedia. Bring a sandwich and grab a bench to watch the newlyweds line up for hours to get their photo taken. *Sumskaya (Сумская) Metro: Arkhitektora Beketova (Архитектора Бекетова)*

Eastern Ukraine

Park Shevchenko
Парк Шевченко

Just off Svobody Square lies the city's park. Founded in 1804 by the same man who founded the University, this park is sectioned into two parts: a botanical garden and a landscape park. It case you're collecting photos of the various Taras Shevchenko monuments, there's one here on Sumskaya (Сумская) Street. *Metro: Universytet (Университет)*

Zoo
Зоопарк, *Zoopark*

Located inside Park Shevchenko is the country's oldest zoo. With over 385 species of animals – one hundred of which are rare or endangered – it can make for a slightly depressing sight to see the animals in small cages or crowded conditions. While the staff seems to care about the animals, by the end of it, you walk away feeling a little worse for wear. Perhaps not the best place to take the kids. *35 Sumskaya (35 Сумская); Open 08:00-17:00; Admission 20UAH adults, Children 5-13 5UAH, Under 5 free; Metro: Universytet (Университет)*

MUSEUMS

Scientific and Educational Museum of Sexual Cultures of the World
Музей сексуальных культур, *Muzyei seksual'nyh kul'tur*

Basically this is a sex museum. The twelve halls cover all aspects of sexuality from ancient sexual taboos and how they treated sexual diseases, to how to tell if you're sexually compatible with your current partner. Located in a private courtyard, this place is a little hard to find – but just listen for the giggling school groups and you'll get here. Mostly presented in Russian, the massive amounts of diagrams help get the point across. *81a Myronosytska (81a Мироносицкая); Metro: Pushkins'ka (Пушкинская); +(38) 057 247 47 66*

Kharkiv Historical Museum
Харьковский исторический музей, *Har'kovskii istoricheskii muzyei*

This museum is broken into four historical time periods that run the gamut from Bronze-era archeological finds to Soviet and German weapons and insignia. *5 Universytet (5 Университет); Open Tuesday-Sunday 10:00-17:00; Admission: 5UAH; Metro: Universytet (Университет)*

Kharkiv Art Museum
Харьковский художественный музей, *Har'kovskii hudozhestvennyi muzyei*

This museum recently celebrated its two-hundredth anniversary and is the pride of the city. Having one of the greatest art collections in the country, the exposition halls can supposedly only hold one-tenth of the museum's collection at a time (the museum has over twenty thousand pieces in storage). Probably its best piece is one of Ilya Repin's renditions of "The Zaporozhian Cossacks Write a Letter to the Turkish Sultan." Well presented and worth a quick trip through. *11 Sovnarkomovskaya (11 Совнаркомовской);*

Open Wednesday-Monday; 10:00-19:00; Metro: Arkhitektora Beketova (Архитектора Бекетова); www.artmuseum.kharkov.ua

Former KGB Building

Located on the corner of Sumskya (Сумська) and Teatralnaya (Театральная) this building was once the headquarters for the KGB in Kharkiv.

CHURCHES

The Annunciation Cathedral
Благовещенский собор, *Blagoveshchenskii sobor*

The main Orthodox church in the city, this gorgeous cathedral was erected between 1889 and 1901. Based upon Istanbul's Hagia Sophia, this candy-cane striped beauty is crowned with an eighty-meter tall bell tower. Hard to miss from Karla Marksa (Карла Маркса) Boulevard.

Assumption Cathedral
Успенський собор, *Uspens'kyy̆ Sobor*

This was the main church in the city until the Annunciation Cathedral came along. Built in the 1820s, it remained the tallest building in the city until the twenty-first century. In 1929, Soviet authorities closed the church and tore down its bell towers. It was restored in the 1970s. *11 Universytetskaya (11 Университетская)*

MARKETS

Kharkiv's Central Market
Центральный рынок, *Tsentral'nyy̆ rynok*

If you're lucky enough to have a refrigerator, or if you need some Soviet knick-knacks, then come here like the locals do. Carrots and beets abound year-round and sometimes other vegetables make an appearance. Make sure to head to the covered part of the market to see a fabulous array of meat being hacked with the largest mallets mankind has ever created. *Metro: Tsentralny Rynok (Центральний ринок)*

Barabashova Market
Барабашово рынка, *Barabashovo rynka*

The fourteenth largest market in the world, this place is a whirlwind of vendors, buyers, foreigners, and pickpockets (be careful!). Seemingly everything under the sun is sold here: from wallpaper, jackets, and fur hats, to furniture, meat, dogs, and porn. *Open Tuesday-Friday 07:00-15:00, Saturday and Sunday 07:00-17:00; Metro: Akademika Barabashova (Академика Барабашова)*

SKIING

Kharkov's Switzerland (Харьковская Швейцария, *Har'kovskaya Shvyeisariya*) Offering two, four-hundred-meter tracks, this place has trails segregated for sledding, children, beginners, and advanced skiers. To get there from Kharkiv take any bus towards "Пятихатки" (Pyatihatki) and get off at the sign that says "база отдыха Фэдовец," (*Basa otdiha Fedovets*, Recreation Fedovets). *Open during the season*

Monday-Friday 13:00-23:00, Saturday and Sunday 10:00-23:00. Pass for a day 150UAH; www.sklon.kharkov.ua

Alpine Valley (Альпийская долина, *Al'piiskaya dolina*) Located fifteen kilometers outside of the city, this is the only ski-resort that makes its own snow, so the runs are open regardless of the weather. In the summertime, this is a popular place for picnicking and "nature excursions." *Ski-packages start at 100UAH; ten lift tickets 40UAH; www.alpdol.narod.ru*

EAT & DRINK

Vienna Café (Венское кафе, *Venskoe kafe*) Recently opened, this coffee shop offers an independent vibe when compared with the chains. With comfy couches, only five tables, and the ever classic home/coffee shop design motif, this one hits all the notes. The staff is friendly and the coffee is real and done well. *15 Chernishevskogo (15 Чернышевского); Coffee from 15UAH, Desserts from 17UAH; Metro: Arkhitektora Beketova (Архитектора Бекетова)*

"**French Bakery**" The entrance to this place is easily spotted as a giant replica of the Eiffel Tower looms in their window. The counter, reminiscent of Paris' pastry shops, can be seen through the glass. While their croissants are best avoided (you'll just be disappointed), their other pastries and sandwiches are delicious enough to attract a devoted following. Don't plan on getting a table; just get it to go. *66 Pushkinskaya (66 Пушкинская); Pastries from 8UAH; Metro: Pushkins'ka (Пушкинская)*

"**Pasta Project**" ("Паста проекта") Each table is segregated in this always popping place into little isolated cubes. A screen is on the back of every booth and you place your order through it (a button on the monitor calls your waitress should you need assistance...or another beer). The food here is good and the focus is on, of course, pastas. Their spaghetti carbonara at 49UAH was worth coming back for. At night, this place turns more into a bar where specialty drinks and hookah pipes abound. *9 Geroev Truda/Pratsi (9 Героев Труда/Праці, third floor of the "Dafi/дафи" shopping complex); Pasta from 35-90UAH, Beer from 15UAH; Mixed Drinks from 23UAH; Open 11:00-22:00; Metro: Geroev Truda/Pratsi (Героев Труда/ Праці); www.pastaproject.com.ua*

Stargorod (Старгород) Russian for "Old City," this lively restaurant prides itself on the beer it brews in-house – their "ten" beer (десятку) being their most popular (ten refers to the alcohol percentage by volume). When sporting matches are on, this place gets crazy, and at night it's a great place to go for a drink and a meal consisting of nothing but meat. If you want to get real crazy, bring your computer and attempt to do work with their free Wi-Fi. But with an atmosphere screaming Octoberfest, good luck. *7 Lermontovskaya (7 Лермонтовская); Beer from 14UAH, Entrées from 28UAH; Open 10:00-till; Metro: Pushkins'ka (Пушкинская); www.stargorod.net*

Khachapurnaya (Хачапурная) Khachapuri to go? Yes, please! Ranging in prices from 10 to 20UAH, you can try all the varieties they offer. The combinations reach a ridiculous level when the late bar crowd rolls in, but this place is busy all day. After all, is there anything better for a hangover than a giant loaf of lavash topped with cheese? Expect a fifteen-minute wait – well worth it. *59 Pushkinskaya (59 Пушкинская); Metro: Pushkins'ka (Пушкинская)*

Pizza Bella (Пицца Белла) You have to include the obligatory pizza place, but luckily the service here sets it apart. Also the pizza is good, they don't skimp on the cheese and the varieties are awesome. The only odd thing is that their "New York Pizza," according to the menu, has almonds on it. *3 Lenina prospect (3 пр. Ленина); Pizzas come in three sizes and range from 28UAH for a small to 74UAH for a large, Beer from 18UAH; Open 12:00-23:00; Metro: Naukova (Наукова)*

SLEEP

Chichikov Hotel (Отель "Чичиков") Centrally located, this small, fifty-two-room hotel will win you over with a smiling welcome in whatever language they guess you might speak (I was slightly disappointed when the girl immediately started speaking English…am I that obvious?). The whole place seems brand spanking new and the complimentary Wi-Fi makes it popular with business travelers. Forget the "dreary" Eastern European hotel idea you have in your head, this place is colorful, bright, and modern. *6/8 Gogola (6/8 Гоголя); Single: 800UAH; Double: 1140UAH, Twin: 1280; Metro: Arkhitektora Beketova (Архитектора Бекетова); www.chichikov-hotel.com.ua*

Aurora Hotel (Аврора Отель) Centrally located, this is good choice if you're on business and don't want any surprises. With an in-house restaurant, complimentary breakfast, stylish interior, free Wi-Fi, and a staff that's well informed and eager to help, you can't go wrong. *10 Artema (10 Артема); Standard Twin: 660UAH, Superior Twin: 892UAH: King: 892UAH; Metro: Universytet (Университет); +(38) 057 752 40 02; hotel-aurora.com.ua*

Hotel Kharkiv Behind this building's omnipresent façade is a polished interior that will shake off any first impressions. If you're a Westerner, they might try to check you into one of their "Luxe" rooms, but their cheaper options – while cramped and un-renovated – will do just fine for those on a budget. Air conditioning, free Wi-Fi, and breakfast make this a great value for the money. *7 Svobody (7 Свободы); Single Standard from 349UAH, Doubles from 499UAH, Suites from 900UAH; Metro: Universytet (Университет); +(38) 057 705 46 74; www.hotel.kharkov.com*

Apartment Rentals

Kharkov Apartment Rentals Renting apartments is easy with Kharkov Apartment Rentals. The website is in English and they accept PayPal and Visa. All the apartments are listed on their website along with address and pictures. Discounts are available for stays longer than five nights. *Single Rooms starting at US$38, Doubles from US$50, "Luxe" Class from US$80; (English speaking) +(38) 099 373 32 00; www.kharkov-for-rent.com.ua*

Poltava (Полтава)

Situated on the banks of the Vorskla River, about 350 kilometers southwest of Kyiv, you'd never suspect this quaint little town to have played host to such a bloody battle as the Battle of Poltava. This battle signaled the end of Sweden's power and Cossack interference, and introduced Russia as the undisputed ruler of this area for the next three hundred years.

TRANSPORTATION

Train

This city has two train stations: the Kyivska Station and the Southern Train Station (Південний вокзал, *Pivdennyy vokzal*). Located on separate sides of the city, most trains go through the Southern Train Station. Daily trains to Odessa (13 hours), Kharkiv (3.5 hours), and Kyiv (7 hours) leave from there along with the occasional train to Moscow (16 hours) and St. Petersburg (30 hours). To get to the city center, take trolley bus #1 which also connects to the Kyivska Station.

Eastern Ukraine

Bus

The Bus Station s located about seven kilometers from the city with daily buses that run everywhere out East and often to Kyiv (4 to 5 hours) and Kharkov (3 hours). Trolley bus #15 connects to the city center.

SIGHTS & ACTIVITIES:

Battle of Poltava Museum

Полтавська битва музей, *Poltavs'ka bytva muzey*

One of the most famous battles of the Great Northern War, when both Sweden and Russia were clamoring for control over the Baltic, the Battle of Poltava took place on June 8, 1709. It's widely credited as signaling the beginning of Sweden's decline as an imperial power and marked the emergence of Russia as a world power.

Perhaps the country most significantly affected by the outcome of the battle was Ukraine. Ivan Mazepa, the Ukrainian Hetman (leader) had been frustrated for years with Russian Tsar Peter I. The Tsar had been adamant that Ukrainian Cossacks join his imperial forces in Lithuania in battle, and yet he refused to send troops to aid Ukraine in defense from Polish attacks. These were both violations of the Treaty of Pereyaslav that former Ukrainian Hetmen Bohdan Khmelnytsky had signed in 1654. So Mazepa broke the treaty that had promised the Cossacks eternal fidelity to the Russian Tsars, and aligned with Swedish King Charles XXI in battle.

The battle raged throughout the early morning, beginning before dawn and not ending till noon. The Cossacks and the Swedish troops were outnumbered three-to-one by the Tsars' forces, so defeat seemed inevitable. Still, the highly trained Swedish army and the unflinching Cossacks charged on, refusing to falter for hours. Finally, just before noon, Charles XXI cried out to his men to retreat, fleeing south. Hetman Mazepa himself also fled, dying soon afterwards.

Peter the Great left a strong military presence in Poltava, scattering the remaining Cossacks to the wind and squashing any notion that a true, independent Ukraine would emerge anytime soon. He also redesigned the city, giving it its undeniable Russian appearance.

Ivan Mazepa's legacy has changed with the political times. At first, he was regarded as a traitor whose own treachery led to his demise. But with Ukraine's emergence as an independent power, his fortune has taken on another meaning. He's now often regarded as a hero, a brave soul who dared to take on Imperial Russia for Ukrainian freedom. He can be seen on the 10 hryvnia note.

Surely Ivan Mazepa would take comfort in the knowledge that unadulterated, clean Ukrainian – the most beautiful of melodies – has sprouted in the streets of Poltava. They may have Russian squares, but this town is Ukrainian through and through.

Located seven kilometers outside of the center (taxi should cost 35UAH, or take bus #4 or #5 to the museum), the Battle of Poltava Museum opened on the two-hundredth anniversary of the battle. Monuments dot the grounds and inside uniforms, maps and paintings tell the story of the battle. *32 Shveds'ka Mohyla*

(32Шведська Могила); Open Tuesday-Sunday 09:00-17:00 (16:00 on Friday); Admission 6UAH adults/ 3UAH children, Tour: 30UAH; www.battle-poltava.org

Monument of Glory
Пам'ятник Слави, *Pam'yatnyk Slavy*

You can't miss this eagle-topped column rising out from the center of Kopusny Park. Built to commemorate the one-hundredth anniversary of Peter the Great's battle victory, the city's website declares it "a symbol of Poltava and its glory" but it seems a little out of place here. Sure the city has its Russophiles, but a symbol of Russia's victory over their beloved Cossacks smack dab in the middle of the town? One can't help but think that constantly seeing this Russian "symbol" every day is why the Ukrainian language took off here.

Exaltation of the Cross Monastery
Воздвиження Хреста монастиря, *Vozdvyzhennya Khresta Monastyrya*

An example of Cossack baroque (did you know there was such a thing?), this monastery was founded in the eighteenth century. Periodically its functions changed (it was used as the Swedish monarch's residence in 1709), but since 1991 it has been run by a community of nuns. Open to tourists, it is popular with pilgrims as it is the only church in the country – apart from St. Michael's in Kyiv – with seven cupolas. Located three kilometers from Kopusny Parkon at 2 Sverdlova (Свердлова).

Museum-Estate Kotlyarevsky
Музей-садиба Котляревського, *Muzey-sadyba Kotlyarevs'koho*

One of the founders of Ukrainian literature, Kotlyarevsky's home and surrounding garden have been restored and opened to the public. In a town full of museums dedicated to its writers, this is the most interesting. Even if you know nothing about Ukrainian literature, this museum is worth checking out as it provides a look into

From Those in the Know – Barbara Trecker

Pigs loom large in Ukrainian life, almost like household demigods. They live in unexpected places, like in backyards and sheds, both urban and rural, across Ukraine.

Swine seem to be especially revered in Poltava, where there are university courses on pig breeding and agriculural and husbandry degrees galore. A statue of a big pig with two young Ukrainians is a feature on the campus grounds of the Agricultural University. Unfortunately, the children – and the pig – were crafted with the empty eyes that some moviegoers might recognize as belonging to *Children of the Corn*, so the effect is more scary than celebratory. But it's a tribute, nonetheless.

A better example of civic pride – and a more successful tribute – is a different monument: a giant bowl of dumplings, strategically perched on a scenic hilltop. These dumpling (*halushka*) are a special local variety which can be ordered at several of the local restaurants. They are indeed very tasty, and very filling. Rib-stickin' good!

Another scene in Poltava is the building formerly known as KGB headquarters. It's a rather marvelous building that looks like a fairy tale mansion – all curlicues and frivolities. Is it possible to tour inside? No one seems to know. But if you do get in, don't inspect the rooms too closely – the walls may still have ears...and eyes.

Ukrainian life over two hundred years ago. With gardens, a barn, and an immaculately cared for interior, this lovely little blossoming farm home should not be missed. *5 Soborna ploshcha (5 Соборна площа); Open: 10:00-18:00 (Spring-Summer), 09:00-17:00 (Autumn and Winter); Admission: 5UAH*

EAT

Restaurants abound along Zhovten (Жовтень) Street and Soborna Ploshcha (Соборна площа) but some to look out for are:

Palazzo (Палаццо) If you're in the mood to splurge, then the restaurant in the Hotel Palazzo does a good take on European and – oddly enough – Japanese fare. The setting is a little too posh and the service perhaps overtly formal, but the food is good, the atmosphere quiet and relaxing, and the sushi…well just stick to the "European" menu. *33 Hoholya (33 Гоголя); Entrées from 80UAH, Beer from 22UAH*

Café Kavaler (Кафе "Кавалер") Just steps from the park, this café has decent coffee and exceptional pastries. Get your afternoon sugar buzz going here. *19 Hoholya (19 Гоголя); Coffee from 20UAH, Pastries from 17UAh*

Café Hutorok (Кафе Хуторок) This café, outfitted like the Ukrainian kitchens of yore, serves up traditional fare at reasonable prices. Popular with the locals, it's seemingly always crowded and a little noisy. *118 Lenina (118 Леніна); Open 11:00-22:00; Entrées from 21UAH, Drinks from 10UAH*

Zoloto (Gold) Pizzeria (Золото Піцерія) Located in the Hotel Gold, this café offers over fifteen varieties of pizza along with the usual Ukrainian salads and beer. Not the best pizza I've ever had, but when you're hungry at ten o'clock at night, it's nice to know this place is open. *17b Pershotravnevyy Prospekt (17Б Первомайский проспект); Pizza from 22UAH, Drinks from 8UAH; Open 11:00-23:00*

SLEEP

Hotel Grand Avenue (Готель Гранд Авеню) Located downtown, this twenty-one-room hotel has free Wi-Fi, twenty-four-hour room service, and a staff that doesn't brush you off. Cute, if small, rooms have everything you need to be comfortable. Ask for the "economy" if you're cash-strapped, otherwise they'll book you a "standard." Breakfast included. *57 Zhovtneva (57 Жовтнева); Economy: 36 Euros, Standard: 46/56 Euros Single/Double, Standard Plus 64/78 Euros Single/Double; +(38) 053 257 97 37; info@alleya-grand.com.ua; www.alleya-grand.com.ua*

Hotel (Gold) Zoloto (Готель "Золото") While not the most fabulous hotel you'd ever imagine (the name "Gold" seems more like an aspiration than a verifiable achievement), the rooms here are clean, cheap, and have everything you need to be comfortable. Air conditioning, TV, friendly staff, and a good, free breakfast make it better. It's located just ten minutes from the center. *17b Pershotravnevyy Prospekt (17Б Первомайский проспект); Single: 350UAH, Double: 550UAH; +38(0532) 613-157; www.gold-hotel.com.ua*

Pallazzo Hotel (Палаццо готель) This swanky joint is the place to stay in Poltava. With lush robes, plush beds, a friendly English-speaking staff, and Wi-Fi, you might not leave the room. The expensive restaurant is located downstairs, but you're just a few steps from the city center and a line of cafés. The hotel bar – replete with purple neon lighting – is the place to meet some local characters. *33 Hoholya (33 Гоголя); Standard: 465/525UAH Single/Double, Standard Plus 485/595UAH Single/Double, Junior Suite 750/810UAH Single/Double; +380 (532) 611-205; www.palazzo.com.ua*

Donetsk (Донецьк, Донецк)

The capital of the coal rich Donbass region, when people hear "Donetsk" images of shaking black dust off their clothes at the end of the day come to mind. But, while the number of factories can be unattractive, it's far from dirty. Ukrainians brag that it's one of the "cleanest industrial cities in the world!" If that doesn't make you want to visit, I don't know what will. Tourists here are an unlikely sight and, if visiting, locals assume you're either here for business or wife hunting. But if you find yourself here be sure to visit the salt mines – a strange journey for sure – and experience a football match at the "Diamond" Arena.

HISTORY

In the 1870s, a steel plant was started here by a Welshman named John Hughes. The town that built up around the plant was subsequently named after him and christened Yuzovka (a Russified version of "hugh"). In 1924 the name was changed to Stalino and, in 1961, during the de-Stalinization process it was christened Donetsk.

With the most pro-Yanukovych billboards in the country (outside of Crimea), it's easy to see that Donetsk is very much a fan of the current President – after all, he was the governor of Donetsk Oblast from 1997 to 2002. After the collapse of the Soviet Union, he solidified his base loyalty here by allocating money to the mines and ensuring that they were not shut down (even though most were losing money). Watch your tongue if you get into political arguments here: you're in Yanukovych territory now.

TRANSPORTATION

Air

Donetsk does have one tiny airport about eight kilometers from the city. For now, all domestic and international flights are crammed into one terminal, but hopefully this will change in 2012 when its second terminal opens. DonbassAero, Aerosvit, and Lufthansa connect Donetsk to destinations like Moscow, Munich, and Kyiv. *Airport Code: DOK; +(38) 062 344 73 22; www. airport.dn.ua*

The cost to get to the center from the airport shouldn't be more than 40UAH. Marshrutka #9 and the (slow) trolleybus that stops in front of the airport go to the center as well.

Train

Donetsk's train station is located on Pryvokzal'na (Привокзальная) Square and has connections to nearby cities as well as Kyiv. Overnight trains to Kyiv (12 hours), Lviv (28 hours), Odessa (15 hours), and Simferopol (11 hours) are available. Shorter trains to nearby towns like Luhansk (3 hours) are also available. *68 Artema (68 Артема); +(38) (0623) 194 450; www.railway.dn.ua*

Eastern Ukraine

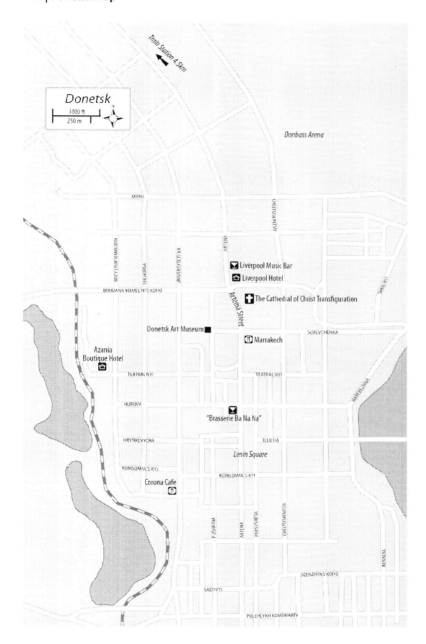

Donetsk

1000 ft
250 m

Train Station 4.5km

Donbass Arena

MYRU

Liverpool Music Bar
Liverpool Hotel

The Cathedral of Christ Transfiguration

BOHDANA KHMELNIS'KOHO

Donetsk Art Museum

Marrakech

Azania
Boutique Hotel

TEATRALNYI

TEATRALNYI

HUROVA

"Brasserie Ba Na Na"

HRYNKEVYCHA

ILLICHA

Lenin Square

KOMSOMOL'S'KYI

KOMSOMOL'S'KYI

Corona Cafe

SCHEVCHENKA

DZERZHYNS'KOHO

SADOVYI

POLEHLYKH KOMUNARIV

To get from the train station to the center shouldn't cost more than 30UAH by taxi. Marshrutka #2 also heads towards the center (25 minutes) as well as trolleybus #2 (40 minutes).

Bus

Only a few international buses come to the **Southern Bus Station** (Южный Автовокзал, Yuzhny Avtovokzal), a twenty-minute walk from the center. To get to it will cost 15UAH for a taxi, or take marshrutka #10 or trolleybus #10. *4 Pl. Komunariv (4 пл. Комунарів); +(38) 062 266 51 19*

Buses from nearby Ukrainian cities – Luhansk (2.5 hours), Kharkiv (6 hours), Dniproprotrovsk (4 hours), and Kyiv (11 hours) – come to the **Putilovskiy Bus Station** (Путиловский Автовокзал). Gunsel and Autolux also have VIP buses here. Marshrutka #25 or #73 will get you to the center. *1 Vzletnaya (1 Взлетная); +(38) 062 312 05 09*

SIGHTS & ACTIVITIES

Lenin Square
Площадь Ленина, *Ploshchad' Lenina*

Concert Hall and the Donetsk Drama Theatre spoon the square and in its center is the requisite Lenin statue. Supposedly, before it was erected, parents buried letters to their future grandchildren underneath the statue. *Ploshcha Lenina (Площадь Ленина)*

Donbass Arena
Донбасс Арена

Locally, the stadium is referred as the "Diamond arena" because the glass walls are designed to make light reflect off it at night so it shines like a diamond. The arena had its grand opening with a sold out Beyonce concert in 2009 (slightly odd, right?), but now it is home to Donetsk's Shakhtar Football Club. It will also host group stage games, one quarter-final, and one semi-final game of the Euro 2012 games. *189 Chelyuskintsiv (189 Челюскинцев); For tickets and info visit www.donbass-arena.com/ru.*

Artema Street
Артема

Locals come to this main thoroughfare to promenade in the summer. With the city's best boutiques, shopping malls, and restaurants along this route, it's always busy. The architecture in this part of town is also the loveliest as the traditional drab Soviet architecture is combined with lighter, more modern buildings. The resulting chaos is nice to appreciate on a summer day.

The Cathedral of Christ Transfiguration
Преображенский собор, *Preobrazhenskiy Sobor*

One of the only churches in the city, the domes of this building pop out over the urban sprawl of Artema Street. Newly restored, the bright colors on the building appear to have been recently painted. The church itself goes back to 1883 when the Council of Yuzovka established an Orthodox church here in place of a wooden temple. Like many churches in the region, it was destroyed in 1933 during the Soviet's anti-religious campaign. Reconstruction began after Ukraine declared independence in 1997 and lasted until 2006. Worth the time, the resulting church is a fantastic beauty. *Artema (Артема) near Liverpool night club.*

Donetsk Art Museum
Донецкий художественный музей, *Donetskiĭ hudozhestvennyĭ muzeĭ*
With an art collection that spans the last three centuries and includes over twelve thousand pieces, the Donetsk Art Museum is especially interesting to those with a love for nineteenth and twentieth century Russian painters. Works by Ivan Aivazovsky, Orest Kiprensky, and Vasily Surikov are among their showcased pieces. *35 Pushkina (35 Пушкіна); Open Wednesday-Sunday 9:00-17:00; Admission 10UAH; +(38) 062 305 37 27*

DAY TRIPS FROM DONETSK

Soledar Salt Mine
Соледар Соляная шахта, *Soledar Solyanaya shahta*
Getting off the bus here it may seem like you're in any other place out East, but you're not here for above-ground entertainment. Three hundred meters below the street is the Salt Mine. While the remnants of a Donbass Region's salt empire may not seem like grand entertainment, you'll be surprised. Carved out by craftsmen, the underground caverns, panels, sculptures, and halls are like massive cathedrals of ice. They are simply amazing.

The salt here is what remains of the Perm Sea, which filled this area 280 million years ago. The resulting mine is now touted as being good for one's health as the warm air infused with salt particles is believed to help with breathing.

Popular with the locals and open to tourists year-round, the mine occasionally hosts concerts as its halls are renowned for their acoustic qualities.

To get here, take a bus from the bus station to the town of "Soledar" (Соледар) and ask to get off at the salt mine (*Solyana shakhta*, Соляна шахта). *The mines are located in Soledar (Соледар) town, Artyomovskiy (Артемовский) rayon, Donetsk oblast.*

EAT & DRINK

Corona (Корона) With cheap Ukrainian and European fair, this three-hundred-seat restaurant is always packed. Dishes include pork ribs, beef stroganoff, and, of course, pizza. The *shashlik* seems to be the thing to get though and averages about 15UAH per 100 grams. At night it can be a little too noisy as the banquet halls are often rented out. But for the price, you really can't complain. *2E Universytets'ka (2e Университетская); Mains from 45UAH, Drinks from 8UAH; Open 11:00-23:00; +(38) 062 348 53 03; www.korona.gorod.dn.ua*

"Brasserie Ba Na Na" This might not be the place to come for the food as the menu boasts an eclectic mix of Brazilian, Cuban, and Portuguese influences (let's be honest, this is Eastern Europe). But the atmosphere is lively and fun; it's worth coming in for a drink. *80a Artema (80a Артема); Entrées from 60UAH; Beer from 11UAH; Open 10:00-23:00; +38 062 312 58 58*

Marrakech Марракеш If you like to smoke hookah (кальян, *kal'yan*), then this is the place to go. With rugs everywhere, pillows to sit upon, and a design that is aimed for an "Istanbul brothel," the atmosphere is chill. Small menu with a decent beer and alcohol selection make for a nice treat (although, pass on the sushi). *127 Artema (127 Артема); Open 11:00-02:00; +(38) 062 381 74 74*

Liverpool Music Bar (Ливерпуль Бар) Clubbing in Donetsk often feels like a scene out of "Eurotrip." Even here the cluttered interior of this swanky club – coupled with the red lighting and pulsing music – can make you feel woozy before you're even had a drink. But the music is cool (The Doors, The Stoke…other "The" bands), and the crowd is a bit more varied than those other "face control" joints. *76 Artema (76 Артема); Beer from 20UAH, full bar; Open 12:00-till; +(38) 062 381 76 76*

SLEEP

Liverpool Hotel (Ливерпуль отель) The funkiest boutique hotel I've seen in Ukraine, the Liverpool Hotel is owned by the same folks who own the nightclub (which is conveniently right next door). The lobby is outfitted with Beatles posters and records, and the staff is friendly. Free Wi-Fi and breakfast, and a concierge service that can book train tickets are a plus. The downside is the rooms are small. *131b Artema (131b Артема); Economy 495/595UAH Single/Double, Executive King 595/643UAH Single/Double; +(38) 062 312 54 74; www.liverpool.com.ua*

Azania Boutique Hotel (Азании отель) If you want to splurge, splurge at this place. With twelve suites that are more like mini-apartments (replete with seating rooms, kitchen, and breakfast in bed), the money is well spent. Each room is resplendent with fantastic little touches and a superb sense of style. *3 Teatralny (3 Театральный); Single: 650-750UAH, Double: 750-850UAH; +(38) 062 349 33 14; azaniahotel@list.ru; www.azaniahotel.com*

Apartment Rentals

In Tours Donetsk Tourism agency In-Tours rents out basic, centrally located apartments ranging from US$50 to US$60 a night. They can also arrange football (soccer) tickets, tours, and transportation. Good for long-term travelers. *+(38) 062 304 71 92; intours2@dn.farlep.net; www.intours.donetsk.ua*

Zaporozhye (Запоріжжя)

Zaporizhzhya's location across the Dnieper River – the town's name itself means "beyond the rapids" – from the island of Khortytsya has solidified it in the hearts of Ukrainians everywhere. This is, after all, the home of their beloved Cossacks, so expect a litany of enthusiastic storytelling to ensue when you mention you're coming here. That being said, the city itself is a mildly depressing stretch of a town, heavily industrialized and not much to behold. Still, for Cossack enthusiasts and Ukrainian history buffs, this area is worth exploring.

Eastern Ukraine

The area's main attractions, the Dneproges Dam and the infamous sixteenth century Khortytsya Island, are located in the northern part of the city. The town's main drag, Lenina (Леніна), stretches the ten kilometers from the train station down to the dam.

TRANSPORTATION

Train
Trains enter the city at the Voksal located at 2 Lenina (2 Леніна). Daily trains head to Kyiv (10 hours), Kharkiv (4.5 hours), Odessa (17 hours) and Dnipropetrovsk (2.5 hours).

Bus
Located not far from the train station, the town's bus station (20 Lenina, 20 Леніна) offers daily buses to Kyiv (9.5 hours) and marshrutkas to Dnipropetrovsk (1.5 hours). Autolux has buses here as well.

SIGHTS & ACTIVITIES

Khortytsya Island and the Zaporizhzhya Sich
Хортиця та Запорізька Січ
The island of Khortytsya was the *sich* (headquarters) of the Cossacks from the sixteenth to the eighteenth century. How it came about and the rise of Cossack power started in 1569 when Poland and Lithuania united and Ukraine came under Polish rule. The Poles, however, were unable to provide enough manpower to stop the devastating Tatar raids that plagued Ukraine. This problem gave rise to the Ukrainian Cossacks; a group of men who recognized the rulers of Poland and yet sought to protect their country. By the beginning of the sixteenth century they had formed a state, declared a Hetman, and pretty much controlled most of southern Ukraine.

It was during this time that the Zaporizhzhya Sich was constructed. Hetman Dmytro Baida organized construction of the Sich in 1553. It was picked because of its location: at a point in the Dnieper River where the water formed dangerous rapids, making it a naturally protected fortress from Polish and Russian authorities. Soon, bands of Cossacks were uniting here with other men from the region who sought to join their cause. This democratic welcoming of men, regardless of social status, is seen by many Ukrainians as the first attempt to form an independent Ukraine. This is perhaps the reason why Cossacks are viewed as such an endearing national symbol.

Tales of the island during its heyday make it sound like "Camelot" in the Monty Python movies. An island full of men (women weren't allowed) who were badass fighters and huge drinkers. It's easy to get carried away in the thought that the place was probably Eastern Europe's first frat house. No wonder Ukraine's most popular brand of Vodka (Khortytsya) is named after it.

But this kumbaya moment in history wouldn't last long. By the end of the sixteenth century Poland sought fuller control over Ukraine, and with it, the Cossacks. Disputes over their persecution of the Orthodox Church led to revolts and to the Cossacks changing their allegiance to the Russian Tsars. That alliance quickly dissolved when the Russians proved to be even more annoying to the Cossacks than the Poles had been. When Hetman Ivan Mazepa had his Cossacks join with the Swedes in the Battle of Poltava in 1709 (see page 216), they shared in the defeat.

Even when the Cossacks were eventually allowed to resettle in their land in 1734, they never won back Russia's trust (the feeling I'm sure was mutual). In 1775 Catherine the Great had the Sich destroyed, scattering the last of Ukraine's true Cossacks to the ends of the empire and stomping all over the notion that there could ever be a true independent Ukraine. It would take over two hundred years before her point was reversed.

Zaporizhzhya Sich Museum
Запорізька Січ музей, *Zaporiz'ka Sich muzey*

Nowadays getting to the island is a quick trip over the Preobrazhensky (Преображенський, Transfiguration) Bridge. The island is now a reserve and home to the Zaporizhzhya Museum. At first, it held mostly Soviet artifacts, but when Ukraine's emerging independence gained momentum, it was changed to the Museum of Zaporizhzhya's Cossacks. Now an ode to the ponytailed men, the museum boasts four dioramas, iconography found around the territory, coins, weapons, and diagrams and drawings of what the island resembled in its heyday. Furthermore, guests are welcome to explore the island which is still dotted with Scythian ruins. Also, a Cossack version of a Renaissance fair seems to take place here daily with "descendants" of the Cossacks working various craft booths and reenacting life as it used to be. *Open: Tuesday-Sunday 09:30-17:00; Admission: 10UAH; www.museum.zp.ua*

Cossacks on Film

While interesting, the island perhaps isn't worth venturing out of your way to see. With the building of the dam, the water surrounding the island is long gone and the "fortress" is hard to imagine. If you're truly interested in seeing it "as it was," then watch Vladimir Bortko's film adaptation of Nicolai's Gogol's *Taras Bulba*. It tells the story of an old Cossack, Taras, and his two sons who join other Cossacks at Khortytsya Island to go to war against Poland. Released in 2009, it was shown all over Ukraine.

Dniproges Dam & Dnieper Hydroelectric Station

Two and half times longer than the Hoover Dam, at 760 meters, the Dniproges Dam sure is a sight – but not a pretty one. Constructed between 1927 and 1932, it is showing its age. At the time of construction, it was the largest Soviet power plant and one of the largest in the world. During World War II this important source of energy was bombed twice: once by retreating Soviet troops, and then again by retreating Germans. But it's still kicking.

EAT & DRINK

Salon de Café (Салон де кафе) This coffee shop has the only bathroom in the city that has a bidet – a fact they are overtly proud of. The walls are decked out with photos of Paris and the Eiffel Tower, but it's the sound of a roaring espresso machine that's the main draw. *12 Dobrolyubova (12 Добролюбова); Coffee from 9UAH, Desserts from 6UAH; Open 10:00-21:00; +(38) 061 213 79 95*

"CrowBar" Located in the InTourist Hotel, this bar's swag can compete with anything Western Europe has to offer. With plush couches, funky decor, fully loaded bars, and a cool mix of people, prepare to spend most of your time in Zaporizhzhya here. Depending on the night, you might have to pay a cover (30UAH) but women are generally admitted free. Stylish dress is encouraged. *135 Lenina (135 Леніна); www.crowbar.com.ua*

Potato House Cheap lunch prevails at this Che Guevara loving chain. With "Mexican" food, like an interesting (but tasty) take on a burrito, this is good place to come for a cheap and filling lunch. *143 Lenina (143 Леніна); Entrées around 30UAH, Drinks from 8UAH; Open 10:30-22:00*

Mediterraneo Zaporizhzhya's newest craze is this seafood and tapas restaurant, and for good reason. The chef (there are rumors he comes from Portugal) offers a fresh take on Mediterranean food for prices that aren't Kyiv outrageous. The grilled lamb with fig sauce is awesome. If you're saving money, try their business lunch (35UAH, includes drink) Monday through Friday from 12:00 to 15:00. *22 Pobedu (22 побіду); Seafood Entrées 79-149UAH (the lobster at 700UAH is the most expensive item on the menu), Meat Entrées 49-109UAH; Open 12:00-22:00; +(38) 061 223 55 11; www.mediterraneo.ws*

SLEEP

Intourist Hotel Zaporizhzhya (Інтурист Готель Запорізька) With a sparkling, (dare I say) "funky" lobby, smiling receptionists, free large breakfast, shiny bathrooms and free Wi-Fi in the bar and lobby, it's a shame all Intourist hotels aren't this good. The hotel's restaurant should also be checked out as their Ukrainian food is the best in town. *135 Lenina (135 Леніна); Standard Single/Double: 810/930UAH, Junior Suite Single/Double: 1140/1620UAH; +(38) 061 223 05 00; reservation@intourist.com.ua; www.intourist.com.ua/en*

Hotel Ukraine (Готель Україна) If you're looking for standard rooms and don't care about all the expensive extras, Hotel Ukraine is for you. With basic rooms, a friendly staff, and a price that won't force you to take third class on the trains from now on, Hotel Ukraine is a good choice for the area. *162a Lenina (162a Леніна); Economy Single/Double: 340/390UAH, Standard Single/Double: 400/450UAH, Two-Room Suite Single/Double: 610/660UAH; +(38) 061 289 04 04; info@ukraine.zp.ua; www.ukraine.zp.ua*

Dnipropetrovsk (Днепропетровск)

Providing a great litmus test for foreigners (try pronouncing this city's name without messing it up), DP, as most expats call it, is the wealthiest city outside of Kyiv. Known for its nightlife, restaurants, and sports cars that crowd its boulevards DP is the stomping grounds for Ukraine's richest and most powerful people.

HISTORY

During the Russo-Turkish Wars, Cossack and Russian armies battled the Ottomans for control of this region. Russia later gained complete control when the Zaporozhian Sich was destroyed in 1775. After Cossacks were out of the picture, Russia started expanding the area and founded DP (which was then known as Yekaterinoslav, meaning "Glory to Yekaterina," or, as you know her, Catherine the Great) just north of where the city is now. Unfortunately the original location chosen was a crappy bog, so Prince Grigory Potemkin had it moved in 1783. He had ambitious plans for the city, but it remained small, even with the river trade, until the industrialization boom of the late 1800s.

In 1926 the city was renamed after the communist leader Grigory Petrovsky. During the Soviet Era and up until the early 1990s, the city was closed and civilians were allowed access only with official permission. A vital part of the arms, space, and nuclear programs in the Soviet Union, the city still plays host to a variety of manufacturing and industrial plants.

> By 1996, 80 percent of all post-Soviet politicians began their career in Dnipropetrovsk, which many Eastern Europeans still refer to as "the rocket closed city."

With so many citizens heavily involved in politics from here (former President Leonid Kuchma graduated from DP's State University), this area is rife with scandal and intrigue. Google "Dnipropetrovsk Mafia" for a night of fun!

TRANSPORTATION

Bus

DP's behemoth of a bus station (10 Kurchatova, 10 Курчатова) lies about ten minutes from the city center. Imposing from afar, inside it is very well organized, if a little chaotic. Autolux and Gusel have "VIP" Western-style bus services that run to Kyiv (8 hours) as well as other large cities. Buses to Crimea (Simferopol, 15 hours) run daily, with buses to closer cities (Donetsk, 4 hours) running hourly. Tickets can be bought from the central kiosk on the second floor.

Train

Arriving here by train feels like entering Moscow. Luckily the electronic message boards and easy-to-understand train platforms make navigating this mess easy. Fast trains to Kyiv (6 hours) happen twice daily as well as the usual slow trains (10 hours). Overnight trains to Odessa (11 hours) and further to Crimea (Simferopol, 7 hours) make DP the busiest commuter city out East.

Train tickets are bought outside the main train station. Exit through the front entrance and the ticket office (108 Karla Marksa, 108 Карла Маркса) will be in the building to your left.

To get to the city center from the station, take trolleybus #1 which runs the length of Karla Marksa.

Eastern Ukraine

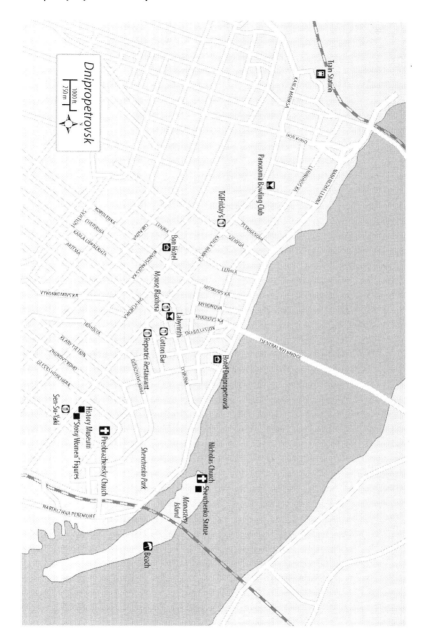

Airport

Traveling here by commercial plane is becoming a common thing, though private jets are still the norm. Dnipropetrovsk International Airport serves Ukraine as well as nearby European cities. It's definitely worth checking out if you're just coming for business. Located fifteen kilometers outside the city center, it also serves as the hub for the Zaporizhia region. A taxi into the city will cost around 75UAH, or you can take tram #60 or #109 to the train station.

SIGHTS & ACTIVITIES

History Museum
Исторический музей, *Istoricheskii muzyei*

Inside this building is a large pyramid – known as the "Pyramid of the Lost Ones" – constructed entirely out of photographs of people who perished here during World War II. In the rear, they have their famed **Diorama** – an 840-square-meter painting of the WWII battles fought along the Dnipro. Continue walking towards the back of the museum and you'll come across the odd collection of helicopters and tanks from WWII.

In the front, on the right side you'll see the unguarded "**Stony Women**" figures. These ancient stone statues are relics of a steppe nomadic tribe known as the Cumans, or Kipchaks, that resided here up until the Mongol invasion. Resembling mini Easter Island statues, their original purpose was to serve as index points for the nomads. *16 Karla Marksa (16 Карла Маркса); Open 10:00-17:00 Tues-Sunday; Admission 10UAH, Diorama: 8UAH*

Preobrazhensky Church
Преображенский

Continue walking down the path behind the History Museum and you'll see the

---

"The Rocket Closed City"

"Secret Cities," or "Closed Cities," were cities established by the Soviet Union beginning in 1940. The cities were often not named but rather simply referred to by their "post box" number, as mail to the cities were addressed to other towns, with the addition of a certain post box number.

The cities were divided into two categories. The first being small communities that dealt with sensitive military information and facilities such as nuclear power research or arms manufacturing. Absolutely no civilians were allowed into these towns without official permission and often times the existence of these towns was denied. Other larger "closed cities" existed that were officially open to citizens of the Soviet Union but closed off to foreigners.

Ukraine had eleven such towns, the most famous being Sevastopol and Dnipropetrovsk. Dnipropetrovsk's Yuzhmash facility "officially" produced agricultural and kitchen equipment, but it was quietly one of the largest missile factories in the Soviet Union. It became closed to visitors in 1959 by the KGB, when over 60 percent of the city's population worked for the plant. It wasn't open to the public again until 1987.

yellow façade of Dnipropetrovsk's holiest church peeking out from behind some tanks. Founded by Grigory Potemkin in 1786, by order of Catherine of Great, the initial plan was to have it surpass the height and grandiosity of St. Peter's Cathedral in Rome. It didn't quite make it. Constructed in Russian Classicalism, its richly decorated interior is definitely worth viewing. Scarves for women are available for use by the front entrance. Men should take off their hats. Donations accepted.

Shevchenko Park
Парк Шевченко

Continue down Karla Marksa, past the History Museum, and you'll come to Shevchenko Park. A pleasant park in the middle of this bustling city, it offers a peaceful retreat. Well into the fall season, old men gather here to play chess, beer tents are set up along the main thoroughfares, and patrons sip espressos at the cafés and restaurants that line its outskirts.

Monastery Island
Монастырский остров, *Monastyrskii ostrov*

If you walk through Shevchenko Park, towards the southern end of Lenina Street, you'll see the bridge that crosses over to this island. The island is named after a Byzantine Monastery that was constructed here around 870 AD and later destroyed by the Mongols in 1240. It now hosts sunbathers who come here for the town's beach.

Crossing the bridge from the park to the island you'll soon run into a massive **Taras Shevchenko Statue**, the size of which truly says…something (perhaps "we love him more!" was what they were going for). Down the path to the left of the statue you'll find the cute **St. Nicholas Church** overlooking the river.

EAT

"Cotton Bar" The owners of this bar are enamored with the music scene of New Orleans and sought to recreate it in Ukraine. The result? A jazz club that looks more like a Wild West saloon, but no one's complaining. Live music on the weekends with special shows throughout the month, make this a place worthy of stopping by for a schedule of performances. Full menu and a well stocked bar (they have Jack Daniels!) seal the deal. *5/7, Sholom-Aleikhema (5/7 Шолом-Алейхема); Beer from 30UAH; Open from 11:00; +(38) 056 744 85 76; www.cotton-bar.com.ua*

Sen-Su-Yaki (Сен-Су-Яки) Dnipropetrovsk is a city all about the latest fads and the sushi craze is showing no signs of fading. Overpriced cafés that serve the stuff abound, so it's nice to find one that's not charging an armful for something that's, well, Ukrainian sushi. *17a Karla Marksa (17 а Карла Маркса); Rolls from 30UAH, Yakitori from 20UAH (per 100 gram), Bento boxes from 70UAH; +(38) 056 236 20 62; www.sensuyaki.com*

TGI Friday's I hate myself for including this, but sometimes you just want a dang hamburger with french fries. Filled to the brim on most weekends with expats who have traversed vast distances for a taste of the familiar, it has everything the West has perpetrated upon its consumers, only more expensive. *2 Serova (2 Серова); Mains from 100UAH; Open from 11:00; www.tgifridays.ru/eng*

Mouse Blaxhera (Мыши Бляхера) Down in a basement (look for a staircase leading down to a wooden door), this was my favorite place in Ukraine. With an eclectic design (the walls are made out of second-hand books) that's worth the trip alone, it's the food that sets this place apart. I had the braised pork with apples one night, and the next day for lunch I just had the hamburger – both were fabulous.

The servers here wear shirts that when put together spell "Бляхера" (the name of the restaurant) but when separate make for a nice tongue-in-cheek joke: "Бля" and "хер" are two amazing curse words in Russian. Reservations recommended. *46 Karla Marksa (46 Карла Маркса); Entrées from 55UAH, Drinks from 15UAH; Open from 12:00; +(38) 056 377 33 77; www.mishi.com.ua*

NIGHTLIFE

Discos keep popping up along the waterway in DP. Regarded as having a better party scene than Kyiv, keep your wits about you and dress to impress.

Labyrinth (Лабиринт) Known as the best place in the city for singles, this club offers a sushi bar (of course), three dance floors and "chill-out" rooms. The obligatory face control and mild attitude is thrown in for free! Girls abound in this place, as do foreigners, but visitors should be cautious as many girls that frequent this place are "pros"…but maybe that's not something you're too worried about. *3 Kharkovskaya (3 Харьковская); Admission: from 30UAH*

Reporter (Репортер) You can't miss this four-story complex. The top floor is a cinema/café that serves food and drinks while guests watch Russian films (fun even if you don't speak the language). The middle floor plays hosts to a restaurant and café that serves an ever-changing menu (like king prawns with white sauce for 145UAH), but the real reason people come here is the basement's "drinking house." Half liters of tasty, cold German beers go down easy here as do any of their other imports. A popular first stop for a night out, don't be surprised if you just end up staying here. With live music on the weekends, it's easy to do so. *2 Barrikadnaya (2 Баррикадная); Beer from 25UAH; +(38) 056 233 75 75; www.reporter.dp.ua*

Panorama Bowling Club (Панорама Боулинг-клуб) For those who like their nights out a little low-key, Panorama Bowling Club offers up American and Russian billiards, bowling – which is very popular in Ukraine – and a bar! Have no fear, the ladies come here too. *1 Stolyarova (1 Столярова); Admission free-10UAH; Lane Rentals: 78-180UAH (per lane, per hour, nights more expensive); Open Tuesday-Sunday from 14:00, Monday from 17:00; www.bowling.dp.ua*

SLEEP

Unfortunately DP offers little in the form of budget accommodations. In a city full of money, its guests are expected to shell it out. Apartment rentals online are available but be careful when booking, pay only through PayPal, and be sure not to pay in-full until you are in the apartment. Average apartment per night is around US$65.

Hotel Dnipropetrovsk (Отель Днепропетровск) What this hotel lacks in charm, it makes up for in great views of the Dnipro. With over three hundred rooms, it's possible to walk in here without a reservation as well. The front desk staff speak English and rooms have everything you need – but perhaps not everything you would want. *33 Naberezhnaya Lenina (33 Набережная Ленина); Standard double: US$46, Two-Room Suite: US$63, Apartment US$100*

Bon (Boutique) Hotel (Бон Отель) I suspect the next big trend to sweep Ukraine will suddenly be to call everything a "boutique" hotel. This place is posh and its style is unquestionably cool. With in-room breakfast service (you order the night before), Wi-Fi, air conditioning, luscious beds, and heated tile bathroom floors all included in the price, this is one of the nicest hotels in the city. Unfortunately the price reflects this. *26 Komsomolskaya(26 Комсомольская); Single: 800UAH, Standard Double: 1000UAH, "Luxe" Suite: 1500UAH; +(38) 056 726 55 55*

Lugansk (Луганськ, Луганск)

Luhansk, Lugansk, or Luhans'k. The variations of this city's name rivals that of Lviv. Located at the convergence of the Luhan River and Vilkhivka River, in the Donets Basin, Luhansk is a very industrialized town. With coal mining, steel engineering plants, and automotive and train factories, Luhansk is often compared to Detroit. And unlike Donetsk, where wealthy, politically-affiliated citizens inject lots of money back into the town to keep it looking nice, the fact that Luhansk is an industrial town isn't concealed. One look and you know.

Not much here to attract the average visitor, but if you find yourself here…

TRANSPORTATION

Trains to Luhansk from Kyiv leave daily and take eighteen hours. The train station is located at 6 Pyatyorkina (6 Пиатьоркина) and can be contacted at +(38) 064 252 10 87.

Buses leave regularly to Kyiv (16 hours) and Donetsk (2.5 hours). The bus station is located at 28 Oboronnaya (28 Оборонная) and can be contacted at +(38) 064 250 71 34.

SIGHTS & ACTIVITIES

St. Peter and St. Paul's Cathedral
Св. Петра и Павла Собор, *Sv. Petra i Pavla Sobor*
Built in the middle of the nineteenth century, this church was the only Orthodox cathedral in the city that survived the Soviet anti-religious campaigns. In the 1930s, it was turned into a cinema and later a disco, but now it's back to being a church. *Kamin Ford (Камень Форд)*

Red Square
Located in the center of town, this square was originally called Cathedral Square because St. Nicholas' Cathedral resided here. During the Bolshevik Era, the cathedral was destroyed and the name changed to that of Moscow's Square. Visiting the square now, you'll see **St. George's Chapel** and the **Chernobyl Memorial**. *Krasnaya ploshchad (Красная площадь)*

Mergeleva Ridge
Мергелева гряда, *Mergeleva gryada*
Located about thirty kilometers from the city of Luhansk, the ridge is the site of an ancient burial complex and temple. It was discovered by a group of school children in 2004. In 2006, Ukrainian archaeologists claimed they had found the remnants of

an ancient pyramid structure that predated the Egyptian pyramids by three hundred years. Other archaeologists have since speculated that what they found was not in fact a pyramid. Now the Ridge's terrain is littered with ancient ruble and the location is popular with school groups and an odd scientist or two. If you fit into one of those categories, then take a bus out to Perevalsk (Перевальськ) to see it. Tour operators also organize trips to the ridge but are overpriced.

SLEEP

Hotel Luhansk (Отель Луганск) This old Soviet hotel is still creeping along. Decent enough, it's popular with businesses and tour groups because they can just book up the whole place and be done with it. *76 Sovetskaya (76 Советская); Standard 340/400UAH Single/Double; +(38) 064 234 47 13; info@hotel-lugansk.lg.ua; www.hotel-lugansk.lg.ua*

Eastern Ukraine

Survival Ukrainian

Ukrainian is understood (sometimes humorously) throughout the country. Ukrainians love when foreigners speak Ukrainian and not Russian; they think it's respectful and, often times, "adorable." The following will get you started on your journey. For those planning to travel extensively, investment in a Ukrainian-English or Russian-English dictionary might be helpful.

PRONUNCIATION

Ukrainian Letter	Approximate sound in English
Аа	a in b**ar**
Бб	b in **b**ook
Вв	v in **v**oice
Гг	h in **h**ow
Ґґ	g in **g**et
Дд	d in **dot**
Ее	e in t**e**n
Єє	ye in **ye**s
Жж	zh in plea**sur**e
Зз	z in **z**one
Ии	y in b**y**te
Іі	ee in m**ee**t
Її	yee in **yea**st
Йй	y in bo**y**

Ukrainian Letter	Approximate sound in English
Кк	k in **k**ey
Лл	l in **l**amp
Мм	m in **m**an
Нн	n in **n**ose
Оо	o in p**or**t
Пп	p in s**p**oon
Рр	r in **r**oof
Сс	s in **s**mall
Тт	t in **t**art
Уу	oo in m**oo**n
Фф	f in **f**ine
Хх	kh in Lo**ch** Ness
Цц	ts in ca**ts**
Чч	ch in **ch**air
Шш	sh in **sh**ine
Щщ	shch in ra**sh ch**oice
ь	no sound, softens previous consonant
Юю	yoo in **yo**uth
Яя	ya in **ya**rd

COMMON PHRASES

Phrase	Ukrainian	Pronunciation
Hello / Good Day	добрий день	dobryy̆ den'
Good Evening	добрий вечір	dobryy̆ vecheer

Phrase	Ukrainian	Pronunciation
Good bye	до побачення	do pobachennya
Hi.	Привіт	pryveet
Yes / No / Maybe	так / ні / можливо	Tak / Nee / mozhlyvo
Please	будь ласка	bud' laska
Thank you	дякую	dyakooyoo
You're Welcome	прошу	proshoo
Sorry / excuse me	вибачте	Vybachte
Nevermind	Нічого	neechoho
May I?	Можна?	mozhna?
How are you?	Як справи	Yak spravy
Good / Bad / Okay	Добре / Погано / нормально	Dobre / Pohano / Normal'no
Who/What/When/Where?	Хто / що / коли / де?	Khto / Shcho / Koly / De?
How/Why?	Як / Чому?	Yak / Chomu?
Repeat please.	Повторіть, будь ласка.	Povtorit' bood' laska
How much (does it cost)?	Скільки коштує?	skil'ki koshtuye?
My name is…	мені звати…	Mene zvaty…
What's you name?	Як Вас звати?	Yak vas zvaty?
Do you speak English?	Ви розмовляєте англійською?	Vy rozmovlyayete anhliys'koyu?

Phrase	Ukrainian	Pronunciation
I'm sorry, I don't understand.	Вибачте, я не розумію.	vybachte ya ne rozoomeeyoo
I want…	Я хочу…	Ya khochu…
I need…	мені треба	meni treba
I love you	Я люблю тебе	Ya lyublyu tebe

EMERGENCIES

Phrase	Ukrainian	Pronunciation
Help!	допоможіть!	dopomozhit!
Where is a hospital?	Де знаходиться лікарні?	De znakhodyt·sya likarni?
I need cops / doctor	Мені потрібна міліція / лікар	Meni potribna militsiya /
I am sick	Я хвора	Ya khvora
Someone Stole…	хтось вкрав…	khtos' vkrav
camera	камера	kamera
bag	сумка	sumka
passport	паспорт	pasport
wallet	гаманець	hamanets

DIRECTIONS

Phrase	Ukrainian	Pronunciation
I got lost.	Я заблукав	Ya Zablukav

Phrase	Ukrainian	Pronunciation
Where is …	Де знаходиться…	De znakhodyt'sya
Hotel "…"	готель	hotel'
bathroom	туалет	tualet
a currency exchange / bank	валют / банк	valyut / bank
an atm	банкомат	bankomat
(to the) right/left	вправо / вліво	vpravo / vlivo
straight	прямо	pryamo
north/south/east/west	північ / південь / схід / захід	pivnich / pivden' / skhid / zakhid
Here / There	Тут / Там	toot / tam

TRANSPORT

Phrase	Ukrainian	Pronunciation
Give me please…	дайте будь ласка	daỷte bud' laska
a ticket to/from	Квиток до / з	Kvytok do / z
Bus station	автовокзал	avtovokzal
The train station	залізничний вокзал	zaliznychnyy vokzal
Taxi	таксі	taksi
Airport	аеропорт	aeroport
Ticket Window	каса	kasa

Phrase	Ukrainian	Pronunciation
Platform	платформа	platforma
(luggage) locker	шафка	shafka
Timetable	розклад	rozklad
First-Class (train)	СВ	SV
Second-Class (train)	купе	kupe
Third-Class (train)	плацкарта	platskarta

HOTEL / HOSTEL

Phrase	Ukrainian	Pronunciation
Do you have an available room?	У вас є вільні номери?	U vas ye vil'ni nomery?
air-conditioner	кондиціонер	kondytsioner
with breakfast	зі сніданком	zi snidankom
Where can I smoke?	Де можна палити?	de mozhna palyty

RESTAURANT

Phrase	Ukrainian	Pronunciation
Table for (one / two)	Столик на (одного / двох)	Stolyk na (odnoho / dvokh)
Give me please…	дайте мені, будь ласка	dayte meni, bud' laska
a beer	пиво	pyvo
wine	вино	vyno

Phrase	Ukrainian	Pronunciation
vodka	водка / горілка	vodka / horilka
a menu	меню	menyu
Check Please	Рахунок, будь ласка	Rakhunok, bud' laska
I am vegetarian (m / f)	Я вегетаріанець / Я вегетаріанка	ya vehetareeanets' / ya vehetareeanka
I am allergic to…	У мене алергія на…	U mene alerhiya na…
Delicious!	Смачно!	smachno!

NUMBERS

Phrase	Ukrainian	Pronunciation
First	Перше	Pershe
Second	другий	druhyy
Third	третину	tretynu
One	один	odyn
Two	два	dva
Three	три	triy
Four	чотири	chotyry
Five	п'ять	p'yat'
Six	шість	shist'
Seven	сім	sim
Eight	вісім	vicim

Phrase	Ukrainian	Pronunciation
Nine	дев'ять	dev'yat'
Ten	десять	desyat'
Twenty	двадцять	dvadtsyat'
One Hundred	сто	sto

Visit us at
www.otherplacespublishing.com

Made in the USA
Lexington, KY
08 February 2013